THE DYNAMICS OF
SUBVERSION AND VIOLENCE
IN CONTEMPORARY ITALY

THE
DYNAMICS OF
SUBVERSION
AND VIOLENCE
IN CONTEMPORARY
ITALY

Vittorfranco S. Pisano

HOOVER INSTITUTION PRESS
STANFORD UNIVERSITY   STANFORD, CALIFORNIA

The Hoover Institution on War, Revolution and Peace, founded at Stanford University in 1919 by the late President Herbert Hoover, is an interdisciplinary research center for advanced study on domestic and international affairs in the twentieth century. The views expressed in its publications are entirely those of the authors and do not necessarily reflect the views of the staff, officers, or Board of Overseers of the Hoover Institution.

Hoover Press Publication 355

First printing, 1987
Manufactured in the United States of America
91 90 89 88 87   9 8 7 6 5 4 3 2 1

Library of Congress Cataloging in Publication Data
Pisano, Vittorfranco S.
   The dynamics of subversion and violence in contemporary Italy.

   Bibliography: p.
   Includes index.
   1. Crime and criminals—Italy. 2. Subversive
activities—Italy. 3. Violent crimes—Italy.
4. Criminal justice, Administration of—Italy.
5. Subversion and violence in contemporary
Italy. I. Title.
HV6992.P56 1987   364'.945 87-13560
ISBN 0-8179-8551-4
ISBN 0-8179-8552-2 (pbk.)

*To my wife
and daughter*

Contents

Preface

It is no secret that Dante's *Inferno* is more widely read than his *Paradiso*. Indeed, human baseness notoriously draws far more attention than virtuous pursuits. As William Shakespeare concisely put it, "The evil that men do lives after them, the good is oft interred with their bones."

The purpose of this book, as the title implies, is to address Italy's contemporary criminal and subversive milieu, rather than the noble manifestations of the human spirit—art, literature, music, or science—all of which are by no means a negligible component of the Italian character. In so doing, the intention of the author is not to overlook Italian achievements, but to review and place in perspective many "newsworthy events" of recent vintage whose significance is frequently lost to a vast public almost exclusively exposed to fragmentary media accounts.

In fact, some examples of events that received limited or even superficial media coverage are the abduction of Italian statesman Aldo Moro and of U.S. Army general James Lee Dozier by the Red Brigades; the abortive attempt on the life of Pope John Paul II in St. Peter's Square by Turkish gunman Mehmet Ali Agca; the various ramifications of the Bulgarian "connection"; overt and covert militancy against the deployment of the cruise missiles in Comiso, Sicily, as part of the modernization of NATO's theater nuclear force; the murder of U.S. diplomat Leamon R. Hunt by the Red Brigades in concert with the Lebanese Armed Revolutionary Faction; the unprecedented exposure of Mafia internal structures and practices by former *mafioso* Tommaso Buscetta; and repeated transnational terrorist attacks in the very heart of the Eternal City as well as at Rome's Leonardo da Vinci International Airport.

The aspiration of this work is therefore to provide background information on Italian criminological and security issues, as well as pertinent detail regarding specific events, so that interested readers from English-

speaking countries may increase their understanding of Italy's complex sociopolitical and criminological setting. The structure of the book is likewise
intended to achieve that end.

Chapter 1, which is in essence an introductory chapter, discusses Italy's
governmental and political institutions and the roots of instability endemic
to Italian public life. Chapter 2 addresses the country's protective structures
in the areas of law enforcement, security, and national defense. Both chapters should benefit the reader who is unfamiliar or insufficiently familiar
with the mechanics of Italian government and society. At the same time,
they should provide a better appreciation for the subject matter covered in
the chapters that follow. Chapters 3 through 7 delve into the principal security and criminological issues that afflict Italy because of their destabilizing effects: overt political violence, terrorism, ideologically motivated abductions, kidnappings for ransom, organized crime, subversive exploitation
of national security matters and of the pacifist movement, and a variety of
hostile intelligence operations conducted by foreign powers and subnational organizations on Italian territory. The stress is on the objectives,
structues, dynamics, and linkages of criminal or hostile forces at work. Although each of these chapters addresses a specific topic, they are all interrelated. Chapter 8 overviews the countermeasures adopted, amidst difficulties, by the Italian state. The appendixes either support the description and
analyses in the body of the text or provide additional detail.

Given the current and fluid nature of the phenomena discussed in the
book, it would be unrealistic to draw definitive conclusions. Rather, the
study at hand serves as a basis to monitor future developments and to assess
future information.

July 1986   Vittorfranco S. Pisano

Acknowledgments

I am particularly thankful to my good friends Alfonso Tarabochia, formerly of the U.S. Senate staff, and Ivaldo Giaquinto, formerly of the Italian Chamber of Deputies staff, for having taught me much of what I know about researching the topics addressed in this book. I would also like to express my appreciation to Dr. Ivan Sipkov and Mrs. Marie-Louise Bernal, two outstanding public servants with the Library of Congress, for their generous and continual assistance in identifying sources.

Abbreviations

AN	National Vanguard
AR	Revolutionary Action
AUTOP	Workers' Autonomy
BR	Red Brigades
CESIS	Executive Committee of the Intelligence and Security Services
CGIL	Italian General Confederation of Labor
CISL	Italian Confederation of Workers' Trade Unions
CISNAL	Italian Confederation of National Syndicates for Workers
COLP	Organized Comrades for Proletarian Liberation
Cominform	Communist Information Bureau
Comintern	Communist International
DC	Christian Democratic Party
DP	Proletarian Democracy
LDU	League for Unilateral Disarmament
LOC	League of Conscientious Objectors
MIR	International Reconciliation Movement
MSI	Italian Socialist Movement
NAP	Armed Proletarian Nuclei
NAR	Armed Revolutionary Nuclei
ON	New Order/Black Order
PCI	Italian Communist Party

PDIUM	Italian Democratic Party for Monarchist Unity
PDUP	Democratic Proletarian Unity Party
PL	Front Line
PLI	Italian Liberal Party
PR	Radical Party
PRI	Italian Republican Party
PSDI	Italian Social Democratic Party
PSI	Italian Socialist Party
SID	Defense Intelligence Service
SISDE	Service for Intelligence and Democratic Security
SISMI	Service for Military Intelligence and Security
UCC	Communist Combat Units
UIL	Italian Union of Labor

CHAPTER ONE

National Institutions and the Problem of Governability

The word crisis is frequently used to characterize Italian public life. Whereas most analyses tend to be more pessimistic than warranted, several factors—both ancient and modern—render confidence in government generally wanting and governability often problematic. This state of affairs not only contributes to the nourishment of antisocial, subversive, and revolutionary aspirations, but also facilitates crime in its common, organized, and political manifestations.

An understanding of Italian institutions and of the causes behind the problem of governability is therefore a prerequisite in order to fully appreciate the significance of the criminological and security issues addressed in the chapters that follow. Interrelated introductory themes include the belated Italian statehood and attendant psychological implications, the parliamentary system and the inordinate preeminence of the legislative branch of government, the multiparty system as fostered by discordant ideologies and proportional electoral laws, the unstable coalition government and concomitant executive weakness, and policymaking based on ideological compromise and political barter outside of the prescribed organs of government. The sociopolitical picture that ultimately emerges is highly complex.

Belated Statehood

Notwithstanding an unrivaled historical record that embraces the glory of ancient Rome and the splendor of the Renaissance, Italy is a latecomer, as a sovereign state, to the community of nations. At the Congress of Vienna of 1815, where the victorious reactionary powers redesigned the political map of post-Napoleonic Europe, Italy was unceremoniously defined "a geographical expression."

The proclamation of an independent and sovereign Italian state did not in fact take place until 1861. It grew out of the progressive territorial expansion of the Kingdom of Piedmont and Sardinia, whose administrative and military posture was the most efficient of all preunification states established or otherwise recognized in Italy. Moreover, complete territorial and ethnic unification under the newly established Kingdom of Italy had to wait until the following century. The Veneto region was incorporated in 1866, Rome in 1870, and the Trento and Trieste provinces only in 1918 after Italy's successful participation in World War I. From an Italian perspective, this conflict was the Fourth War of Independence against the Austro-Hungarian empire and the culminating point of the *Risorgimento,* or process of unification begun in 1848.

Formally, if not substantially, political unification temporarily vested the new kingdom with the status of a world power, but this was not sufficient to nullify the deeply entrenched traditions of popular disunity, on the one hand, and collective distrust of government, on the other. Realistically, the Risorgimento must be acknowledged as the aspiration and accomplishment of Italy's liberal elite of the era; in no way did it resemble a mass popular movement.

To be sure, after the fall of the Roman empire the national character had been forged under the influence of a multiplicity of negative and converging factors: recurrent foreign intervention—Germanic, Arabic, Spanish, French, and Austrian—ranging from mass invasion to military occupation to political meddling; endemic rivalry and warfare among domestic city-states and local dynasties; geographical dissimilarities accompanied by sociological and linguistic cleavages; and, not least, unending conflict between temporal and ecclesiastical authority, the roots of which can be traced to the days of Peter the Apostle who, in selecting Rome as the seat of Christianity, made the Catholic Church and, indeed, the Papacy an integral part of the Italian scene. Throughout the centuries, mastering the art of survival rather than achieving civic participation had been the guiding principle of Italian life, both public and private.

Count Cavour, the chief architect of Italian unification under Piedmontese hegemony, is quoted as having said: "We created Italy, let us now mold the Italians." This ambition was shared, albeit in dissimilar ways, by Benito Mussolini's Fascist regime, which governed Italy with royal consent from 1922 to 1943. Cavour died too soon to see this aspiration—the "molding" of Italians—fulfilled, and the Fascist regime simply failed. Nevertheless, anti-Fascist sentiment served as a catalyst, among otherwise discordant forces, in shaping post–World War II Italy into a substantially modern and potentially democratic state.

The Constitutional Structure

The downfall of the Fascist regime in July 1943 and of the monarchy itself under the weight of a pro-Republic popular referendum in June 1946 necessitated the writing of a new constitution. Italy had been governed by the Albertine Statute, a constitutional charter granted by the liberal Charles Albert to his Kingdom of Piedmont and Sardinia on March 4, 1848. This document had remained in force through the subsequent stages of Italian unification and even during the Fascist regime up to the proclamation of the Republic of Italy on June 2, 1946 (subsequently celebrated every year as Republic Day). The longevity of the Albertine Statute is attributable to its flexibility, since it could be modified by Parliament with the passage of ordinary legislation. There was no requirement for a special amending process.

The new Constitution of the Republic was drawn up in 1947 and became effective on January 1, 1948. It is the reflection of compromises reached by the discordant forces that made up the Constituent Assembly. The delegates included representatives of the Christian Democratic Party, the Italian Socialist Party for Proletarian Unity, the Italian Communist Party, the National Democratic Union, the Common Man's Liberal Democratic Front, the Italian Republican Party, the Sicilian Independence Movement, the Sardinian Action Party, and the National Coalition for Liberty— in other words, Catholics, Marxists, conservatives, moderates, progressives, separatists, and, ironically, royalists all took part.

Little beyond their anti-Fascist sentiment accounted for the unity of the creators of the Constitution. In fact, after the signing of the armistice on September 8, 1943, between the Kingdom of Italy and the Anglo-American powers, all delegates to the Constituent Assembly had supported or participated in the War of Liberation against the German occupation forces. These forces, together with Fascist loyalists, had given birth to the so-called Italian Social Republic (Repubblica Sociale Italiana), a short-lived puppet state in northern Italy under Nazi control.

The Constitution of 1948—which is a rigid document, as opposed to the flexible nature of the Albertine Statute—opens with the declaration that "Italy is a democratic Republic founded on work. Sovereignty is vested in the people and shall be exercised in the forms and within the limits of the Constitution."[1] By providing that the Republic be "one and indivisible,"[2] it attributes to the nation the character of a unitary state, instead of a federal one.

With respect to the dynamics of government, the fundamental constitutional directives establish a parliamentary system, rather than a presidential democracy. This is not surprising. On the one hand, Italian political tradition since 1861—albeit interrupted by twenty years of Fascism—had consistently called for unbridled pluralism. On the other hand, the diversity of the political forces present at the Constituent Assembly and their still-vivid memories of the Fascist era were sufficient motivation for wanting to control closely the powers of the executive branch of government, which had become dominant during the Fascist dictatorship.

The Italian Constitution thus paved the way for an overwhelming preeminence of the legislative branch of government and set up cumbersome procedures in place of a streamlined and ultimately healthier system of checks and balances among the executive, legislative, and judicial branches of government. Moreover, this combination of pluralistic tradition and anti-Fascist preoccupation that permeates the spirit of the Constitution has contributed to the perpetuation of centrifugal forces in Parliament and the nation and, consequently, to the endemic weakness of the national executive.

The following are the principal organs of government comprised in the constitutional scheme of 1948: the president of the Republic, the Parliament, the prime minister, the Council of Ministers, the judiciary, the Constitutional Court, and the intermediate and local bodies of government.

The President

According to the Constitution, "The President of the Republic is Head of State and represents the unity of the Nation." [3] The president is not, however, the chief executive; that role is assigned by the Constitution to the prime minister, who is also referred to as head of government. In essence, the presidency of the Republic stands apart from the three traditional branches of government.

Political doctrine classifies the powers of the president as either substantive or formal. The substantive powers include the appointment of the prime minister and, upon the advice of the latter, the appointment of other ministers; the dissolution of one or both chambers of Parliament prior to the expiration of their normal term in order to call new elections; the returning of a bill to Parliament for a second debate; the sending of messages to the chambers of Parliament; the appointment of five lifetime senators and five Constitutional Court justices; and the exercise of functions as chair of the Supreme Council of Defense and of the Superior Council of the Judiciary.

The formal powers, less charitably but realistically referred to as "notarial," include promulgating laws, ratifying treaties, calling elections, commanding the armed forces, granting pardons and commutations, calling Parliament into special session, and authorizing the introduction of bills by the ministers before Parliament.

Although in theory the president exercises discretion and initiative in connection with the substantive powers inherent to the office, the fact remains that constitutionally "no act of the President of the Republic is valid unless countersigned by the Ministers who proposed it and who must assume full responsibility for it."[4] Moreover, the constitutionally prescribed procedure for the election of the president by Parliament deprives the head of state even of the moral and psychological power deriving from direct investiture by the people. The president serves for a term of seven years and may be re-elected.

Parliament

The Constitution instituted a bicameral Parliament composed of the Chamber of Deputies and the Senate of the Republic. Parliament is the only organ of Italian central government that is directly elected by the people. In turn, it elects the president and approves the composition of the Council of Ministers by means of a vote of confidence expressed, in separate session, by each chamber. If the Council of Ministers—which is usually referred to as the government—does not obtain this approval, it cannot remain in office. This is the most salient aspect of the parliamentary system consecrated in the Republican Constitution and a major cause of governmental instability.

The attribution of the same powers and functions to the two chambers of Parliament has engendered criticism to the effect that each chamber is in essence a duplication of the other and that any differences are purely formal. Moreover, the existence of two nearly identical representative organs in a unitary state, which by definition is exempt from the requirements of federalism, is viewed as unjustified.

Both chambers are elected for a term of five years, which can be shortened if the president dissolves one or both chambers in order to call new elections. However, this is a power that he cannot exercise during the last six months of his tenure, as a precaution against undue influence he might otherwise exert if seeking re-election. The dissolution of Parliament, after which national elections are mandatory, is regarded by constitutional scholars as appropriate when the composition of Parliament no longer represents the actual will of the political forces that make up the nation, or when the government is no longer manageable because of the lack of a solid political majority in Parliament. Since the start of the 1970s, early dissolution of Parliament has become a standard practice; both chambers were dissolved in 1972, 1976, 1979, and 1983. In no case, however, did a solid political majority emerge, nor did the government become substantially more manageable.

Worth noting also is the comparatively large number of deputies and senators (630 and 315, respectively) in a country with just 57 million inhabitants. The number of senators is, in practice, even larger, since each president may appoint for life five exceptionally meritorious citizens in the social, scientific, artistic, and literary fields of endeavor. Moreover, former presidents automatically become lifetime members of the Senate. Parliamentary structures and procedures are rendered even more cumbersome by the provision that joint sessions of the chambers may be held only in the few and infrequent cases specified by the Constitution.

The Constitution provides for the collective exercise of the legislative function by the two chambers of Parliament. A bill, regardless of its nature, may be introduced into the chambers by any deputy or senator. Bills may also be introduced by the National Economic and Labor Council, a specialized agency in that field, by the Regional Councils, or by a petition of 50,000 voters.

Once a bill has been voted into law—as originally introduced or subsequently modified—by both chambers, it is signed by the president of the Republic or returned to the chambers for reconsideration. If confirmed, the president has no choice but to sign it.

Parliament can also declare a state of war, and it confers with the attendant powers on the Council of Ministers, authorizes the ratification of treaties by the president, approves the budget submitted by the Council of Ministers, and makes inquiries into matters of public interest.

The Council of Ministers

The Constitution states that the "Government of the Republic shall consist of the President of the Council and the Ministers, who together constitute the Council of Ministers."[5] This president of the Council—that is, the prime minister, also referred to as the premier—is appointed by the president of the Republic, who also appoints the ministers. Within ten days of appointment, the council must present itself before Parliament to receive a vote of confidence. Failure to receive or retain this confidence, which can be withdrawn by Parliament at its pleasure, will cause the members of the Council of Ministers to resign. The instability of this organ is reflected by the succession of 41 governments since the Constitution went into effect in 1948.

The primary function of the prime minister is to direct the general policy of the government. This individual serves as head of government or chief executive and, as such, must maintain "unity of political and administrative control" by promoting and coordinating the activities of the ministers.[6] Members of the Council of Ministers are jointly responsible for the acts of the council and are also individually responsible for the specific ministry each of them heads. Twenty ministries currently constitute the basic structure of Italy's public administration. Within the council there are frequently also ministers without portfolio, who are not ministerial heads but are responsible for nondepartmental matters of interest to the government.

In addition to its executive and administrative responsibilities, the Council of Ministers is enabled by the Constitution to contribute to the legislative function by introducing draft bills in the Parliament. Moreover, it can constitutionally issue decrees in accordance with specific delegation by the Parliament or on its own authority in "exceptional cases of urgency and necessity."[7] In the first instance, the Council of Ministers issues legislative decrees; in the second, it issues law decrees, which lose their validity retroactively unless converted into law by the two chambers of Parliament within 60 days of publication.

The collegiate nature of the Council of Ministers renders policymaking more complex and reduces the leadership role of the prime minister, who is thus frequently regarded as a *primus inter pares*—first among equals— rather than as a chief executive in the strict sense.

The Judiciary

In order to insure the independence of the judiciary, particularly from the executive branch of government, the Constituent Assembly established an organ named the Superior Council of the Judiciary. The responsibility of this body is "to designate, appoint, transfer, and promote judges and to adopt disciplinary measures regarding them, in accordance with the rules of the judicial organization."[8] The Constitution also sets forth, as a general rule, that judges be appointed on the basis of a competitive examination.

The Superior Council of the Judiciary is chaired by the president of the Republic and consists of 24 members. Except for the chief justice and chief prosecutor of the Supreme Court of Cassation (the highest court of appeal) who are ex officio members, two-thirds of all other members are elected from among the judiciary. Parliament in joint session elects the remaining third from among law school professors and attorneys who have practiced for at least fifteen years. Unfortunately, this method of selection contributes to politicalization of the judiciary, in contrast with the intentions of the Constituent Assembly.

The judicial system is unified and part of the central government. Ordinary courts are headed by the Supreme Court of Cassation, which passes judgment on points of law rather than on fact. Italian courts are not bound by the rule of precedent, which is peculiar to the Anglo-American legal system. At the same time, they may not rule a law or statute unconstitutional, but must refer that issue, if it arises during court proceedings, to the Constitutional Court.

The Constituent Assembly, not satisfied with traditional constitutional guarantees, introduced an additional safeguard: the Constitutional Court. This body judges disputes regarding the unconstitutionality of state and regional legislation and settles conflicts of jurisdiction between state authorities, between the state and the regions, or between regions. It also has jurisdiction over charges of misconduct against the president and the members of the Council of Ministers. The findings of the Constitutional Court may not be challenged. However, of its own initiative it may not render advisory opinions or institute proceedings.

The Constitutional Court comprises fifteen justices, one-third appointed by the president, one-third by Parliament in joint session, and one-third by the highest ordinary and administrative courts. Critics have argued that the system of appointment of the Constitutional Court is responsible for politicizing its role.

Local Government

The Constitution provides for the exercise of certain forms of local autonomy and self-government through the establishment of regions (currently twenty) and the reaffirmation of provinces (95) and municipalities (8,085). The powers of the regions, as intermediate bodies of government, and of the provinces and municipalities, as local ones, are specifically listed in the Constitution itself. In the design of the Constituent Assembly, these bodies of government were to carry out social and productive functions peculiar to their geographic area and sociological environment. The institution of the regions was also intended to decentralize governmental functions and thus provide a more direct form of democratic participation. Five of them are organized under special charters principally because of ethnic characteristics.[9]

The preceding survey of the structure of Italian government would not be complete without expanding on the direct exercise of popular sovereignty. It has been noted that the two chambers of Parliament are elected by the people and that a petition of 50,000 voters is one of several procedures for the introduction of bills. The people also elect regional, provincial, and municipal councils for terms of five years. Moreover, at the request of 500,000 voters, popular referendums may be held for the repeal of legislation. Excluded from this provision are fiscal and budgetary laws, amnesties and pardons, and laws authorizing the ratification of international treaties. A popular referendum was called for the first time in 1974 and nine have since been held; none, however, have succeeded in obtaining the absolute majority required to repeal a law.

The drawbacks of the parliamentary system and of the other convoluted procedures consecrated in the Constitution are magnified by the presence in Italy of numerous parties that enjoy representation in Parliament, but none of which are able to poll a sufficient number of votes to obtain an absolute majority of seats in the two chambers of Parliament.

The Multiparty System

The collapse of the Fascist regime and its one-party system triggered the legal and public re-emergence in 1943 of many political parties and their ancillary organizations. Although some party labels have since been modified following absorption or mergers and new parties have appeared on the Italian scene, basically the same heterogeneous political/ideological forces represented at the Constituent Assembly of 1946–1947 are still active in the country, in the Parliament, and, frequently, in the government.

The Constitution itself specifically prescribes the right of citizens to form and join political parties. Although the Constitution requires political parties to contribute "by democratic means"[10] to the determination of national policy, it imposes no democratic requirements with respect to internal party structures. Thus, the Italian Communist Party, which practices the democratically debatable principle of democratic centralism, is free to operate within the framework of the Republican Constitution.

Major and minor parties that enjoy countrywide electoral support and representation in Parliament currently include the Christian Democratic Party, the Italian Communist Party, the Italian Socialist Party, the Italian Social Movement–National Right, the Italian Republican Party, the Italian Social Democratic Party, the Italian Liberal Party, the Radical Party, and Proletarian Democracy. All but two successfully ran candidates, under their present party name or a similar one, for the Constituent Assembly in 1946 and for Parliament in all subsequent elections. The sequence in which these parties are listed above reflects their importance in terms of the electoral returns obtained in the 1983 parliamentary contest. However, except for the top four, their electoral standings have varied over the years. Appendix 1 reflects the electoral returns of all principal parties in the Chamber of Deputies since the Constitution went into effect.

The Christian Democratic Party

The Christian Democratic Party (Democrazia Cristiana; DC) came into being in 1943 as the heir of the Italian Popular Party (Partito Popolare Italiano), founded in 1919 as a party of Catholic social orientation and with close ties to the ecclesiastical hierarchy. The Popular Party was substantially, though not formally, able to coexist with the Fascist dictatorship because of its operational ties to Catholic Action (Azione Cattolica), a Catholic laymen's organization that formed the cadres of what was to become the DC. Mussolini's less than all-pervasive totalitarianism did not interfere with the pastoral and social ministry of the Catholic Church. It was in fact the conclusion of the Lateran Agreements of 1929 by the Fascist regime with the Holy See that settled the so-called Roman Question, which had been pending since 1870 when the Kingdom of Italy forcibly took over the city of Rome from the Papacy in the pursuit of Italian unification. The Lateran Agreements normalized relations between Church and State.[11]

Virtually from its birth, the DC has been plagued by internal factions that represent, more often than not, power-related interests rather than clear-cut ideological differences. It is nonetheless correct to speak in terms of "left" and "right" within the party. The left wing has traditionally sought centralized economic planning and economic intervention by the state, allegedly to promote social justice. The right wing has favored laissez-faire economics. Since the 1970s, in particular, the distinction between the two wings has also reflected their conflicting attitudes regarding cooperation with the Communist Party. On the whole, however, the past and current image projected by the DC is that of a moderate party inbred with Western and Catholic values and ambitious to govern.

Whereas no party has ever attained an absolute majority in the Senate, the DC is the only one to achieve that standing in the Chamber of Deputies, albeit only in the parliamentary elections of 1948, the first under the Republican Constitution. Thereafter, it continued to carry out the role of a governing party as the relative-majority partner in various multiparty coalitions. Its success through the decades—over 40 percent returns in the 1950s and close to 40 percent in the 1960s and 1970s—has been largely proportional to the fear of communism by the Italian electorate. Limiting factors, however, include the DC's inability to cure internal factionalism and to prevent the corruption, patronage, and inefficiency associated with its uninterrupted governance at the national level and at many local levels since the end of World War II. At the parliamentary elections held in 1983, the DC experienced its worst electoral performance, drawing 32.9 percent of the vote. Nevertheless, it still ranked above all competitors.

DC party congresses, which are convened at irregular intervals, afford a fair reflection of Italian political trends and internal Christian Democratic differences. In 1946 the first party congress formalized the role of the DC and expressed majority support for the republican form of government; this was done in anticipation of the imminent national referendum that abolished the monarchy. In 1947 a congressional majority favored the ouster of the Socialist and Communist ministers with whose parties the DC had been sharing the fortunes of the War of Liberation as well as political power since 1944. That congress may be viewed as a prelude to Italy's pro-Western alignment, which was to translate into unwavering NATO commitment. The congresses of 1949, 1952, and 1954 witnessed the intensification of DC factionalism. Those of 1956, 1959, 1962, and 1964 paved the way for and approved renewed collaboration with the Socialists, and those of 1967, 1969, and 1973 attested to the malaise of the center-left coalition with the Socialists. The congresses of 1973 and 1976 contemplated a constructive relationship with the Communist Party. Finally, those of 1979, 1982, and 1984 coincided with the return to a substantially adversary relationship with the Communists.

The Communist Party

The Italian Communist Party (Partito Comunista Italiano; PCI) was founded in 1921 as an offshoot of the Socialist Party. Forced underground or into exile by the advent of Fascism in 1922, its exponents re-emerged in 1943 and played an active role in the War of Liberation and in the drafting of the Republican Constitution. From a party of cadres, the PCI rapidly expanded into a mass party. As early as the 1946 elections for the Constituent Assembly, the PCI polled 18.9 percent of the vote, as compared to 35.2 and 20.7 percent attained by the DC and the Socialist Party, respectively. Thereafter the PCI consistently took second place to the DC in all parliamentary elections, and it progressively increased its returns to an all-time high of 34.4 percent in 1976, four percentage points behind the DC. This was an enormous leap, since it entailed an unprecedented increase of 7.2 percentage points with respect to the previous elections of 1972. However, in 1979 the PCI's share dropped to 30.4 percent and in 1983 to 29.9 percent.

Undeniably Marxist-Leninist in ideology, the PCI has also been influenced by its early leader Antonio Gramsci, who died in the 1930s. Gramsci held that the PCI should pursue a strategy aimed at the conquest of "civil society" before undertaking to control the state as a political entity. This approach explains not only the PCI's successful infiltration of structures such as the media and cultural institutions, but also its willingness to exploit formal, if not substantial, cooperation with "bourgeois" parties. Two examples are particularly significant. In 1944 Palmiro Togliatti, then PCI secretary-general, agreed to cooperate with the non-Marxist forces that participated in the anti-Nazi and anti-Fascist resistance movement, or War of Liberation. In 1973, then PCI secretary-general Enrico Berlinguer proposed a "historic compromise" between the "democratic popular forces of the nation"—in other words, between the Communist, Socialist, and Christian Democratic parties. Although the historic compromise was never consummated in terms of PCI participation in the Council of Ministers, the PCI informally participated in the decisionmaking process, particularly in the wake of its highly favorable 1976 electoral returns.

The influence of the PCI, which is the largest nonruling communist party in the world, is attributable to several factors, none of which necessarily take precedence over the rest. Simply put, the PCI is well organized, motivated, and disciplined—at least in comparison to its competitors.

The use of democratic centralism in the PCI's decisionmaking process virtually neutralizes factionalism, a characteristic that is readily apparent in the DC and to a lesser degree also plagues the other Italian parties. Moreover, the PCI expels dissenters who jeopardize party interests; most notorious is the expulsion of the Manifesto group in 1969. The PCI's capillary structure is further strengthened by a number of efficient ancillary organizations fully or largely controlled by the party.[12] They include the Italian Communist Youth Federation (Federazione Giovanile Comunista Italiana), the Union of Italian Women (Unione Donne Italiane), party-owned producers' and consumers' cooperatives, and the Italian General Confederation of Labor (Confederazione Generale Italiana del Lavoro; CGIL). The PCI also has a research, information, and training center whose wealth of data rivals that of the Ministry of the Interior. In addition to membership dues and self-financing channels traceable to the cooperatives, the PCI taxes the salaries of affiliated members of Parliament. The PCI is endowed with an enthusiastic and energetic rank and file currently in the range of 1.6 million, as opposed to the roughly equivalent but comparatively inert number of card-carrying DC members.[13]

The PCI also exploits its opposition role at the national level by capitalizing on all causes of discontent, and, when in control of local bodies of government, the party clearly strives toward providing efficient and social-services-oriented administrations. In February 1985 it held an absolute majority in the councils of 431 municipalities. The recipient of the largest number of votes from the working class, the PCI draws traditional geographical support from the so-called Red Belt, that is, the north-central regions of Emilia-Romagna, Tuscany, and Umbria. Since the mid-1970s the PCI has attempted with some success to broaden its electoral appeal by insisting on its commitment to a pluralistic society and independence from Moscow. However, its blatantly pro-Soviet record and its current ambivalence over international security matters, both of which will be discussed in subsequent chapters, understandably continue to foster distrust within the majority of the electorate.

The Socialist Party

The Italian Socialist Party (Partito Socialista Italiano; PSI) was founded in 1892.[14] It is said to possess two "souls," one doctrinaire (formerly revolutionary) and communist fellow traveler, the other reformist and autonomist. The PSI also holds the distinction of having given birth to several offshoots. Besides the PCI, the Italian Social Democratic Party and the Italian Socialist Party for Proletarian Unity are among the political formations originally part of the socialist fold.

In 1947 the PSI joined the PCI in a "unity of action pact," which failed at the national polls the following year when the two parties ran together as the Popular Democratic Front (Fronte Democratico Popolare). In the mid-1950s, particularly after the Soviet repression of Hungary's bid for freedom, the PSI began to move away from the PCI and by the early 1960s was already supporting or participating in DC-led governments. Its reunification with the Social Democratic Party during the second half of the 1960s was of brief duration. Because of its long-established status as the third largest party at the polls, the PSI is considered to be the "needle of the scale" in the formation of coalition governments. At the 1976, 1979, and 1983 parliamentary elections, it polled approximately 10 percent of the vote.

The importance of this party as a political force is attested to by the fact that PSI secretary-general Bettino Craxi is one of two non–Christian Democrats to have headed the Council of Ministers since the Constitution went into effect. After assuming PSI leadership in 1976, Craxi has been instrumental in enhancing the moderate and Western-oriented image of the party and in easing away from the more procommunist elements of the doctrinaire wing. Nevertheless, the PSI still fails to constitute a leftist alternative to the much stronger PCI.

Minor Parties

The remaining parties that enjoy nationwide support and parliamentary representation are correctly classified as minor, but they contribute nonetheless to the formation of a parliamentary majority or carry out a parliamentary opposition role. Frequently called "opinion parties" to distinguish them from the mass parties, they are as much a product of the Italian character as they are bearers of a political philosophy. Few of them poll more than 5 percent of the vote. They are often a receptacle for Italy's roving vote and, from time to time, a vehicle for the expression of discontent about the policies of the mass parties. Occasional efforts toward mergers or coalitions of minor parties as an alternative to the DC or the PCI—the two major poles of attraction in Italian politics—have borne no fruit to date.

The Italian Republican Party (Partito Repubblicano Italiano; PRI) traces its origins to a patriotic organization of the early Risorgimento called *Giovine Italia* (Young Italy) and headed by Giuseppe Mazzini, an advocate of the republican form of government for a unified Italy. Secular, progressive, and economic-policy oriented, the PRI participated in the War of Liberation and in most postwar parliamentary/governmental coalitions. In contrast to the PSI, the PRI has supported Italy's Western commitment from the start.

The Italian Liberal Party (Partito Liberale Italiano; PLI) also traces its heritage to the nineteenth century and, indeed, to the Risorgimento. Count Cavour himself was an exponent of the liberal platform of his day. The PLI, whose classic liberalism is founded on political freedom, secularism, and laissez-faire economics, is in essence a conservative party. It participated in the War of Liberation and thereafter successfully ran candidates for the Constituent Assembly as part of the National Democratic Union (Unione Democratica Nazionale) and for Parliament in 1948 as part of the Common Man's Liberal Democratic Front (Fronte Liberale Democratico dell'Uomo Qualunque). Since 1953 it has been active in politics and in Parliament under its present name. PLI participation in coalition majorities has been selective and largely conditioned by the PLI's conservative and pro-Western stance, which has clashed with PSI attitudes. Over the years, PLI electoral returns have dwindled generally to the benefit of the DC and the PRI.

The Italian Social Democratic Party (Partito Socialista Democratico Italiano; PSDI) was formed in 1947 when it broke away from the then PCI-aligned Socialist Party. Moderately leftist, the PSDI is strongly West-oriented. In 1966 it merged with the PSI, only to break away again in 1969. It has been part of most parliamentary/governmental coalitions since 1948.[15]

The Radical Party (Partito Radicale; PR) traces its recent origins to a left-wing faction that deserted the PLI in December 1955; however, its inspiration and name go back to the classical European concept of radicalism. Progressive but non-Marxist, the PR has been active in libertarian causes and has used tactics such as picketing, sit-ins, and hunger strikes to propagandize its political and civil-rights battles. Various efforts to combine forces with the PSI have failed to produce appreciable results. The PR has enjoyed a modest representation in Parliament since 1976.

Proletarian Democracy (Democrazia Proletaria; DP) is the most extremist Marxist-Leninist party currently represented in Parliament, where it won seats for the first time in 1976. It originated as an electoral front comprising several kindred groups. Although it is the longest-lived formation to the left of the PCI to enjoy parliamentary representation, DP does not constitute the first case of this nature. Its predecessors were eventually absorbed by the PCI or went on to enlarge the ranks of extraparliamentary organizations.[16]

The Italian Social Movement–National Right (Movimento Sociale Italiano–Destra Nazionale; MSI-DN) has been politically active under that denomination since 1972, when the MSI and remnants of the Italian Democratic Party for Monarchist Unity (Partito Democratico Italiano di Unità Monarchica; PDIUM) joined forces. The MSI had been founded in December 1946 by former minor officials of the deposed Fascist regime and by exponents of the short-lived Italian Social Republic. The PDIUM, on the other hand, had been the successor of the National Monarchist Party (Partito Nazionale Monarchico) founded after the abolition of the monarchy in June 1946. Frequently termed neo-Fascist because of its heritage, the MSI-DN stands on the far right of the Italian political spectrum. Though a minor party, it has consistently taken fourth place in parliamentary elections. While it continues to attract the support of the few remaining admirers of the Fascist regime, it draws its electoral strength from a variety of sources because of its professed nationalism, catholicism, anticommunism, and socioeconomic reformism. It often benefits from protest votes at the national and local levels. The MSI-DN, like the MSI and PDIUM before the merger, votes from time to time with the parliamentary majority on specific issues, but substantially constitutes the rightist opposition. In this sense, it parallels the Communist opposition role.

Also represented in Parliament are some regional parties, whose support is obviously not nationwide. The South Tyrolese Popular Party (Suedtiroler Volkspartei), which represents the Germanic ethnics in the region of Trentino-Alto Adige on the border with Austria, has been present in Parliament since 1948. In some respects, it is the local equivalent of the DC. In 1983 parliamentary seats were also won by the Sardinian Action Party (Partito Sardo d'Azione), which had not been represented in Parliament since 1948; by the Union Valdotaine (Valdaosta Union), which had already achieved representation in the 1958, 1963, and 1979 elections; and, for the first time, by the Venetian League (Lega Veneta).

Finally, there are many more parties that have repeatedly failed to obtain parliamentary seats or that make an ephemeral appearance during specific national or local elections. For example, parties that met with failure at the 1979 and 1983 parliamentary contests include the National Retirees Party, the European Labor Party, To Live Liberation, Christian Party for Social Action, Friuli (region) Movement, Slovene Union, Struggle Slate, National Tenants Party, Sicilian National Front, Sardinian Ecological Movement, Movement for the Independence of the Free Territory of Trieste, New United Left, and the Association to Increase Individual Worth. As their names often imply, they are bearers of specific class interests, ethnic/separatist aspirations, perceived moral values, or discontent with existing parties of similar ideological persuasion.

The multiparty system is largely but not exclusively attributable to the ideological fractionalization of Italian society. It is also the result of other factors, sociological as well as technical. For example, there are benefits to be derived by individuals and classes of individuals from the patronage afforded at the national and local levels by well-entrenched political parties. Proportional electoral laws, which by definition tend to make election to Parliament or to regional, provincial, and municipal councils comparatively easy, encourage the multiparty system. The large number of seats available in these bodies further enhances the chances of obtaining some representation. Under Italian electoral laws, any individual seeking election must be accepted on an existing party slate or form a new party. Moreover, a roving vote—consisting of several million ballots—from one election to the next makes it possible even for minor parties to reap unpredictable fruits.

The Public Sector

The politicization of Italian society because of ideological choice or material gain tends to create strong links between parties and other institutions whose purposes are not or should not be intrinsically political. This state of affairs broadly applies to economic organizations and, in a more subtle fashion, to professional circles.

In conformity with the decision of the Constituent Assembly to set up a mixed economy system, the Constitution states that "for purposes of public advantage, the law may reserve from the outset or may transfer . . . to the State, to public bodies, or to communities of workers or users, undertakings related to essential public services, sources of energy, or monopolies that are of outstanding public interest." [17] Today over half of the economy, including virtually all large industrial concerns and the major banks, has taken the form of state holdings.

A survey conducted in 1983 shows that the principal positions in the public sector are filled in accordance with political quotas. In industry, 51 percent of those positions were the preserve of the DC, 22 percent of the PSI, and 1.5 percent of the PCI. In banking, 74.2 percent went to the DC, 12.3 percent to the PSI, and 0.4 percent to the PCI. In the service industries, 37 percent went to the DC, 21 percent to the PSI, and 21 percent to the PCI. In the cultural field, 40, 26, and 22 percent went to the DC, PSI, and PCI, respectively. The remaining positions within those fields of the public sector were assigned to nominees supported by the less important coalition parties in different proportions.[18] Beneficiaries of this system are clearly the ruling coalition members as well as the Communist opposition.

The right to unionize freely is sanctioned by the Constitution. In a population of 14.5 million workers—almost six million white-collar and slightly less than nine million blue-collar—approximately 9.1 million are reportedly unionized, but of these only about 338,550 belong to unions unconnected to parties.[19]

Italy's major unions were founded by political parties. At the end of World War II, organized labor was concentrated in the PCI-dominated CGIL. By 1948, Christian Democrats, Socialists, and Republicans began to desert the CGIL, which nevertheless maintains to this day a Socialist minority. In 1950 the Italian Confederation of Workers' Trade Unions (Confederazione Italiana Sindacati Lavoratori; CISL) and the Italian Union of Labor (Unione Italiana del Lavoro; UIL) were formed to counteract the CGIL's hold on labor. Since then the CISL has remained close to the DC and the UIL to the PSI, PSDI, and PRI. At about the same time, the MSI gave birth to the comparatively weak Italian Confederation of National Syndicates for Workers (Confederazione Italiana Sindacati Nazionali Lavoratori; CISNAL). The CGIL is traditionally the strongest group, with a reported membership of 4,476,020 workers. The CISL and UIL claim 2,976,880 and 1,356,000 members, respectively.[20]

Ties between organized labor and political parties have increased the power of the latter, often under the guise of serving the interest of labor, and have even resulted in the attribution of a political role to the unions. Two examples are significant. The Constitution states that "the right to strike shall be exercised within the limits of the laws regulating it";[21] however, regulatory laws—unwelcome to the unions—have never been passed by Parliament, thus engendering the abuse of an instrument meant to protect the workers as the weaker party in contractual relations, not meant to serve as a weapon for political purposes, such as general strikes and solidarity strikes. Nevertheless, the CGIL in particular did carry out an important political function as a surrogate of the PCI until 1975, because previously the political climate made it impossible for the DC and its coalition partners to deal directly with the PCI.

As mentioned above, the relationship between political parties and professional circles is more subtle. Politicized members of these circles, depending on their moderate-conservative or progressive-Marxist inclination, tend to create organizations that identify themselves as "independent" or "democratic." The more prolific are the democratic ones, as exemplified by such groups as "Democratic Psychiatrists," "Democratic Physicists," "Democratic Editors," and "Democratic Journalists"; some professions emerge under both rubrics, such as "Independent Magistrates" and "Democratic Magistrates." Independent groups generally entertain links with the conservative wing of the DC and the non-Marxist opinion parties; democratic ones generally side with the PCI.

Coalition Government
and Governmental Weakness

The constitutional requirement that the government enjoy a parliamentary vote of confidence makes it necessary for the heterogeneous parliamentary forces to coalesce in order to form a voting majority. Coalition formulas since 1948 may be summarized as follows: centrist, including the DC, PLI, PSDI, and PRI, from 1948 to 1962; center-left, including the DC, PSI, PSDI, and PRI, from 1962 to 1972; a brief return to centrism in 1972–1973; resumption of the center-left coalition from 1973 to 1976; PCI support short of participation in the Council of Ministers from 1976 to 1979; and, since 1979, a pentagonal arrangement that precariously holds together the DC, PSI, PSDI, PRI, and PLI.

Participation in a parliamentary coalition does not necessarily entail party representation in the Council of Ministers, but may take the form of external support for the government or, less frequently, benevolent abstention from the vote of confidence. Appendix 2 lists the political composition of the 41 governments formed under the Republican Constitution. Notably, all prime ministers except Republican Giovanni Spadolini and Socialist Craxi have been members of the DC.

The parliamentary elections of April 1948 gave the DC an absolute majority of seats in the Chamber of Deputies (see Appendix 1) and nearly similar returns in the Senate.[22] This feat, unrivaled and unrepeated in post–World War II Italian parliamentary history, finds an explanation in the political climate of 1948, which was characterized by Stalinism, Soviet expansionist designs, the Cold War, reconstruction, and unprecedented American prestige. These international factors were matched by influential domestic ones, such as the desire for a Western style of life, the role of Christian Democratic leader and outstanding statesman Alcide De Gasperi, and the religious hold and organizational assets of the Catholic Church, which actively supported the DC.

Fully aware that the 1948 vote was the reflection of popular concern rather than the expression of a homogeneous political philosophy, Prime Minister De Gasperi opted for coalition government with the centrist parties, a formula that remained viable until 1962, even though internal coalition problems had surfaced early on. The centrist era was responsible for what has been praised as the Italian "economic miracle" and for Italy's entry into NATO and the European Economic Community, but failed to carry out suitable social programs concomitant with unprecedented industrialization, urbanization, and heavy migration from south to north.

Criticism of the centrist policies frequently overlooks the fact that they were in response to the desires of a broad electoral majority anxious to bury the memory of the deposed Fascist dictatorship and the disastrous consequences of its economic policy of autarky and military involvement in World War II on the side of Nazi Germany. This electoral majority was distrustful, at the same time, of collectivist ideologies. Centrist policies therefore stressed economic reconstruction and expansion as well as foreign trade. Because of domestic conditions, Italian aspirations for modernization and development could be achieved only by importing raw materials and exporting finished products. Cheap labor and know-how were Italy's only assets of those years, and its most realistic course of action was indeed to meet the economic demand of the international market.[23]

The *apertura a sinistra,* or opening to the left, came about through several factors: the progressive weakening of the centrist coalition even in terms of electoral returns; the perceived improvement in East-West relations during the Kennedy-Khrushchev era; the new ecumenical attitude of the Catholic Church as manifested by Pope John XXIII and the Second Vatican Council; and the increasing domestic demand for social structures and reforms. The change was accomplished by replacing as coalition partners the rigidly centrist Liberals with the Socialists, who had in the meantime renounced their opposition to NATO and withdrawn from their formal alliance at the national level with the PCI. As a gesture of goodwill toward the Socialists, the electric power plants were nationalized.

Although the opening to the left dates back to 1962, its official birth took place in 1963 with PSI participation in the Council of Ministers. The first years of the center-left coalition, 1963–1968, bore no appreciable policy changes. The desired social reforms did not come about and, ironically, the nationalization of electric energy proved to be economically unsound. On its part, the PSI emulated the DC by exploiting its privileges at the national level. In essence, the governments of this period were characterized by their inertia.

In 1968 the Italian scene was set ablaze by a Marxist-inspired "cultural revolution" propelled by the youth in the universities and subsequently in the secondary schools. Its target was the entire establishment, but traditional family discipline and the academic system turned out to be the main casualties. The demands of the students included "group exams," choice of texts and examination questions, guaranteed passing grades, diplomas, and degrees, and the establishment of political collectives in the schools. To show their strength, these students would seize school premises and perpetrate various forms of vandalism and violence. Their idols were formations such as Al Fatah and the Viet Cong and individuals such as Ho Chi Minh, Fidel Castro, and Ernesto "Che" Guevara.

The workers' "hot autumn" (*autunno caldo*) of 1969, which coincided with the expiration of the national collective bargaining agreements, can be regarded as the spillover effect of the cultural revolution. From their previously moderate stance, the unions resorted to forms of unrest ranging from political demonstrations and unbridled strikes to civil disorders and episodes of industrial sabotage and physical violence. This behavior did not cease even after substantial gains were made by labor with the signing of the new collective bargaining agreements.

Trends generated by the cultural revolution and, more so, by the "hot autumn" have been long lasting. So have their damaging effects. Over 302 million working hours were lost because of strikes in 1969; between 1970 and 1976, annual statistics ranged from losses of 103,590,000 to 177,634,000 working hours.[24] The consequent loss of productivity obviously aggravated the incidence of the 1973 oil crisis, which deeply affected the national economy because of Italy's reliance on imports for 80 percent of its energy needs. Moreover, abuses perpetrated during labor unrest were often sanctioned by politicized judges who applied Marxist-oriented "juridical sociology" to labor disputes, rather than applying the rule of law.

Under the pressure of those events, the center-left coalition awoke from its torpor. However, from 1969 through the end of its fragile cohesion in the mid-1970s, it responded to the state of siege with the passage of indiscriminate and rash reforms that damaged the (albeit obsolete) educational system, slanted labor relations in favor of salaried labor and labor unions to the detriment of the national economy, lessened the severity of criminal legislation and procedure to the detriment of law and order, reduced the efficiency of the armed forces and the police agencies, and emasculated the intelligence services. Throughout this period, the PSI systematically assumed positions adverse to the governmental coalition it was part of and frequently joined with the PCI at the regional, provincial, and municipal levels even when it was possible to form local coalitions with its national-level political partners.

The dissatisfaction of large sectors of the population over public disorder and governmental weakness was clearly expressed in the parliamentary elections of 1972, whose outcome included the near doubling of the rightist MSI-DN parliamentary seats. As a result of those elections there was a brief return to centrism in 1972–1973; however, acts of violence perpetrated by, or attributed to, the extreme right and rumors of projected Fascist coups led to the resumption of the center-left coalition with the negative consequences outlined above.

The center-left formula even failed to achieve its other alleged original aim: the isolation of the PCI. In fact, during this period the PCI improved its structures, refined its propaganda machine, and became the recipient of the protest vote at both the regional elections of 1975 and the parliamentary elections of 1976 in massive proportions that dimmed the popular discontent that had favored the right in 1972.

The numerical difficulties and political impossibility of returning to centrism or to yet another multiparty alliance including the Socialists were overcome with new and imaginative formulas. The DC, as the relative-majority party, formed a one-party government in August 1976 with the benevolent abstention from the vote of confidence by the PSI, PSDI, PRI, PLI, and PCI; the PCI was rewarded with the presidency of the Chamber of Deputies and the chairmanship of seven parliamentary committees. This accommodation was called the "no nonconfidence," or *non sfiducia*. In July 1977 the PCI advanced one more step by entering into a "programmatic agreement" with the DC and the other abstention parties. In March 1978, under the trauma of the abduction of DC president Aldo Moro by the Red Brigades, the DC, PSI, PSDI, PRI, and—for the first time since 1947—PCI coalesced into a parliamentary majority (exclusive of the PLI) that gave birth to another all–Christian Democratic Council of Ministers.

The collaboration with the PCI, which came to be known as the second opening to the left, turned out to be short-lived. This was because of the anomalous power-sharing within the alliance, the objective difficulty of keeping together an even more discordant political alliance than the ones entered into previously, and, ultimately, the 1979 parliamentary electoral returns—confirmed by those of 1983—that set PCI support back to pre-1976 levels.

Numerical considerations as well as the ostensible absence of other solutions account for the coalition that exists as of mid-1986. It has been in force since 1979 and encompasses the DC, PSI, PRI, PSDI, and PLI. The fact that this coalition, like all preceding ones, has been kept together by several succeeding governments is indicative of its precarious equilibrium.[25]

The Decisionmaking Process and Its Participants

The complexity of Italy's system of government, coupled with the presence of heterogeneous political forces and their ancillary organizations, weigh heavily on the decisionmaking process, which all too frequently occurs outside of the constitutionally prescribed organs of government.

Parliamentary coalitions—needed not only to express the vote of confidence for Italy's chronically unstable governments but also for the passage of legislation—are formed by way of interparty agreements well before any coalition or voting bloc materializes on the floor of either chamber of Parliament. The same can be said with respect to decisions that constitutionally belong to the Council of Ministers.[26] Party headquarters are therefore a natural stage for ideological compromise and political barter over legislation as well as over policies that often clash with campaign promises made to the electorate.[27] However, the most typical interparty agreements address the distribution of ministerial posts and undersecretariatships (whose number frequently increases to satisfy the demands of all coalition participants), parliamentary committee chairmanships, and directorships and top managerial positions of public entities. The division of the spoils must also take into account the demands of individual factions within each party. It is incidentally worth noting that factions of one party often ally themselves with other parties, rather than with other factions of their own party, to achieve certain political results.[28]

Prior to 1969, the three principal labor unions—CGIL, CISL, and UIL—had respected the wall of separation between the role of government and their own; after the "hot autumn," however, they became participants in the political decisionmaking process to the point of being dubbed "the second branch of government." Labor legislation has since been preliminarily agreed upon with them, and periodic meetings have been held between the government and these unions to discuss policy matters. In March 1980 their representatives were received by the president to address the topic of unemployment. These labor unions, just like the political parties, now have a voice in the appointment of a large number of board directors of public entities with decisive influence on economic policies, given the above-noted expansion of state holdings in Italy.[29]

Conversely, the influence exercised by the Catholic Church in the political sphere has dramatically diminished. The first substantive indication of the secularization of Italian society emerged in 1974, when the DC promoted a referendum to repeal the divorce legislation enacted four years earlier. Almost 60 percent of the electorate voted in favor of its retention. Similarly, in 1981 a majority of the electorate voted against the repeal of the recently enacted abortion law. Current statistics further attest to the waning hold of the Church on the population, over 90 percent of which is nominally Catholic. In 1984 the average family consisted of the parents and not quite two children (statistical average: 1.5); 15,000 divorces took place, as opposed to 700 Canon Law annulments. Moreover, 1985 statistical findings reflect that only 30.8 percent of the population attends Sunday Mass and an even lower percentage, 14.7, is willing to contribute to Church support.[30] Notably, the new agreement of November 15, 1984, which amended the Lateran Agreements of 1929 between Italy and the Holy See, limits Church support by the state to 0.8 percent of the personal income tax; this money must be specifically designated for that purpose by the individual taxpayer. The waning influence of the Church has been accompanied by that of the family, which was formerly the other cohesive factor in Italian society.

Migrations from south to north and from rural areas to the cities during the post–World War II reconstruction and industrial expansion era brought about profound changes in the make-up of the country. Statistics are eloquent. In 1958–1963, over five million people left their original residence area. Between 1951 and 1981, the agricultural sector lost five million workers, while the industrial and the other sectors of the economy acquired 1.9 and 5.4 million more workers, respectively.[31] The resulting urban congestion was accompanied by shortages of dwellings, schools, hospitals, and overall social services. Subsequently, even the new employment opportunities in industry and commerce dwindled. This metropolitan state of affairs, which remains to be fully cured, generated notable material discontent and psychological apprehension. Moreover, the uprooting of society also caused the near disintegration of the traditional extended-family structure, which had served as a source of material as well as moral support.

Departure from traditional values—particularly the religious ones, but also those pertaining to the family as an institution—contributes to the loss of ground by the DC. It can no longer effectively count on its former pillars of support: Catholic Action, the Civic Committees (Comitati Civici), and even spiritually kindred labor or trade organizations such as the Christian Associations of Italian Workers (Associazioni Cristiane dei Lavoratori Italiani; ACLI), the CISL, and the General Confederation of Agriculture (Confederazione Generale dell'Agricoltura). In fact, the CISL generally pursues common objectives with the PCI-oriented CGIL and the secular UIL, while the ACLI often embraces radical causes. The DC's relative-majority standing today is therefore only partially due to its confessional character. More incisive factors are the fear of communism[32] and the DC's patronage capability at the central and local levels of government.

The continuing absence of a homogeneous and solid parliamentary majority, accompanied by endemic governmental instability, can be expected to perpetuate a system whose viability rests upon ideological, political, and material accommodation in direct contrast with the democratic spirit of Italy's Republican Constitution and electoral laws. Moreover, this state of affairs adversely affects societal relations and increases the country's vulnerability to criminal and subversive designs.

CHAPTER TWO

Law Enforcement and National Defense

Law-Enforcement Agencies

In Italy, crime prevention and law enforcement are a primary responsibility of the Ministry of the Interior, which statutorily serves as the leading agency in this field. Decentralization is accomplished with the appointment of a prefect in each of Italy's 95 provinces. The prefect represents the Ministry of the Interior and the central government locally in a variety of administrative matters, including crime prevention and law enforcement. Another key official at the provincial level is the police superintendent (*questore*), who is subordinate to the prefect and is specifically responsible for police matters.[1]

In addition to municipal police forces, whose tasks generally encompass traffic control and comparatively minor administrative matters, Italy has five national police forces with countrywide functions. They are: (1) the State Police (Polizia di Stato); (2) the Carabinieri (Arma dei Carabinieri or Carabinieri Arm, but normally referred to simply as Carabinieri in the plural); (3) the Finance Guard (Guardia di Finanza); (4) the Confinement Police (Corpo degli Agenti di Custodia); and (5) the Forestry Police (Corpo Forestale dello Stato).

The State Police, formerly a militarized police force called Public Security (Pubblica Sicurezza), is the law-enforcement branch of the Ministry of the Interior. A number of central offices and specialized units of the State Police operate under the immediate supervision of the ministry itself, whereas decentralized offices and units are directed by the provincial police superintendents and other subordinate officials, all of whom are employees of the same ministry. In addition to multiple police duties, the State Police is specifically tasked with the issuance and control of police-related administrative licenses and permits.

The Carabinieri, Italy's military police, are vested with both military and civil jurisdiction. With respect to organizational structure, personnel management, and military duties, the Carabinieri constitute an integral element of the Italian Armed Forces. In the exercise of civil jurisdiction, the Carabinieri have full police powers over the civilian population throughout the national territory. For purposes of law enforcement, the Carabinieri have a pyramidal, territorial structure, to which 80 percent of the force is assigned. Headed by the general headquarters in Rome, the territorial echelons include three divisions—in northern, central, and southern Italy, respectively—with subordinate brigades, legions, groups, lieutenancies, and stations. In the vast majority of cases, there is one legion in each region and one group in each province.[2] There is at least one Carabinieri station in nearly all municipalities. Companies and lieutenancies generally constitute intermediate headquarters between the provincial and municipal echelons.

As opposed to the State Police and the Carabinieri, whose law-enforcement responsibilities are quite broad, the Finance Guard is specifically tasked with the prevention and repression of crimes related to tax evasion. The Finance Guard operates under the direction of the Ministry of Finance and has a pyramidal structure similar to that of the Carabinieri's territorial organization.

The two smaller national police forces are the Confinement Police and the Forestry Police. Like the Finance Guard, they too have a specific law-enforcement mission. The Confinement Police operates penitentiaries under the direction of the Ministry of Justice. The Forestry Police, under the direction of the Ministry of Agriculture and Forestry, carries out functions similar to those of the U.S. Park Police.

Because of the statutory role of the Ministry of the Interior, this ministry—and its subordinate officials at the provincial level—exercises operational control over all national police forces when conducting public order, security, and safety functions.[3] However, those elements of the national police forces tasked with the investigation and repression of crimes operate under the direction of the judiciary. In the performance of this mission, such elements are termed "judicial police" (*polizia giudiziaria*), which is a police function rather than a police force. The same term also refers to the professional status of law-enforcement personnel as judicial police officers and agents.[4]

Intelligence and Security Services

Italy's intelligence and security services are currently governed by a reform law that was enacted in October 1977.[5] Major factors behind the reform include the actual, alleged, and/or perceived abuses of intelligence and security functions by key personnel and/or political patrons of the former services—the Armed Forces Intelligence Service (Servizio Informazioni Forze Armate), in existence from 1949 to 1965, and the Defense Intelligence Service (Servizio Informazioni Difesa; SID), its successor, in existence from 1965 to 1978.

The 1977 reform introduced four major innovations: (1) a more stringent supervision of the intelligence and security services by the Council of Ministers and, for the first time, oversight by Parliament; (2) the creation of two separate services—the Service for Military Intelligence and Security (Servizio Informazioni Sicurezza Militare; SISMI) and the Service for Intelligence and Democratic Security (Servizio Informazioni Sicurezza Democratica; SISDE); (3) separation of intelligence and security functions from law-enforcement functions; and (4) new regulations governing state secrecy.

Pursuant to the reform law, the intelligence system now works in the following manner. The prime minister, who is responsible for intelligence and security policies, supervises the newly instituted services with the assistance of the Interministerial Committee on Intelligence and Security (Comitato Interministeriale sulle Informazioni e la Sicurezza; CIIS), consisting of the ministers of foreign affairs, the interior, justice, defense, industry, and finance. The two services, SISMI and SISDE, are coordinated by the Executive Committee for the Intelligence and Security Services (CESIS), which is chaired by the prime minister or an under secretary delegated by him. The composition of CESIS is determined by the prime minister, except for the SISMI and SISDE directors, who are both statutory members. The structure of CESIS includes a general secretariat headed by a public official of the highest administrative rank, who is appointed by the prime minister with consultation of the CIIS.

SISMI is responsible for all intelligence and security functions pertaining to military defense, including collection and counterespionage. It is subordinate to the minister of defense, who exercises supervision in accordance with the directives of the prime minister and appoints SISMI's director, subject to the concurring opinion of the CIIS. SISMI must keep both the minister of defense and CESIS abreast of all intelligence information and analyses in its possession and of all its operations.

SISMI's internal structure, which is delegated to the minister of defense, is believed to comprise the office of the director and the secretariat, the office of the deputy director, operational offices/divisions tasked with collection, counterintelligence, and analysis, and support offices/divisions tasked with matters pertaining to personnel, finance, communications, science/technology, logistics, security control, and foreign affairs. The collection office/division reportedly has subordinate stations abroad, whereas the counterintelligence office/division has decentralized offices within the national territory.[6]

SISDE is responsible for all intelligence and security functions pertaining to the preservation of democracy and the protection of the institutions established by Italy's Republican Constitution of 1948. It is subordinate to the minister of the interior, whose duties and prerogatives in relation to SISDE are analogous to those of the minister of defense in relation to SISMI. SISDE is subject to the same reporting requirement incumbent upon SISMI, and the internal structures of the two are also reportedly similar.[7]

Personnel assigned to CESIS, SISMI, and SISDE may not hold or retain the status of judicial police officers or agents for the duration of their assignment. However, the directors of the services must report—to the pertinent organs of the judicial police—information and evidence that could constitute criminal offenses. Delay in so doing is permissible only with the consent of the prime minister when necessary to perform institutional functions. On their part, law-enforcement officers having judicial police functions must cooperate with the intelligence and security services.

The Council of Ministers must report in writing every six months to Parliament as a whole on the intelligence and security policies as well as on their results. The parliamentary oversight committee monitors the application of the principles set forth in the reform law and is entitled to request basic information on the structure and activities of the services from the prime minister and the CIIS. Whenever the prime minister uses the power to claim the need for state secrecy, which must be briefly substantiated, the parliamentary oversight committee may refer the matter to each chamber of Parliament for the necessary political evaluation.

Though not directly governed by the intelligence reform law, Italy's intelligence community includes additional organs that are part of the armed forces and of the law-enforcement agencies. Each one of the three services— army, navy, and air force—has its own Operational Analytical Intelligence Service (Servizio Informazioni Operativo Situazione), whose limited mission, as opposed to SISMI's, combines elements of strategic intelligence, combat intelligence, and security. The Carabinieri and the Finance Guard have organic offices concerned with police intelligence and security. Other intelligence and security functions are carried out by the Ministry of the Interior through central and decentralized offices/divisions.

The Military

Italy's peaceful intentions toward the community of nations are consecrated in its Constitution of 1948. Article 11, which is part of the introductory *Fundamental Principles*, specifically states:

> Italy repudiates war as an instrument aimed at violating the liberty of other peoples and as a means of resolving international disputes; consents, under

conditions of equality with the other States, to the limitations of sovereignty necessary [to establish] a system that insures peace and justice among Nations; promotes and favors international organizations that have said purpose.

This declaration of principle is complemented by Article 52: "The defense of the Fatherland is a sacred duty of citizenship. Military service is obligatory in accordance with the limits and modalities established by law ... The organization of the armed forces must respect the democratic spirit of the Republic."

These two articles are largely the product of the historical climate in which the Constitution was drafted. Despite pronounced ideological differences among themselves, all political forces represented at the Constituent Assembly of 1946–1947 had participated in the resistance movement against the Fascist regime, which they unanimously held responsible for having suppressed democracy in Italy for over twenty years and for having caused unjust bloodshed and destruction abroad with the seizure of Ethiopia, the annexation of Albania, the intervention in the Spanish Civil War in support of the Falangist forces, and the aggressive role in World War II on the side of Nazi Germany.

Ties to the West

In 1949, one year after the Constitution went into effect, the Italian government, headed by Christian Democratic prime minister Alcide De Gasperi, was among the twelve original signatories of the North Atlantic Treaty. However, notwithstanding the purely defensive nature of the treaty, the process of ratification by the two chambers of Parliament was a hurdle that the government overcame with difficulty, not only because of the Communist and Socialist opposition but also because of the fears of the parliamentary majority coalition that Italy might be drawn into yet another undesired military conflict.

Although the Italian government has never wavered in its ideological commitment to the West, the historical and political climates referred to above have contributed in a lasting manner to Italy's low-key participation in NATO from 1949 through the end of the 1970s. In fact, Italy's defense budget has consistently been one of the lowest in the Atlantic Alliance. In terms of per capita military spending, only Luxembourg, Portugal, and Turkey generally rank behind Italy. (Iceland, though a member of NATO, has no military forces and therefore no military budget.) Moreover, in terms of gross national product, only Denmark and Luxembourg have a record of lower defense spending than Italy.

Italy's most significant contribution to the Alliance lies, rather, in the availability of its territory for the establishment of important NATO headquarters and installations. In this respect, a U.S. Senate report defines Italy as "essential to military control of the Mediterranean."[8] Major NATO facilities on the Italian peninsula include the headquarters of the Allied Forces Southern Europe in Naples and of the Allied Land Forces Southern Europe in Verona, the homebase of the Fifth Allied Tactical Air Force in Vicenza, and ten Air Defense Ground Environment early warning sites in select strategic areas from North to South. U.S. troops and equipment tasked with NATO and/or mutual security missions are also stationed in Italy, and the ports of Naples and Gaeta house major support complexes for the U.S. Sixth Fleet and its flagship, respectively. Finally, as of March 1984, a NATO cruise-missile installation became operational in Comiso, Sicily.

In addition to placing its territory at the disposal of NATO, Italy has been a participant in the Defense Planning Committee and the Nuclear Planning Group. Its armed forces have also been tasked with two NATO missions. The army and air force are responsible for defending the northeastern frontier of the peninsula, while the navy contributes to the protection of the Mediterranean communication routes and provides antisubmarine and antiair warfare capabilities in the waters and straits of the peninsula. These missions, however, entail substantially circumscribed area defense.

Consistent with its peaceable attitudes, Italy has always refused to consider the adoption of a national nuclear capability for military purposes. In fact, in January 1969 the Italian government signed the Nuclear Non-Proliferation Agreement, which was subsequently ratified by Parliament in April 1975.[9] Moreover, Italy has renounced all resort to chemical and biological weapons.

Likewise, through the end of the 1970s the Italian military role outside of national territory was hardly noticeable. Pursuant to a U.N. fiduciary mandate, Italy maintained a task force in its former colony of Somaliland (currently Somalia) from 1950 to 1960. Besides insuring that African country's orderly transition to national independence, the military police element of the Italian task force was specifically responsible for training the Somalia police force. Over a partially overlapping period of time, Italy participated—always under the authority of the United Nations—in the Korean War by sending a field hospital unit. Toward the end of the 1970s Italian military policy, though unquestionably still respectful of constitutional dictates, assumed a more visible and indeed more dynamic role not only within NATO itself but also in a broader Mediterranean context.

The Mission of the Armed Forces

Current defense policy assigns to the Italian armed forces five basic missions that substantially coincide with Italy's role in NATO: (1) defense of the northeastern frontier; (2) defense of the southern air and maritime frontiers and sea communications; (3) air defense; (4) territorial defense; and (5) peacekeeping, security, and civil-protection operations.[10]

Defense of the northeastern frontier is particularly sensitive, since a potential attack by the Soviet Union and its Warsaw Pact satellite against Italy or NATO's entire southern flank would assign priority to this geographical sector. According to NATO estimates, ten Soviet and Hungarian divisions, including approximately 2,340 tanks and 1,560 artillery pieces, are earmarked for deployment against Italy's northeastern frontier. Those forces are reinforceable by seven divisions, including 2,000 tanks and 1,300 artillery pieces, stationed in the Kiev Military District. The Italian military effort in this sector is principally an army and air force responsibility.

The southern sector is also important because of Italy's peninsular position, with a coastline of over 8,000 kilometers, and the country's dependence on maritime transportation for the supply of indispensable raw materials. The mission of the Italian armed forces, which in this sector is primarily a navy and air force responsibility, is to keep open the sea lanes, control and protect the merchant marine traffic, and defend the coast from potential enemy sea landing and airborne operations.

The third mission calls for air defense in the strict sense, that is, neutralization of enemy aircraft while in flight before they reach their objectives on Italian territory; it also calls for counterair, that is, neutralization of enemy aircraft even before takeoff. Air superiority, though limited in space and time, is considered to be a prerequisite for the conduct of all military operations: land, naval, and air. In this context air defense in particular is interrelated with all other assigned missions. It encompasses aircraft, missile, and artillery systems.

The territorial defense mission entails the defense of all national and insular territory with the exception of the northeastern sector—in other words, defense of the communications zone that, in case of war, would support the Italian armed forces operating in the northeastern and southern sectors and in the Mediterranean Sea. This area could even become an objective of secondary actions during conflicts in the Mediterranean region not directly involving Italy. Territorial defense is principally, but not exclusively, an army responsibility.

The fifth and final mission addresses peacekeeping, security, and civil-protection operations. Security operations bordering on collective defense include Italian participation in NATO's standing Allied Mobile Force and Naval On-Call Force Mediterranean. Civil-protection tasks call for military assistance during the organizational and execution phases of relief operations in response to natural calamities such as floods and earthquakes. As opposed to security and civil protection, peacekeeping operations represent a recent defense-policy development that has afforded the armed forces unprecedented visibility in post–World War II Italy. Operations of this nature began in 1979 in collaboration with other governments or under the aegis of the United Nations.

Italian contingents have taken part in the U.N. Interim Forces in Lebanon since July 26, 1979; in the multinational peacekeeping force in Lebanon from August 26 to September 12, 1982, and again from September 26, 1982, to February 26, 1984;[11] in the Multinational Force and Observers—whose administrative headquarters are in Rome—on the Sinai Peninsula since April 25, 1982;[12] and in the multinational minesweeping operations in the Red Sea from August 22 to October 7, 1984.

In conjunction with Italy's defense and security posture of recent years, reference must also be made to the Treaty of September 15, 1980, between Italy and Malta, pursuant to which the former committed itself to protect the neutrality of the latter. Most significant, however, is Italy's support for the 1979 NATO decision to modernize the European theater nuclear force in response to the deployment of the Soviet SS-20 missiles; this modernization includes the deployment of 112 cruise missiles in Italy. The selection of the Sicilian town of Comiso (Ragusa) as the pertinent missile site was subsequently made by the Italian Council of Ministers on August 7, 1981, and part of the overall number of cruise missiles to be deployed in Comiso became operational in March 1984.[13]

CHAPTER THREE

Domestic Terrorism

What is terrorism? Neither the Italian Criminal Code nor its complementary statutes define this crime. There is, nevertheless, sufficient consensus among Italian police officials, prosecutors, and judges to the effect that terrorism constitutes politically motivated violence perpetrated by clandestine organizations. This working definition, which is particularly applicable to the Italian experience, effectively differentiates terrorism from other forms of criminal behavior, specifically common crime and political violence in its broadest connotation.

It is in fact political motivation that sets terrorism apart from common crime; perpetration of the latter usually reflects economic goals or uncontrolled instincts and emotions. The same criterion differentiates terrorism from organized crime, which is nothing other than a more sophisticated manifestation of common crime in the economic sphere. Concurrently, the clandestine nature of terrorism's structures and dynamics distinguishes it from ordinary political violence, whose perpetration follows an overt process. Notably, the degeneration of political rivalry or ideological discordance into violent clashes between adversary groups lacks the covert characteristics peculiar to terrorism. The same holds true with respect to the violent behavior of a politically motivated mob, notwithstanding its potential terrorizing effect. Though related, political violence and terrorism are not synonymous terms.

Factors and Precedents

Political violence in its broadest connotation is deeply embedded in Italian history. The twentieth century began with the assassination of King Umberto I by anarchist Gaetano Bresci, who simply walked up to the monarch's carriage and shot him. In the aftermath of World War I, bloody clashes took place in Italy's major urban centers between the followers of Mussolini's Fascist doctrines and militants of the Socialist and Communist parties. Between the rise and fall of the Fascist regime, Benito Mussolini himself was the target of a number of abortive assassination attempts. Yet even after the restoration of democracy, the tactics of violence continued to attract a variety of political groups on both the right and the left.

Terrorism, however, is a more recent phenomenon. That is, it is more recent in the sense of serving as an intermediate step toward revolution. Although the student and labor unrest of the late 1960s acted as a catalyst, terrorism is the end product of a combination of factors, environmental as well as cultural. Environmental factors include societal inadequacies, political contradictions, and governmental instability, all of which have been addressed above.

Whereas these three interrelated factors undeniably produce a fertile environment for discontent and the formulation of extremist solutions, they are not sufficient by themselves to bring about terrorism. To these factors must therefore be added a fourth and overriding one: the presence of a subversive and revolutionary culture, which has been part of the Italian scene—albeit in dissimilar proportions—on both the rightist and leftist poles of the political spectrum.

The Constitution bars the "reorganization, in any form whatsoever, of the dissolved Fascist party."[1] This dictate was subsequently implemented with the passage of ordinary laws establishing pertinent penalties. Despite these legislative enactments, a small minority of the population, including individuals who experienced life under the Fascist regime and younger elements lacking direct knowledge thereof, continued to cling to Fascist doctrines and even attempted to set up suitable structures in order to orchestrate the restoration of a Fascist-inspired system of government.

In fact, well before the outburst of contemporary terrorism, elements of the rightist Italian Social Movement (MSI) periodically conspired to transform that party, its youth branch (Fronte della Gioventù), and/or its subordinate structures into revolutionary formations. As these designs failed, expulsions and desertions from the MSI followed. Right-wing extremists also created for the same purpose organizations lacking an official connection with the MSI or its youth branch. Principal organizations of this nature include New Order (Ordine Nuovo; ON), founded in 1953 as an offshoot of the MSI, and National Vanguard (Avanguardia Nazionale; AN), founded in 1962.[2] However, until the outburst of contemporary terrorism in the late 1960s, right-wing extremism generally entailed open violent clashes with, and "punitive" or "retaliatory" raids against, leftist counterparts. These practices are reminiscent of the *squadrismo*, or "squad tactics," associated with the precursors of the defunct Fascist regime.

Because of a greater numerical following and better organizational ability, the leftist revolutionary milieu—whose matrix is Marxist-Leninist—has been more menacing than the rightists through the decades. Until the early 1960s the Italian Communist Party (PCI) was virtually its sole apostle, although it can be argued that only a minority of the Communist leadership and rank and file planned, carried out, was aware of, or condoned unlawful actions.[3] In practice, however, various forms of political violence and sporadic terrorist acts were perpetrated by elements of communist inspiration long before the current wave of terrorism.

One of the goals of communist participation in the resistance movement or War of Liberation of 1943–1945 had been the creation of an Italian Soviet republic. When the war came to an end without ushering in the desired regime, many communist partisans stored their weapons away for future opportunities. Other groups formed paramilitary and more-or-less covert structures parallel to the official PCI organization.

Reliable estimates indicate that between 13,000 and 30,000 persons were summarily executed in Italy in the name of "popular justice" during the six-month period following April 25, 1945—Liberation Day from Nazi-Fascism.[4] A large number of these murders occurred in the Milan area and in the Emilia-Romagna region, both characterized by an appreciable presence of communist partisans. Only a fraction of the victims may properly be considered Fascist criminals. The remainder were simply "class enemies." Their nameless corpses could be found at dawn abandoned along the road. In other cases, at times involving entire families, the corpses were recovered years later. Additional victims were either wounded or subjected to degrading "punishments."[5]

The most notorious of the communist paramilitary units was the Red Strike Force (Volante Rossa), which operated out of Gallarate (Milan province) from 1945 through 1949 under the guise of a recreational/athletic organization utilizing PCI premises. In addition to personnel and weapons, it had uniforms, identification cards, and even a banner and an anthem. The Red Strike Force murdered or otherwise "punished" enemies such as former Fascists and industrialists. At least twice it acted openly. On November 28, 1947, the Prefecture of Milan was seized and access thereto was forcibly blocked by communist and socialist demonstrators—including former partisans mobilized regionwide for the occasion—in order to protest against the decision of the Rome government to remove the last of the prefects originally appointed by the Liberation forces. Other actions were taken by the Red Strike Force in the days following the July 14, 1948, abortive attempts on the life of then–PCI secretary-general Palmiro Togliatti by rightist student Antonio Pallante.[6]

The attempt on Togliatti also led to the retrieval of hidden weapons and to insurrectional activity by a large number of PCI activists that lasted three days. Public buildings and factories were seized and the red flag was hoisted, Christian Democratic and Social Democratic party offices were devastated, barricades were raised, and the police forces were assaulted with firearms and hand grenades. The most seriously affected provinces were those in the North.[7] In terms of human suffering, this insurrection caused twenty deaths and approximately 600 injuries.[8]

Throughout these early years of the Republic, the PCI disclaimed party involvement with violent and unlawful formations. Yet its actions were, to say the least, ambivalent. For example, PCI lawyers generally represented former partisans on trial for the aggressions committed in the aftermath of Liberation Day.[9] The Red Strike Force was deployed during the Sixth Party Congress of 1948 to provide security and even served as an escort for French Communist Party secretary-general Maurice Thorez and the Soviet delegates.[10] The seizure of the Milan Prefecture was led by then–regional secretary Giancarlo Pajetta, now a member of the national leadership.[11] On the evening following the attack on Togliatti, Luigi Longo, who later became his successor, declared: "Let's see how things go. If the protest wave increases, we will allow it to increase. If it decreases, we will block it." The next day, Longo and fellow hard-liner Pietro Secchia stated before the party's central committee: "The insurgent forces are concentrated in the large cities of the North, but even in the North the campaign is not certain; communications among the cities would be uncertain. The rank and file are saying: 'We have the factories in our hands; we have the cities in our hands.' Let the comrades reflect: for the time being neither the police nor the army has intervened. If they will do so, they will have cannon and tanks against which it is impossible to resist."[12]

In the early 1960s, notable political violence erupted once again in the cities. In the summer of 1960, the Council of Ministers headed by Christian Democrat Fernando Tambroni, who had accepted the parliamentary support of the MSI, resigned under the pressure of communist-inspired disorder in Genoa, Licata, Rome, Reggio Emilia, Palermo, and Catania. Clashes with the police caused eight deaths and several hundred injuries. In Genoa alone, where the MSI had attempted to hold its party congress, 162 policemen and 40 leftist rioters were wounded on June 30, 1960.[13] Two years later, in July 1962, new unrest broke out in Turin in the industrial sector. Executive employees were physically prevented from going to work and clashes with the police followed. The Turin uprising, as it has been called, was largely the work of the new and less politically disciplined urban proletariat, even though PCI leaders, including Pajetta, were present among the demonstrators. As in the past, the PCI denied party responsibility for the violence.[14]

The Turin uprising coincided by and large with the emergence of new groups to the left of the PCI. Between 1961 and 1967 a plurality of revolution-oriented organizations revolved around such periodicals as *Quaderni Rossi* (Red notebooks), *Quaderni Piacentini* (Piacenza notebooks), *Classe Operaia* (Workers' class), *Giovane Critica* (Young criticism), *Falce e Martello* (Sickle and hammer), *Classe e Stato* (Class and state), *La Sinistra* (The left), *La Voce Operaia* (The workers' voice), *La Classe* (The class), and *Nuovo Impegno* (New commitment). These groups, whose attitudes toward the parliamentary parties ranged from polemical to hostile, contributed to the revolutionary culture out of which student and labor unrest of the late 1960s and, ultimately, contemporary Italian terrorism were born.

The Emergence of Contemporary Terrorism

Contemporary Italian terrorism does not have an official date of birth. Its emergence closely coincides with the opposition to the establishment and to the system itself, which was expressed for the first time on a large scale through extraparliamentary or noninstitutional channels in the late 1960s and early 1970s. As noted above, the so-called cultural revolution in Italy exploded in the universities in 1968 and its contagion on labor, the "hot autumn," came about the following year. In response to the Marxist-Leninist slant of this phenomenon, actions were called by the less numerous but equally revolution-oriented rightist milieu.

What could otherwise have been a peaceful national renovation process was marred from the start by violence and unlawfulness. Between 1969 and 1971, 83,327 crimes were committed in the course of public demonstrations or were, in any case, motivated by political designs.[15] An integral part of this climate was the birth and infancy of contemporary Italian terrorism.

To understand its growth and vitality, particular attention must be devoted to the ideological components of the terrorist spectrum and to the principal terrorist formations within each ideological component. Worth noting preliminarily are the statistical incidence and trends of the phenomenon as a whole.

As opposed to less than 150 terrorist incidents recorded in 1968, several hundred per year took place between 1969 and 1975, over 1,000 in 1976, and over 2,000 per year from 1977 to 1979. A downward yearly trend ranging from over one thousand to several hundred incidents has been recorded thereafter, but the annual number of serious incidents—that is, murders and woundings—has remained relatively constant. In this respect,

TABLE 3.1

TERRORIST INCIDENTS, 1968–1985

Year	All Incidents	Murders	Woundings	Abduction
1968	147	—	—	—
1969	398	17	96	—
1970	363	2	3	1
1971	514	4	14	—
1972	580	2	11	2
1973	422	40	73	4
1974	590	27	166	4
1975	682	5	19	5
1976	1,203	8	11	1
1977	2,067	10	45	1
1978	2,498	25	74	1
1979	2,384	22	149	—
1980	1,275	120	288	1
1981	862	26	71	5
1982	628	26	85	1
1983	421	2	16	—
1984	339	19	134	—
1985	426	20	147	—
TOTALS	15,799	375	1,402	26

however, allowances must be made for the increasing incidence of major acts of transnational terrorism on Italian territory since 1980, a matter that raises the issue of international connections; this will be treated at length in Chapter 7.

Table 3.1 reports the official annual statistics pertaining to all terrorist incidents and to specific categories of terrorism-motivated crimes recorded in Italy from 1968 through 1985.

Also worth noting is the conventional labeling of domestic terrorism as leftist or rightist, even though a larger number of more narrowly classifiable components is discernable. The leftist-rightist distinction stems from practical considerations. On the one hand, it facilitates the compilation of statistics, chronologies, and other data lists; on the other, it is objectively difficult to draw a rigid line of demarcation between terrorist formations whose ideologies and/or objectives at times overlap. Considerations of this nature explain why official reports abide by that conventional distinction.

The Terrorist Left

Nearly all terrorist formations of the left profess the Marxist-Leninist faith and pursue strictly communist goals, regardless of the nature of their physical or material targets. The remaining groups intertwine Marxism-Leninism with other political goals that range from anarchism to pacifism and from internationalism to feminism. Equally inspired by Marxist-Leninist dogma are the terrorist formations that seek Sardinian independence from Italy. Out of 297 leftist formations that have claimed responsibility for terrorist attacks, 259 are classifiable as strictly communist, twelve as anarchist, five as ecological/antinuclear/pacifist, seven as internationalist, six as feminist, and eight as separatist.

Although the terrorist left as a whole has displayed considerable capability in perpetuating itself despite internal discordance and schism, on the one hand, and defections and successful law-enforcement operations, on the other, only a few formations reflect continuity. Foremost among the latter are the Red Brigades (Brigate Rosse; BR), characterized by their resiliency and ability to absorb less viable formations. In fact, the BR are normally referred to as an "organization," in contrast to the term "formation" that categorizes terrorist bands more loosely held together.

The Red Brigades.   The BR are an offshoot of the Metropolitan Political Collective (Collettivo Politico Metropolitano; CPM) of Milan, which was founded on September 8, 1969. The avowed objective of the CPM was to set up "indispensable work structures to solve in a nonindividual manner the necessary problem of the revolutionary organization in the metropolis." [16] The CPM published a series of so-called struggle sheets; twice these were titled *Proletarian Left* (Sinistra Proletaria), which, by July 1970, became the new name of the CPM.

On November 1, 1969, well before this development took place, leading members of the CPM and other extremists from various areas of the country had met at the Stella Maris, a Catholic facility in Chiavari (Genoa), under the pretext of holding a conference sponsored by the Catholic organization Student Youth (Gioventù Studentesca). On this occasion Renato Curcio, reputedly the principal founder of the BR, proposed recourse to the armed struggle. In the months that followed, divergent views arose between those who favored less violent social clashes and those who regarded the armed struggle as the main road toward communism. A second conference, held in October 1970, marked the final split between the two factions. That same month a Proletarian Left struggle sheet announced the official birth of the BR, which adopted as their symbol an unevenly traced five-pointed star.

A widely held misconception stresses the Catholic roots of what is known as the historic nucleus of the BR. The nucleus consisted of seventeen members of diverse origins, but whose common denominator was Marx-ism-Leninism. These founding fathers, most of whom first banded together in the CPM or in Proletarian Left, had previously been active in extrapar-liamentary groups during their student days in the sociology department of the University of Trent, in the Italian Communist Youth Federation of Reggio Emilia, or in the extremist Study Groups (Gruppi di Studio) and Rank-and-File Unitary Committees (Comitati Unitari di Base) of the major Milan factories. In fact, the latter two—together with other student-worker groups of the left—constituted the backbone of the CPM.

The group from Trent comprised Renato Curcio, Margherita "Mara" Cagol, who later became his wife, and Giorgio Semeria, the reputed inventor of the BR's complex logistical structure. Curcio was illegitimate and had actually been raised by his Protestant mother, but he married Mara in a Catholic church. Before joining the CPM, he was a militant of the Marxist-Leninist Communist Party of Italy (Partito Comunista d'Italia–Marxista-Leninista) of Maoist observance. The group from Reggio Emilia consisted of Alberto Franceschini, Prospero Gallinari, Lauro Azzolini, Roberto Ognibene, Fabrizio Pelli, and Tonino Loris Paroli, all former militants of the youth federation of the PCI, except for the very young Ognibene, whose family background was nonetheless communist. The third group was made up of individuals who had sundry leftist extraparliamentary experiences. Some of them, such as Paolo Maurizio Ferrari, had also received a Catholic upbringing; others, such as Pietro Morlacchi, had been associated with the PCI. Of particular importance among the members of this group was Mario Moretti, who until his capture in 1981 was responsible for the BR's international connections.

The BR's communist ideology and objectives are no mystery. As far back as the 1969 Chiavari conference, Curcio had stated: "The city must become a treacherous terrain for the enemy, for the men who exercise today an ever increasing hostile power extraneous to the interest of the masses. All their gestures must be observed, all abuses must be denounced, all collusion between the economic and political power must be uncovered . . . The long revolutionary march in the metropolis . . . must begin here today." [17] The BR have remained faithful to this programmatic speech, as evidenced by the recurrent themes of their revolutionary literature. The following excerpts are to the point:

The State, even in the most democratic republic, is only an oppressive machine used by one class against another . . . In the capitalistic social formations, the State, its juristic ideology, and its law are nothing other than instruments through which the bourgeoisie exercises its dictatorship over the proletariat . . . The only language that the servants of imperialism have demonstrated to understand is the language of arms and it is in this language that the proletariat is beginning to speak . . . No objective, no matter how militarily protected, is unattackable by a guerrilla force . . . Proletarian power must be affirmed even through the concretization of its own justice, through the capability of trying, passing judgment on, [and] convicting the enemies of the proletariat . . . To construct the system of proletarian power means to fight against the power of the opposing class.[18]

In their declared war against the "imperialist state of the multinationals," the BR view themselves as the vanguard of the proletariat. In this capacity they stress Leninist military discipline and oppose spontaneity, a position that sets the BR apart from other groups of the same ideological component.

The history of the BR may be broken down into three principal phases. The first, 1970–1974, coincides with their birth and adolescence under the leadership of the historic nucleus, whose actions were more demonstrative than violent. The second phase, 1975–1981, marks the advent of the armed struggle in the most violent sense of the term—that is, willful murders and woundings. It also marks the emergence of second and third generations of less intellectually refined militants. Since 1982 the third and ongoing phase has been characterized by unprecedented setbacks, but it also reflects the BR's will to reconsolidate and strike back at "the heart of the state."[19]

By 1980 the BR had developed a clandestine structure, based on operational and territorial criteria, that presumably still influences current organizational concepts despite signs of restructuring after the setbacks of recent years. What might be termed the classical structure of the BR calls for a strategic directorate, an executive committee, several columns, and a number of fronts. Present in these bodies are regular and/or irregular militants; the former are full-time terrorists who live in absolute clandestinity, whereas the latter are part-timers with regular jobs and nearly normal lifestyles.

The column is the basic self-sustaining unit of this clandestine and compartmentalized structure. Composed of regulars, the column has a specific geographical area of responsibility known as a pole, which usually coincides with a municipality or an entire region. At least seven columns exist, the best known of which operate in Milan, Turin, Genoa, the Veneto region, Rome, Naples, and the island of Sardinia. The columns, each of which has a single leader, enjoy a vast degree of operational autonomy and supervise subordinate brigades, which consist in general of no more than five irregulars. One or more regulars may be present in each brigade for liaison with the column. Brigades are termed logistical or mass brigades, depending on their mission. As the qualifier implies, logistical brigades are concerned with procurement, falsification, communications, codes, medical assistance, billeting, and similar support activities. Mass brigades are responsible for intelligence and operations. They are normally present in the factories or are assigned specialized missions in relation to political parties, the judiciary, and the law-enforcement agencies.

As of mid-1980 there were two fronts: the logistical front and the mass front, both having nationwide and often overlapping functions. Their purpose was the coordination and approval of operations or campaigns to be conducted by the columns and brigades.

The executive committee is regarded as the "government" of the BR, whereas the strategic directorate, the BR's supreme organ, may be considered their "parliament." The executive committee, whose membership comprises four or five regulars, is particularly important because it carries out the political and military decisions of the strategic directorate, which meets as a rule no more than twice a year and includes a larger number of both regulars and irregulars. Moreover, the executive committee oversees the more demanding operations of the organization.[20]

The first BR column was constituted, naturally enough, in Milan. By 1972, thanks to contacts dating back to the early days of the historic nucleus, a second one was operating in Turin. Four subordinate brigades were eventually organized within the FIAT plants: Meccanica, Rivalta, Presse, and Lingotto. BR appendages also came into being in the Veneto region at about the same time. In 1974, when the BR extended their sphere of action from industry to the state itself, it became necessary to think in terms of a national structure along the lines described above. This decision was prompted by the BR's logistical and operational problems experienced in connection with the abduction and prolonged captivity of Assistant State Attorney Mario Sossi of Genoa. By 1976 a column had also become operational in Genoa and another in Rome; earlier efforts in the capital had failed because of insufficient external support. The Naples and Sardinian columns came into being, at least at the incipient level, in the late 1970s. Revolutionary committees, which are anomalous bodies with respect to the classical BR structure, appeared in the Tuscany and Marches regions.

The Rome column deserves particular attention. In addition to the traditional importance and large size of that column, Rome remains to this day a noteworthy pole, or geographical area of responsibility. Moreover, as opposed to the other columns, whose origins are closely tied to agitation in the factories, this column has drawn its manpower and support from peripheral neighborhoods—which are journalistically referred to as "BR City"—and from the services sector of the economy. The most recent report in the public domain describes the Rome column as consisting of "area" and "functional" brigades. The area, or neighborhood, brigades were Primavalle, Montespaccato, Tirburtina, Cinecittà, Valmelaina, and Quarticciolo. An additional one was set up in Ostia, Rome's ancient seaport. The functional brigades were named after the work environment or in relation to other missions: for example, hospital personnel, railroad personnel, mechanical works, and propaganda. The Rome brigade structure atypically called for one or more nuclei of four or five militants.[21]

Following the setbacks beginning in early 1982, the BR structure is believed to have experienced some changes. The stress now appears to be placed on irregular membership to reduce the risk of identification and arrest. Although a strategic directorate and executive committee may still be in existence, the geographical boundaries of what remains of the classical columns are likely to be less well defined. Moreover, areas where BR members can hide have probably acquired more importance than in the past.

Nevertheless, there has been no substantial change in targeting techniques. The BR select a target because of its symbolic value and comparative vulnerability. Typical human targets include representatives of the capitalist system of production, political figures associated with the relative-majority Christian Democratic Party, members of the judiciary and law-enforcement agencies, and journalists and academics accused of supporting the establishment. Typical material targets include property, public or private, in any way related to the classes of individuals referred to above. Attacks on property are either complementary to attacks on persons or serve as training and testing of recruits.

There are four standard targeting techniques: the use of explosive devices, the ambush attack, the raid, and the abduction. The ambush attack and the raid, which normally require the deployment of three to five and four to twelve militants, respectively, are hit-and-run operations based on surprise and speed; they fall within the mission of brigades and columns. The raid serves the purpose of either reaching a victim not accessible outdoors or accomplishing the acquisition of documents.

Before attacking a person, his habits are closely studied and, whenever feasible, information is collected by planted informants ("points of contact," in BR parlance). If an ambush is involved, it is conducted at a well-surveyed site at a pre-established time. At least one female member frequently participates in the action, as part of either the assault team or the back-up team. The attackers are generally disguised. Most often the attack team closes in on the victim on foot, but vehicular attacks are also on record.

Ambush attacks and raids have frequently occurred in cluster form to intensify their terror effect. Pertinent patterns include attacks on a specific category of targets within a brief time span in the same city or in cities far apart, rotation of category attacks, and stepped-up rhythm of violence against specific categories of targets. Principal victims of these cluster methods have been industrial figures, Christian Democratic politicians, and journalists.

Moreover, victims are often selected because they individually represent a plurality of enemy institutions at the same time; for example, one person may represent the state, the Christian Democratic Party, and the educational system or the judiciary and the prison system. For purposes of intimidation, the timing of attacks frequently coincides with events of public interest, such as political elections, criminal trials, and labor disputes. Some victims are targeted to retaliate against the institution they represent or are singled out because of their role in that institution. This is particularly applicable to law-enforcement personnel.

Abductions require greater planning and expenditure of human and material resources than the other BR targeting techniques. Besides serving political and, occasionally, self-financing purposes, they often constitute full-scale campaigns that reflect specific periods of BR history. Because of their particular nature, abductions will be dealt with in the next chapter, but a few preliminary observations are in order here. Armed escorts do not necessarily deter terrorist abduction plans. There is no preferred specific time or place; however, only in a minority of cases have the victims been snatched from their residences. A van is employed in nearly all cases, and various disguises are resorted to by the snatchers. Abductions afford the terrorists prolonged media coverage, since they subject their captives to "interrogations" and "trials" that are publicized through communiques.

As of mid-1986 the BR have been responsible for 171 major incidents involving murders, woundings, and abductions. All of them are listed in chronological sequence in Appendix 3, which reflects cluster patterns.

As opposed to revenue-raising ventures, which are not always publicized, politically motivated actions are followed by BR responsibility claims, generally in accordance with a standard procedure. Responsibility is first claimed by a telephone call to the media shortly after the action. Verbal confirmation is then provided in court by red brigadists standing trial for previous crimes. The third and final claim is issued in writing by the organization as a whole or by the specific column responsible for the action. The media are advised by telephone where the pertinent leaflet may be found. This procedure is normally accomplished within three days. The written claim generally provides a "résumé" of the victim's career and outlines the political reasoning behind the attack. Only occasionally does one leaflet claim responsibility for multiple actions.

Responsibility claims are not the BR's sole mode of literary expression. In addition to writings for internal consumption, the BR issue communiques, strategic resolutions, and other comparable tracts. Communiques are issued during trials of BR members by the defendants themselves or by elements of the organization during their management of political kidnappings. Strategic resolutions, which serve programmatic, analytical, and propaganda purposes, are authored or approved by the strategic directorate. The actual drafting is at times delegated to imprisoned red brigadists. The distinction between strategic resolutions—twenty as of mid-1986— and comparable documents—approximately one dozen—is not clear cut. BR writings that address the same topic are generally given a progressive numeration.

Recruitment most often takes place in extraparliamentary circles connected to the factories, the service industries, or the academic environment. Prison inmates are also a recruitment source, as is the absorption of less viable terrorist formations. With few known exceptions, the average age of the BR militant, regular or irregular, ranges from early twenties to mid-thirties. Family background is largely middle class or lower middle class. The female presence in the ranks is a minority, but there appears to be no discrimination as to leadership roles. Nearly all the militants hold at least a high-school diploma.

Domestic training for recruits is conducted by veteran militants. Financing is at least in part the product of thefts, armed robberies, and kidnappings. Official statistics covering the period from 1974 through mid-1980 reflect that more than 2.1 billion lire were acquired by the terrorist left through major armed robberies,[22] a portion of which went into the BR coffers. Weapons and other equipment are stolen, seized, or procured through nonclandestine and clandestine channels. The BR's logistical apparatus is credited with highly developed forging capabilities.

All organizational and personal behavior is regulated by detailed security norms that govern movement, rendezvous, code names, acquisition and maintenance of bases, and every other aspect of clandestine militancy.[23] Failure to abide by rigid compartmentalization criteria peculiar to the structure of the organization has in fact facilitated law-enforcement operations, particularly since 1980 when a number of captured red brigadists began to cooperate with the authorities. Previously, upon arrest, militants would invariably declare themselves "political prisoners" and remain silent. BR rules do call for continued militancy in the prisons as well as in the courtrooms. Liaison between members at large and captured ones has been kept by family members and ideologically committed defense counsel, such as Edoardo Arnaldi and Sergio Spazzali, who were in fact considered BR members by the organization itself.[24]

Appendix 3 dolefully reflects the sustained rhythm of the BR onslaught during the period 1976–1982 and its exceptional momentum in 1977–1981. Those years mark the adulthood and maximum expansion point of the organization, on the one hand, and its failure to graduate from terrorism to civil war, on the other. From 1983 to 1985 the BR were unable to field more than one major successful operation per year, apart from self-financing ventures. However, in February 1986 two serious attacks were recorded eleven days apart. Neither the BR nor the governmental authorities regard this type of unconventional warfare as having come to an end.

Despite the dramatic drop in operational rhythm, BR actions continue to display sophistication. After a period of decadence, the BR's situational analyses and propaganda have also resumed a notable degree of sophistication. Moreover, apprehensions carried out in 1984–1985 have failed—even where those arrested were willing to cooperate—to bring about further law-enforcement inroads into the organization. This is indicative of improved compartmentalization between the logistical and operational echelons of the organization. A tentative reconstruction of the post-1982 BR order of battle rests on data in the government's and the judiciary's possession. BR forces are believed to be concentrated primarily in Rome, but they also have appendages in Milan, Turin, Genoa, Naples, and the Tuscany and Veneto regions. Overall strength comprises a few hundred militants, including regulars, irregulars, and points of contact. Recruits tend to be rather young and have clean police records. Availability of weapons does not appear to be a problem.[25]

There are no fully reliable indications as to the current status of dissent within the organization. Prior to the capture of Mario Moretti in 1981 and of Giovanni Senzani in 1982, a controversy divided the "militarist" wing, subsequently called the Combatant Communist Party (Partito Comunista Combattente), and the "movementist" wing, subsequently called the Guerrilla Party (Partito della Guerriglia), of the organization. Both regarded the BR as the vanguard of the proletariat. However, the "movementist" wing tended to be more favorable toward mass participation and wanted to serve as the interpreter of the needs of the masses; in other words, it stressed the social sector. A more recent difference of opinion between the two wings concerned the methodology of the armed struggle. The Combatant Communist Party stood for relentless warfare, whereas the Guerrilla Party stressed clamor-inducing actions, even if somewhat less violent.

Four major post-1982 operations have been claimed by the BR as the Combatant Communist Party. The last serious attack to date, perpetrated on February 21, 1986, was claimed by the previously unheard-of Communist Combatant Union (Unione dei Combattenti Comunisti), an apparent BR faction or spin-off. Although there is little divergence in ultimate goals, the controversy between BR wings has contributed to reducing operational efficiency.

Front Line. Second only to the record of the BR is that of another communist formation, Front Line (Prima Linea; PL), whose self-image and structure reflect an alternative to the BR model, although ultimate political ends and terrorist methods do not differ. PL came into being in 1976 in the Milan and Turin areas as the progeny of violent elements formerly associated with the extraparliamentary parties Ongoing Struggle (Lotta Continua) and Workers' Power (Potere Operaio). Its first leaflet stated: "Front Line is not a new communist combat nucleus, but an organization born of the union and synthesis of various guerrilla units that until now acted using individual acronyms."[26] PL's onslaught came to an end in the early 1980s, but its model remained available for emulation.

As opposed to the BR's mind-set as the "vanguard of the proletariat," PL always regarded itself as a proletarian "service structure." In fact, PL never adopted the pyramidal, compartmentalized, and rigidly territorial structure peculiar to the BR. PL militants tended to be irregulars, unless forced into clandestinity by the police dragnet. Their double lives enabled them to combine political action with the armed struggle. PL's structure allowed greater operational flexibility to individual militants and to organic units and satellites, which were frequently called fire groups, squads, or patrols. In its heyday, PL possessed a national executive responsible for major decisions of political, military, and logistical nature and for liaison with other terrorist formations of the left. Also part of the overall organization was a national command that represented and coordinated the various affiliations.

PL has claimed responsibility for 32 major actions, all listed in Appendix 4. However, there is evidence that additional attacks have been carried out under different names or as the result of joint operations with minor groups such as the Communist Combat Formations (Formazioni Combattenti Comuniste).

In April 1983 PL officially announced its dissolution. The announcement was made in court in Bologna by high-ranking members on trial. Nonetheless, the Organized Comrades for Proletarian Liberation (Compagni Organizzati per la Liberazione Proletaria; COLP) are believed to be a surviving affiliation of PL. In addition to the goal inherent to their very name, COLP objectives include the reorganization of PL and the development of new "social guerrilla models."

Other PL assets have been absorbed by the BR, as have the remnants of two additional formations that predated PL and more closely paralleled the rigidly clandestine BR model: the Partisan Action Groups (Gruppi di Azione Partigiani; GAP), active in northern Italy from 1970 to 1972, and the Armed Proletarian Nuclei (Nuclei Armati Proletari; NAP), active in Naples and Rome from 1974 to 1977. The GAP, a small group of former communist partisans, unemployed extremists, and common criminals, was the creature of multimillionaire, publisher, and would-be revolutionary Giangiacomo Feltrinelli, who was obsessed by the specter of an impending Fascist coup and intended to preempt it through classical partisan warfare, a military approach that clashed with the urban guerrilla principles of the BR and thus made an early merger impracticable. The GAP did not survive Feltrinelli's accidental death on a power pylon he was attempting to dynamite in March 1972. (Earlier the GAP had absorbed the October XXII Circle, a similar band founded in 1969.) The NAP, in contrast, was the product of an alliance between former Ongoing Struggle militants and former prison inmates. Its objective was to link up the revolution inside and outside the prisons. A few joint BR-NAP operations actually preceded the absorption process. Whereas the GAP is credited with no major actions, the October XXII Circle and the NAP are credited with two and thirteen, respectively.[27]

Minor Formations. The remaining terrorist formations of communist persuasion, the vast majority of which have made an ephemeral appearance on the scene never to be heard from again, constitute what is normally referred to as spontaneous or diffused terrorism. These minor groups are nevertheless dangerous. They are aggregately responsible for over 100 major terrorist attacks perpetrated nationwide since 1975 against targets similar to those of the major formations. Moreover, they serve as an "experienced" recruitment pool for the better established terrorist formations and contribute to broadening the front of the armed struggle through the perpetration of less serious, though extremely numerous, terrorist actions directed against public and private property.

With respect to these groups, some additional observations are in order. Despite the BR's condemnation of revolutionary spontaneity, their militants, especially the irregulars, frequently cross over from the BR to minor formations and vice versa. The Rome column, for example, was largely formed by absorbing elements from the Armed Communist Formations (Formazioni Armate Comuniste) and the Communist Combat Units (Unità Combattenti Comuniste; UCC). Historic nucleus member Corrado Alunni left the BR to form the Communist Combat Formations, a band close to PL. PL itself, whose mind-set accepts spontaneity, has regularly encouraged this sort of diffused terrorism, as has, to a degree, the "movementist" wing of the BR. Other formations, such as the March 28 Brigade for Communism (Brigata 28 Marzo per il Comunismo), came into being as the result of its founders' intent to prove their suitability for BR membership.

Terrorism of the left, whether structured or spontaneous, could not survive were it not for the support of a sufficiently vast extraparliamentary and revolution-oriented stratum of the politically active population. This subversive element is generally referred to as "the Movement." Its more militant and, indeed, more violent segment is called "the Autonomy."[28] An effective definition of the Autonomy is provided by one of the many publications that constitute its ideological backbone: "By proletarian autonomy we mean the practical and daily reality of the anticapitalist and antistate struggle manifested by revolt and class struggle . . . by the break of ties with bourgeois law and morals."[29] A further distinction separates the Autonomy as a whole, whose members are collectively termed autonomists, from Workers' Autonomy (Autonomia Operaia; AUTOP); AUTOP is also occasionally called Organized Workers' Autonomy (Autonomia Operaia Organizzata) in homage to its tighter structures that render it a pole of aggregation or point of reference for the multitude of collectives and groups present in the Autonomy and in the broader Movement.

AUTOP is the heir of the self-dissolved Workers' Power, a similar organization in existence from 1969 through 1973. Indicative of AUTOP's ideology are several slogans such as "Work is not a manner of living, but the obligation to sell oneself in order to live." From agitation within the factories for "guaranteed wages," AUTOP expanded its propaganda and militancy to include the unilateral reduction of rent payments by tenants and of public utility rates by consumers, seizure of unrented dwellings, resistance against eviction, and "proletarian expropriations" in supermarkets. It has also attacked the school system as "the school of unemployment, selectivity, and repression."

AUTOP and, somewhat similarly, the rest of the Autonomy maintain double structures: an overt one for subversive propaganda and agitation and a covert one for urban guerrilla warfare, armed robberies, and occasional acts of terrorism. A tactical objective of the autonomists is the degeneration, through infiltration, of public demonstrations. As will be seen in Chapter 6, they are active, for example, in the pacifist movement. To the autonomists can also be ascribed several acts of violence against embassies and commercial interests of select foreign countries as a form of commitment to proletarian internationalism.

It is significant that the BR consider the various Autonomy groups as the Proletarian Movement for Offensive Resistance, a term they write in capital letters.[30] According to "repentant" red brigadist Antonio Savasta, BR militants have covertly been active in extraparliamentary aggregations for purposes of influence, intelligence collection, and selective recruitment.[31] Moreover, within AUTOP itself, projects were drawn up to channel the leftist extraparliamentary forces, including terrorist formations, toward a controlled and unitary revolutionary strategy. The most ambitious of these projects, which envisaged the control of the BR, was called "Metropolis" from the name of an AUTOP publication.[32]

Autonomists are estimated by the government to number tens of thousands and are concentrated in the key regions of Latium, Veneto, Lombardy, and Campania.[33] Particularly disconcerting is AUTOP's entrenchment in academic circles. In fact, the University of Padua has been its traditional stronghold as well as the home base of charismatic Professor Antonio (Toni) Negri, AUTOP's foremost ideologue. Negri, who was sentenced in absentia by the Court of Assizes of Rome to a 30-year prison term in June 1984, is currently enjoying asylum in France. Together with 56 other defendants, including a number of his academic colleagues in the School of Political Science, Negri was convicted of crimes ranging from subversion to abduction to murder. The court defined Negri as "an individual who for a decade propagandized everywhere messages of hatred and violence and advocated the necessity to constitute an organization having a twofold program of aggression against the State: the incitement of the masses (to commit unlawful) appropriations, on the one hand, and (the launching) of a vanguard attack, on the other." The verdict also states: "He was the instigator, the principal, the organizer of those choices that characterized a long season of violence."[34]

While the trial was still in progress, the libertarian Radical Party decided to run Negri on its slate for the June 1983 parliamentary elections. He was elected to the Chamber of Deputies in all three districts in which his candidacy was submitted, which is a dramatic reflection of AUTOP's political following. Negri obtained 13,521 votes in Milan, 26,389 in Rome, and 11,480 in Naples.[35] The total exceeds 50,000 votes, a confirmation of the governmental estimate of AUTOP's strength. Before the Chamber of Deputies could strip him of parliamentary immunity in order to return him to prison, Negri fled.

Of the anarchist groups cataloged under the heading of terrorism of the left, one deserves attention: Revolutionary Action (Azione Rivoluzionaria; AR). It appeared on the scene in the early 1970s and remained active through the end of the decade, during which it claimed responsibility for two serious actions that entailed woundings. AR's "charter" states that "our cultural experience can be defined as anarchist-communist." The late Gianfranco Faina, a former professor of political doctrines at the University of Genoa, was AR's reputed historic leader. His political background included militancy in the PCI's youth organization, conceptualization of the periodical *Quaderni Rossi* together with Toni Negri, and authorship of "A Ray of Light in the Darkness," a pamphlet dedicated to Ulrike Meinhof of Germany's Red Army Faction. According to "repentant" AR militant Enrico Paghera, "Revolutionary Action introduced itself as an alternative to other organizations, which, in the conduct of the armed struggle, had a precise ideological and organizational scheme . . . [AR] was made up of affinity groups connected among themselves . . . Each nucleus operated in a territory [and] was autonomous."[36] According to press accounts, a 1985 intelligence report voiced concern over AR's ongoing reorganization.[37]

With respect to Sardinian separatists that express their aspirations through terrorist actions, the most notorious formation was Red Barbagia (Barbagia Rossa), a group from the Barbagia area in the province of Nuoro, which was largely absorbed in the late 1970s by the Sardinian column of the BR. Red Barbagia had been responsible for three major incidents that caused deaths and injuries. Of the remaining seven formations that have claimed responsibility for terrorist attacks under names that combine separatist and communist goals, only one perpetrated a serious action. Currently most active on the island is a group called the Sardinian Armed Movement (Movimento Armato Sardo). However, this group is believed to be common-crime oriented despite political ambiguities. Support for separatist violence issues primarily from extremist or renegade elements of the leftist Sardinian Action Party.

Indirect indications as to the numerical strength of the terrorist left may be drawn from the latest governmental statistics in the public domain on imprisoned terrorists and identified terrorists at large. The prison population includes 1,100 terrorists of the left.[38] Those on the wanted list number 295.[39] To these figures should be added 142 more individuals of the same fold who have been released because of the lapse of the authorized pretrial confinement term.

The Terrorist Right

Although the extreme right has been responsible for numerous terrorist attacks, it lacks the necessary assets and sophistication to qualify as a close competitor of its leftist counterpart. Organic to the terrorist right are three components, which can be classified as neo-Fascist, separatist, and nationalist/counterseparatist. The neo-Fascist component is the most menacing one in terms of overall numerical strength, number of individual formations, and level of violence. The other two components pose a marginal threat, largely because of their circumscribed operational sphere.

The neo-Fascist terrorist formations are perhaps better characterized as neo-Nazi, since their cultural points of reference appear to lie so far outside of the humanist tradition. In fact, their symbols and terminology are extensively borrowed from Nordic history and mythology. These groups, whose members frequently merge political aspirations with common crime, contemplate the violent uprooting of the Western system of government and its replacement by a totalitarian regime based on a combination of nationalistic and socialist principles allegedly in contrast with both capitalism and communism. However, what ultimately emerges from their incoherent and often grammatically impeachable writings is an extremely hazy ideology.[40]

Until the late 1970s, neo-Fascist targetings were predicated on the indiscriminate use of explosives in the presumable belief that chaos would enhance the revolutionary cause. Trains and public places were favorite targets. Thereafter, neo-Fascist extremists began to imitate with inferior sophistication the selective methods of the terrorist left, including the use of firearms against specific persons, but these were limited to magistrates, police officials, leftist adversaries, and individuals considered traitors to the cause.

Regrettably, all trials, appellate proceedings, and re-trials through mid-1986 have failed to establish the material paternity of four massacres generally attributed to the extreme right. If these massacres were in fact of neo-Fascist inspiration, they evidence the intent of combining indiscriminate and selective tactics. These massacres were caused by the detonation of explosives in a Milan bank in December 1969 (sixteen deaths and 90 injuries), in a Brescia city square during a demonstration in May 1974 (eight deaths and 100 injuries), on the Italicus rail express in August 1974 (twelve deaths and 44 injuries), and in the Bologna railroad station in August 1980 (85 deaths and 181 injuries). A potential fifth massacre failed in August 1983, when an explosive charge did not dislodge the railroad tracks in the proximity of Vernio (near Florence). The intended target was the Milan-Palermo train with 1,000 passengers aboard. As it turned out, only two machinists were slightly wounded by flying glass.

Since the late 1960s, six aggregations of neo-Fascist extremists have been particularly visible: ON, Black Order, AN, Third Position, the Armed Revolutionary Nuclei, and the Popular Revolutionary Movement. ON and AN originally came into being as extremist organizations and subsequently degenerated into terrorist bands. Less notorious aggregations include the Revolutionary Action Movement (Movimento d'Azione Rivoluzionaria), the Mussolini Action Squads (Squadre d'Azione Mussolini), the Organic People's Communities (Comunità Organiche di Popolo), and Let's Construct the Action (Construiamo l'Azione). The former two groups claimed responsibilities in the late 1960s and early 1970s for a series of bombings. All told, approximately 64 formations have claimed responsibility for terrorist actions, usually minor ones entailing damage to property. Different names do not necessarily reflect the existence of different organizations, since denominational changes are often made for tactical deception.

New Order/Black Order. ON was founded in the 1950s by a group of hard-liners who deserted the Italian Social Movement (MSI). In 1969, shortly before the Milan massacre, the majority of these schismatics returned to the MSI fold. Notable exceptions include Clemente Graziani, Elio Massagrande, and Salvatore Francia, who were arrested in 1971 after the police seized arms caches and documents indicative of subversive designs. Seventy-three ON members were brought to trial in Rome on charges of reconstitution of the outlawed National Fascist Party (Partito Nazionale Fascista); 30 of them were convicted and given prison terms ranging from one to five years. Consequently, ON itself was forcibly dissolved at the end of 1973, at which time its reported strength amounted to 2,500 members.

A presumably small percentage of ON militants went underground and the organization resurfaced as a clandestine formation under the name of Black Order (Ordine Nero, still ON). ON's leadership remained the same and for some time published a periodical, *Anno Zero* (Zero year), edited by Salvatore Francia. ON's reconstituted ranks drew new manpower from former militants of AN, the Mussolini Action Squads, and the Revolutionary Action Movement.

Bomb attacks perpetrated by ON between 1974 and 1978 caused one death and eight woundings, plus damage to property. Moreover, two gun attacks resulted in the wounding of a communist militant and in the death of Assistant State Attorney Vittorio Occorsio in Rome on July 10, 1976. Occorsio had served as prosecutor during the trial that led to the banning of New Order in 1973.[41]

National Vanguard. AN was organized in Rome in 1962 by Stefano Delle Chiaie and subsequently reached a peak strength of 600 members. AN's philosophy refuted egalitarianism and the parliamentary system in favor of "natural selection," and it advocated "revolutionary action" to bring about "natural order." In 1976 it was forcibly dissolved on the same legal grounds as ON had been earlier. It is uncertain whether remnants of AN are still in existence, either dormant or as behind-the-scene elements of more recent terrorist formations. In any case, there is evidence that a substantive portion of AN's cadres merged with ON in the mid-1970s.[42]

Third Position. Third Position (Terza Posizione) made its appearance in the late 1970s under the leadership of Roberto Fiore and Gabriele Adinolfi, who eventually fled to England but maintained their subversive contacts in Italy. The group draws its denomination from a defunct periodical that circulated under the same name. Its political objectives appear to coincide with those of ON—namely, the creation of a "movement that organically represents the will of the people" and the overcoming of the "restrictive concept of the ballot as the sole and deeply indirect contact between the people and those who govern."

By the end of 1980, Third Position's structure in Rome comprised a central nucleus and various nuclei at the neighborhood echelon, including the Talenti, Balduina, Montemario, Parioli, Tuscolano, and EUR nuclei. The somewhat more autonomous Trieste neighborhood was referred to as the Trieste Neighborhood Revolutionary Committee (Comitato Rivoluzionario Quartiere Trieste). In essence, Third Position was intended to serve as a recruitment and support pool for neo-Fascist terrorism in general and for the Armed Revolutionary Nuclei in particular. Third Position's structural model is the leftist Autonomy. However, its current structure and numerical strength are difficult to assess because of successful police operations that have at least temporarily crippled all rightist terrorist formations.

The Armed Revolutionary Nuclei. The Armed Revolutionary Nuclei (Nuclei Armati Rivoluzionari; NAR) appeared on the scene at approximately the same time as their reservoir, Third Position. Characterized by violent spontaneity, the NAR are not believed to have a hierarchical structure. In fact, the name NAR is reportedly used by several groups of extremists in claiming responsibility for terrorist crimes. At the same time, their actions tend to be selective. Firearms, grenades, and explosives are the NAR's revolutionary tools. Between 1977 and 1982, the NAR's most active period, NAR spokesmen claimed responsibility for fifteen murders and 47 woundings. Most of the victims were preplanned targets. In other cases, murders and woundings were incidental to armed robberies or gun-fire exchanges with the police. Of these woundings, 23 resulted from the detonation of a single explosive device planted in a PCI section office in Rome in June 1979. Six months earlier, five radio station operators had been injured during a NAR submachine-gun and grenade attack on the leftist extraparliamentary transmitter Radio Città Futura.

Like Black Order before them, the NAR are believed to fall within the clandestine succession of New Order. NAR's spearhead figures, G. Valerio Fioravanti and Francesca Mambro, are currently serving life sentences for murder and other crimes. Judicial investigations into NAR activity reflect a multifaceted political and operational scheme: armed robberies and thefts for the acquisition of weapons and explosives; domestic training on the use of weapons and explosives and foreign training in Lebanon; armed robberies for self-financing and assistance to imprisoned comrades; liaison with common crime circles for the acquisition and storage of arms and for channeling stolen goods; perpetration of common crimes as a form of revolutionary training and rejection of the bourgeois state; attacks against persons and property belonging to adversary political organizations, attacks against public utilities, and violent actions to create a climate of terror; organization of structures and channels for the laundering of funds, clandestine expatriation, and falsification of documents; and demonstrations intended to degenerate into political violence and riots.

The Popular Revolutionary Movement. The Popular Revolutionary Movement (Movimento Popolare Rivoluzionario) belongs to the same generation of neo-Fascist terrorism as Third Position and the NAR. Its principal actions, which are circumscribed to the city of Rome and the year 1979, entailed bomb attacks on material structures: City Hall, the Regina Coeli Prison, the Superior Council of the Judiciary, and the Ministry of Foreign Affairs. The Popular Revolutionary Movement, the Organic People's Communities, and Let's Construct the Action are all considered part of the NAR clan and, as such, offshoots of New Order.[43]

Trends and General Rightist Activity. As evidenced by neo-Fascist terrorist activity from 1983 through 1985, Rome, Milan, and the Veneto region continue to be principal settings, although its operational rhythm has slowed down considerably. Paternity of two gun attacks that caused two deaths and one injury during this period was claimed or attributed to the NAR. The arson of a theater on January 12, 1985, where the MSI was to hold a meeting the following day, was also accompanied by a NAR responsibility claim.

The most recent trends of neo-Fascist terrorism are schematically described in the 1984–1985 semiannual intelligence reports of the prime minister to Parliament. They point to continuing linkages between neo-Fascist extremists and common criminals. They attest to the ideological influence of the dissolved ON and AN on more recent formations, and they specifically note the crossover of militants from one formation to another or even their simultaneous presence in various neo-Fascist formations. They also detect the NAR's reorganizational efforts, particularly in Rome and the Veneto region. The reports voice concern over the interest that neo-Fascist elements are displaying for Islamic extremism and and view this development as a potential source of linkage between neo-Fascist and leftist formations.[44] An earlier semiannual intelligence report indicated unprecedented availability on the part of the terrorist left to open up to the overtures of its rightist counterpart.[45]

Apart from purely ideological considerations, the overall lack of revolutionary and operational refinement on the part of neo-Fascist terrorism would exclude the possibility that links were ever formed with the principal formations of the left—that is, with the BR and PL. Besides, the absence of such a relationship is corroborated by police investigations and judicial proceedings. Conversely, there is evidence of political and logistical cooperation between groups that fall under the umbrella of the leftist Autonomy and neo-Fascist terrorist formations. This explains, at least in part, occasional responsibility claims issuing from both the right and the left after comparatively minor terrorist attacks. For example, the above-reported arson of January 12, 1985, was claimed by both the NAR and the Anti-Fascist Territorial Groups (Gruppi Antifascisti Territoriali).

An indirect indicator of the comparatively limited human resources on which neo-Fascist terrorism can count is once again provided by official statistics on rightist terrorists in prison and identified ones at large. The former amount to 180.[46] The latter number 68.[47] To these figures should be added 40 individuals of the same fold who have been released because of the expiration of the authorized pretrial confinement term.

The reconstruction and analysis of events related to neo-Fascist terrorism are rendered more complex by recurrent allegations of involvement by members of sensitive governmental agencies. The most grievous accusations have been leveled against the intelligence community, but an accusing finger has also been pointed at law-enforcement agencies and the military. The fundamental allegation holds that neo-Fascist formations, at times disguised as leftist ones, are parallel structures of the intelligence services tasked with destabilization missions in order to set back the democratic process or even to orchestrate a rightist coup. However, parliamentary investigations and judicial proceedings completed to date reflect no evidence of such designs.[48] Those investigations still in progress hope to establish whether or not there are responsibilities on the part of governmental functionaries.[49]

With respect to the allegation that terrorism of the right disguises itself as terrorism of the left, the very record of the terrorist left tends to contradict that theory. For example, very rarely—and never on account of their political allegiance—have Communists been physically attacked by the terrorist left.[50] A BR document even defines the PCI as "a great democratic force that coherently pursues a strategy exactly opposed to our own."[51] Of significance also are the judgments of individuals at one time associated with, or influenced by, the PCI. In commenting on the doctrine, objectives, and parlance of the terrorist left, Rossana Rossanda, formerly of the PCI and then of the Manifesto group, stated: "It's like leafing through a family album."[52] More incisive is a statement by jailed red brigadist Ognibene: "We built the fire with the ideological wood that we had: we have taken Marxism-Leninism, its theory on imperialism we learned from the PCI catechism, and we adapted it to the capitalism of the multinationals."[53]

Another analytical problem is the result of increasing indicators of links between neo-Fascist terrorism and elements of organized crime; this matter will be addressed in subsequent chapters.

In contrast to that of neo-Fascism, the motivation behind violence perpetrated by the separatist and nationalist/counterseparatist components of the terrorist right is clear. The separatist component is active in the ethnically Germanic South Tyrol area of the Trentino-Alto Adige region. Formations such as Befreiungsausschuss Suedtirol, Heimatbund, and Tirol seek independence from Italy and the establishment of an authoritarian form of government of Nazi inspiration. Terrorist attacks by these groups have been limited to material targets since the resurgence of their militancy in the late 1970s. The nationalist/counterseparatist component is also active in the same area and consists of Italian formations such as the Italian Adige Movement (Movimento Italiano Adige) that conduct retaliatory attacks against the property of their Germanic counterparts and of Austrian and German tourists. Similar nationalist formations, such as the Nuclei for the Territorial Defense of Trieste (Nuclei Difesa Territoriale Triestina), have carried out minor terrorist actions in that area to protest against territorial concessions to Yugoslavia and other concessions to Slavic ethnics on Italian territory.

The Kidnap Industry

The "kidnap industry" is a colorful term coined in journalistic circles to characterize the wave of abductions that has afflicted nearly all regions of the country since the early 1970s. To be sure, kidnappings are not new to the Italian scene. This practice dates back to preunification days and became particularly visible in the latter part of the nineteenth century in the central and southern areas of the country, which were infested not only by common criminals but also by externally supported insurgents battling against the newly established Kingdom of Italy.

Italy's current Criminal Code, drawn up in 1930, defines kidnapping as "the deprivation of someone's personal liberty." [1] Subsequent amendments render the offense more grievous if committed "for purposes of extortion" or "for purposes of terrorism and subversion." [2] Both amendments were introduced during the 1970s in response to the increased number of abductions by crime syndicates and, for the first time in contemporary Italy, by terrorist formations. In order to simplify and speed up investigations, the Code of Criminal Procedure was also amended during the same period to vest with territorial jurisdiction the court of the place where the abduction is perpetrated, rather than the court of the place where the victim is ultimately returned to liberty, as previously established. [3]

However, neither the stricter penalty for kidnappings committed for purposes of extortion, terrorism, or subversion—25 to 30 years of imprisonment—nor the streamlining of the pertinent procedural rules have obliterated this type of crime. The reasons are obvious. To organized crime circles, kidnappings for ransom generally produce high profits with comparatively little risk and provide quick capital for "clean" reinvestment. To terrorist formations, abductions afford intensive and prolonged media coverage. In either case, the perpetrators select the victim(s) and determine the

TABLE 4.1

KIDNAPPING INCIDENTS, 1960–1985

(Total = 636)

1960–1972		1973–1985	
Year	Number of Incidents	Year	Number of Incidents
1960	2	1973	17
1961	—	1974	40
1962	—	1975	62
1963	2	1976	47
1964	—	1977	75
1965	2	1978	43
1966	12	1979	59
1967	13	1980	38
1968	14	1981	40
1969	3	1982	50
1970	10	1983	39
1971	15	1984	29
1972	7	1985	17

time and place of the abduction, thus capitalizing on the elements of initiative and surprise.

Statistics on abductions are difficult to compile and therefore constitute a less than fully accurate record. Fear for the fate of a loved one may cause relatives to pay a ransom or give in to other demands of a criminal organization without informing the police authorities that the abduction took place. In other cases, the ransom payment is kept secret even if the occurrence of the kidnapping is public knowledge. As opposed to common criminals, terrorists tend to publicize their actions, particularly ideological abductions. However, qualified observers believe that terrorist kidnappings for self-financing—as frequently happens in the case of robberies perpetrated for the same purpose—are not always followed by a responsibility claim.

Table 4.1 lists kidnapping incidents on record but does not take into account multiple victims in the few cases where two or more persons were abducted simultaneously. It nevertheless provides an indication of trends from 1960 through the end of 1985.[4]

The vast majority of kidnappings perpetrated in Italy is for extortion purposes. A comparatively small number is attributable to terrorist or subversive designs, and still other kidnappings reflect a combination of criminal, sociological, and political factors. Finally, there are indications pointing to occasional joint ventures in the kidnap industry between organized crime and terrorist formations. Lines between these components are not always clear.

Politically Motivated Abductions

Political abductions draw the most extensive coverage. Consequently, a great deal of information is available regarding the motivation behind each individual case and the pertinent operational modalities. Political abductions are classified as "ideological" when directly related to political aims and as "pragmatic" when conducted to acquire funds or other instrumentalities for the revolutionary cause. Ideological kidnappings intended to be purely demonstrative are usually of short duration. Ideological kidnappings aimed at challenging the authority of the state in a substantive manner tend to extend over time and encompass a variety of interconnected revolutionary techniques.

Since the outbreak of contemporary terrorism, 26 political abductions are known to have been perpetrated in Italy: 24 were carried out by the Marxist-Leninist left and two by the neo-Fascist right. Although the rightist and a negligible fraction of the leftist operations were comparatively unimportant, political abductions most often entail a high degree of sophistication and are the expression of carefully planned terrorist campaigns. In this respect, they differ from a number of terrorist actions of complementary nature or of nuisance value.

The largest number of political kidnappings is the work of the Red Brigades (BR), which have claimed responsibility for eighteen of them. Fifteen are classifiable as ideological and three as pragmatic. Since BR kidnappings tend to display cluster characteristics, caution must be exercised not to inject them with too much significance. To reduce this risk and examine in depth their modi operandi, it is beneficial to review these operations individually within each presumable cluster.

The BR are not the initiators of political abductions in contemporary Italy, but they are the terrorist formation that has systematically resorted to them and progressively refined their perpetration to the point of turning abductions into the most effective terrorist tool. The first BR kidnapping occurred in 1972 and the last (as of mid-1986) occurred in 1982. Throughout that decade, the BR made it clear that they view abductions primarily as politico-military operations and only marginally as revenue-gathering initiatives.

The initial six BR kidnappings—recorded in 1972–1974—clearly constitute a well-coordinated cluster that coincides with the territorial expansion of that terrorist organization from Milan to the industrial triangle of the North comprising Milan, Turin, and Genoa. This cluster also reflects the broadening of the BR offensive from "capitalist" and "fascist" targets to targets that embody the authority of the state.

Their first victim was Idalgo Macchiarini, 43 years of age, personnel manager of Sit-Siemens. He was abducted in Milan on March 3, 1972, at 7:05 P.M. Three men wearing workers' overalls overpowered him a short distance away from the plant as he was walking to his car. Macchiarini was forced into a stolen FIAT-750 van, tied, gagged, and taken for a 30-minute ride, during which he was photographed with a BR poster around his neck. He was ultimately abandoned inside the van in the suburbs of Milan. He suffered two blows on the face when he first reacted against his aggressors and one more, while in the van, when he made a second fruitless attempt to free himself. Responsibility was claimed in a leaflet dropped off in the van itself. Two days later the BR confirmed this action in a communique sent to the news agency ANSA and accompanied by Macchiarini's picture.

Equally brief was the second abduction of this cluster. Bartolomeo Di Mino, 44, a blue-collar worker and deputy secretary of the Cesano Boscone (Milan) section of the rightist Italian Social Movement (MSI), was overpowered ten days later inside the MSI section offices, where he was working alone after an evening meeting. Four masked attackers, including one woman, struck him on the head with the grip of a pistol, tied and gagged him, and then photographed him. Before leaving the premises they conducted a search, collected a number of files, and spray-painted "Red Brigades" on the walls. The following day, the BR confirmed their action with a leaflet and a photograph.

The third and fourth kidnappings went beyond the simply demonstrative level. Apart from their longer duration, they reflect the beginnings of the "people's trial" terrorist approach. Bruno Labate, 30, a FIAT clerical employee and provincial secretary of the Italian Confederation of National Syndicates for Workers (CISNAL) metalworkers, the MSI-connected labor union, was kidnapped in Turin on February 12, 1973, at 9:30 A.M. as he was walking to work. Two men seized him, hit him on the head and mouth to overpower him, and pushed him into yet another stolen van, where two additional men were waiting. According to a bystander attracted by Labate's shouts, the two attackers were wearing workers' overalls. The victim was driven to a garage, subjected to a haircut, and photographed. An unprecedented feature of the case was that Labate was also interrogated for five hours regarding FIAT's hiring practices and CISNAL's numerical strength in the area. At 3:25 P.M. he was driven to the FIAT Mirafiori plant, dropped off near gate no. 1 in his underwear, chained to a light pole, and left there with a poster around his neck indicating his identity. A BR responsibility claim was followed by a transcript of the interrogation.

Four months later, on June 28 at 8:30 P.M., Michele Mincuzzi, 56, an executive employee of Alfa Romeo's production division, was kidnapped in Milan as he was parking his car in front of his residence. After suffering a broken nose in an attempt to resist, Mincuzzi was forced into a stolen van, taken to what he subsequently described as a "hall," and subjected to a "people's trial," which the victim recalled to be "a rather subdued ideological discussion." He was abandoned in a field near the corporate plant in Arese (Milan) at 11 P.M. with a poster around his neck depicting the BR symbol. According to the leaflet left with the victim, Mincuzzi was one of the many executive employees "who try to shift the cost of the crisis onto the blue-collar workers by using such instruments as extortion, high cost of living, terrorism, [and] provocation; that is to say, antiproletarian violence." It is interesting to note that members of an extremist workers committee within the plant had suggested to the BR the abduction of Mincuzzi.

With the fifth and sixth kidnappings, which conclude this cluster, the BR fully mastered political abduction techniques. Their sixth kidnapping also marked the expansion of BR targeting from the private sector to governmental figures.

On December 10, 1973, at 7:30 A.M., Ettore Amerio, 56, FIAT's personnel manager for the automobile sector, was kidnapped in Turin while on his way to the garage where he habitually parked his car for the night. Physically lifted into a van stolen from the telephone company and transferred en route into a sedan that took him to a safe house for the "people's trial," Amerio was held in captivity for eight days. His abduction coincided with the negotiations for the periodical renewal of national bargaining agreements. Amerio's "trial" included further probings into FIAT's hiring and other personnel practices.

For the first time the BR exploited repeated media coverage by issuing communiques connected to the phases of the "trial." One of them was accompanied by a picture of the victim with the BR banner behind him. Amerio's release took place in Turin on December 18 at 6 A.M. The victim subsequently testified that he was interrogated three hours per day by a well-educated male, whom he later identified to be historic-nucleus member Renato Curcio. Between these sessions he was allowed to read or listen to music but had no access to newspapers; his watch was likewise removed to reduce his awareness. He claims to have been "treated with kindness" and summed up his captivity as follows: "This too is an experience in life and, like all other experiences, it causes us to mature and reflect more pro-foundly." After his release, not only did he resign as personnel manager, but he did not even attempt to seek redress in the criminal proceedings against the BR.

The last target of this cluster was Mario Sossi, 43, the assistant state attorney of the tribunal of Genoa who had prosecuted the terrorist forma-tion known as the October XXII Circle. Sossi was kidnapped on April 18, 1974, at 9 P.M., as he was returning home from the Court House. Once again, a stolen van was used. Previously no public official had been the target of any BR action. Sossi was held captive for 35 days, during which he was interrogated and "tried." The BR issued eight communiques to prop-agandize the "trial" and disseminate the record of the interrogation. For the first time, letters from a BR kidnap victim were sent to family members and professional associates. In exchange for his freedom, the BR demanded the release of eight convicted terrorists of the October XXII Circle. The court having pertinent jurisdiction granted a provisional release, which was blocked by an appeal filed with the Supreme Court by Chief Prosecutor Francesco Coco. The BR nonetheless released Sossi in the belief that the state's authority had been sufficiently compromised. On May 23 at 11 P.M. they dropped Sossi off in a park in the suburbs of Milan. Coco, however, was murdered in Genoa two years later by a BR commando unit.

By releasing Sossi in Milan, the BR displayed knowledge of the proce-dural rules still in force at the time and their intention to hinder the inves-tigation. Procedurally, territorial jurisdiction should have passed from Genoa to Milan. Yet Sossi immediately and secretively returned to Genoa and thus foiled the BR; he then actively assisted the investigators. His deci-sion to return to Genoa may have been influenced by the suspicion of pos-sible BR contacts with the Milan "establishment" in view of certain value judgments expressed by his jailers regarding Milan magistrates. Sossi testi-fied that he had received humane treatment despite a broken rib when forced into the van and the loss of five kilograms during captivity. Sossi's behavior throughout and after this experience was consistent with his con-servative convictions.

As opposed to one month's preparation for Amerio's abduction, BR planning for Sossi's kidnapping took a full year. Moreover, this action re-flected compartmentalization techniques that parallel those used by orga-nized crime during kidnap ventures. The necessary intelligence gathering in the Genoa area was performed by BR regulars without disclosing to sup-porting elements that Sossi was the intended target. The plan also required that the kidnap team turn the victim over to the "jailers," who were the only ones to know where the "people's prison" was located—a villa in the mountainous area of Tortona purchased at the beginning of 1974 with false identity documents.[5]

This first cluster was followed by a second one loosely held together by less significant kidnappings, four in all, between 1975 and 1977. Two were for self-financing and the others were hardly more than demonstrative. They are nevertheless important because they coincide with the emergence of a second generation of red brigadists that replaced the historic nucleus, most of whose members had been or were being captured by the police forces. The new generation injected willful bloodshed into BR operations. In fact, the kidnappings of the second cluster took place in a terrorist setting characterized by woundings and murders, in contrast with the actions against property that had accompanied the first cluster of abductions.

On June 4, 1975, at 3:30 P.M., wine producer Vittorio Vallarino Gancia, 43, was abducted by five men and one woman in Canelli (Asti), while driving away from his villa. A male disguised as a road maintenance worker stopped him by waving a danger flag. A masked man then approached, forced him out of his car at gun point, and ordered him into a van, which in the meantime had pulled behind Gancia's car. This successful abduction turned out to be an abortive revenue venture. At about noon of the following day, even before the issuance of the ransom demand, a Carabinieri patrol ran into the BR country hideout at Spiotta di Arzello, near Acqui Terme (Alessandria), where Gancia was being held captive. In the gun-fire that ensued there were casualties and injuries on both sides, but Gancia was freed. Mara Cagol of the historic nucleus lost her life in this fight.

Two demonstrative abductions followed. Enrico Boffa, 41, manager of the Singer plant at Leinì, was seized in Rivoli (Turin) on October 21, 1975, as he was locking the garage door upon his return home. Three armed men suddenly appeared, made him kneel, hung a BR poster around his neck, photographed him, and fired two pistol shots, one of which wounded Boffa's right leg. This action coincided with ongoing labor unrest at Boffa's plant generated by a projected reduction in the number of workers. In their responsibility claim, the BR defined Boffa as a "reactionary" and a supporter of the policies of the "American bosses."

The next day, Vincenzo Casabona, 47, personnel manager of Ansaldo Meccanica Nucleare, was likewise seized in front of his residence in Arenzano (Genoa) upon his return home. After being forced into a van he was held captive for one hour, beaten, subjected to a haircut, questioned on corporate policies, and finally dropped off in Recco (Genoa). A written responsibility claim issued by the BR the following day connected this incident to the earlier Amerio abduction. However, the kidnappers who attempted to interrogate Casabona on corporate policies displayed a lack of the most elementary knowledge regarding labor relations at the Singer plant.

This cluster came to an end with the abduction of 42-year-old ship-owner Pietro Costa on January 12, 1977, at 8 P.M., in front of his residence at Belvedere Montaldo (Genoa). Armed men forced him into a FIAT-132 sedan that ultimately took him to a hideout located in an apartment near Genoa's Principe Railroad Station, where he was held in captivity for 81 days. Following a ransom payment of 1.5 billion lire settled in a park in Rome, Costa was released on April 3 on the outskirts of Milan near the superhighway. The BR justified this action as "taxation of a multinational."

The original demand entailed a ransom payment of ten billion lire, but since the victim was insured against kidnappings with Lloyd's of London for only 1.3 billion lire, negotiations were reportedly drawn out to make the ransom coincide as closely as possible with the insurance coverage. Moreover, a contractual clause made payment contingent upon captivity in excess of 40 days. One year later, a portion of the proceeds would be used to cover the logistical costs relative to the Moro abduction.[6]

The kidnapping of Aldo Moro, former five-time premier and incumbent president of the Christian Democratic Party (DC), stands by itself because of its operational sophistication and because of the ambitious project it embodied. As far back as April 1975, a strategic resolution of the BR had identified the DC as the principal enemy to be annihilated. Moro was at the time the most influential figure within the DC and a comparatively acces-sible target, largely on account of his rigid patterns. In fact, after an initial inquest—the term used by the BR for surveillance and assessment opera-tions—then-premier Giulio Andreotti and then-president of the Senate Amintore Fanfani, both Christian Democrats, were discarded as possible targets because they were too well protected. The decision to kidnap Moro was made by the strategic directorate in the fall of 1977 and the operation was delegated to the Rome column under the supervision of the executive committee. Material preparation lasted three months.

The abduction took place in Rome on March 16, 1978, at approxi-mately 8:55 A.M., as Moro was riding on the Via Fani in his ministerial-assigned, nonarmored FIAT-130 sedan. Moro's habitual pattern entailed departure from his residence before 9 A.M., attendance at Mass at the Parish Church of Santa Chiara, and travel on the same route to the center of Rome, where he conducted his political and academic activities. On the day of his abduction he was headed for the Chamber of Deputies, of which he was a member, to participate in the vote of confidence for the newly appointed Council of Ministers. Aboard his sedan were also a Carabinieri senior non-commissioned officer (NCO), who served as escort commander, and a Carabinieri trooper at the steering wheel. The car was followed by a back-up vehicle with three Public Security guards, including one NCO.

At the corner of Via Fani and Via Stresa, a stolen white FIAT-128 bearing separately stolen diplomatic license plates suddenly blocked Moro's car by maneuvering to its front. Failure on the part of the Carabinieri driver to take evasive action resulted in boxing Moro's sedan in between the FIAT-128 and the back-up vehicle, which crashed in from behind. The occupants of the FIAT-128 got out and fired their pistols against Moro's driver and escort commander from each side of the statesman's car. At the same time, four men in Alitalia (Italian Airlines) flight uniforms, who had been waiting on the left side of the street by a snack bar, pulled out submachine guns from a large bag and fired on the Carabinieri in Moro's car and on the Public Security guards in the back-up vehicle. Only one escort member— a Public Security guard—managed to draw his pistol, get out of the back-up vehicle, and fire some shots, but he was almost immediately hit and killed, together with the remainder of the escort force, by two members of the commando hidden behind parked cars. At least two more red brigadists were "covering" the road, one along the Via Fani and the other, a woman, at the corner of Via Stresa. It is believed that nine persons formed the core of the attack force.

Moro himself, only slightly wounded, was snatched from his sedan and placed into a blue FIAT-132 that had pulled up in accordance with the plan. This vehicle, as well as two FIAT-128s, departed the scene with the commando members aboard. There is some doubt as to whether a Honda motorcycle was also part of the fleeing convoy. During the attack, traffic had been held off by supporting elements who used stolen police directional batons and fired their weapons as a warning. Moro was subsequently transferred into a van that took him to the "people's prison," which may have been located in an apartment on the Via Montalcini in Rome's southern section, an aspect of the abduction that remains to be established.

There is evidence that the night before the attack the BR had, elsewhere in town, slashed all four tires of a florist's pick-up truck that was usually parked during business hours at the abduction site. Its presence would have been an encumbrance. Moreover, the telephone lines in the area were probably tampered with by BR support elements who infiltrated Italy's telephone service in order to prevent emergency calls.

At the site of the attack, police found 84 ammunition casings (9-mm and 7.65-mm), twelve fragments of pertinent rounds, a 9-mm submachine-gun magazine, an Alitalia flight-officer cap, a German-made black leather bag with an Alitalia sticker on it (not part of Alitalia issue), and a theatrical mustache. The white FIAT-128 with diplomatic license plates was left behind at the site, whereas the other three vehicles used on the Via Fani by the terrorists—all of which turned out to be stolen—were abandoned on the same day or during the days immediately thereafter on the Via Licinio Calvo, which is part of the same neighborhood.

Aldo Moro's captivity lasted 55 days and ended tragically on May 9. During this period he underwent the classical "people's trial" and related interrogations, as reflected in nine BR communiques, two accompanied by a picture of the statesman. From his prison Moro wrote a number of letters to his wife, his associates, political figures, Pope Paul VI, U.N. secretary-general Kurt Waldheim, and other dignitaries. Of these letters, 24 are known to have been received by their addressees. However, material confiscated on October 1, 1978, in a BR safe house on Milan's Via Monte Nevoso discloses that at least 38 letters were written by Moro. Some of them appear to be alternative texts. In the same safe house, the Carabinieri found the photocopy of a so-called memorial, which is presumably the text of Moro's "confessions." Although undoubtedly written under close scrutiny and delivered (or discarded) at the BR's discretion, these letters reflect Moro's unique and highly nuanced writing style. It is virtually certain that the statesman was actively attempting to negotiate his own release.

The first six communiques bear BR ideological propaganda as well as reports regarding Moro's "confessions" and the stages of the "trial," which ended with his "conviction." From these communiques and from the "memorial" it is possible to conclude that the BR were seeking revelations regarding what they term the "imperialist state of the multinationals." It turned out to be a frustrated expectation, since the desired details—largely imagined in the BR's view of capitalist society and U.S.–West European relations—failed to emerge. An exchange of prisoners for Moro's release was demanded for the first time in communique no. 7 and thirteen names were subsequently listed in communique no. 8: those of ranking members of the BR historic nucleus, members of the October XXII Circle and of the Armed Proletarian Nuclei (NAP), politicized common criminals, and even a red brigadist who had participated in the murder of an assistant warden shortly after Moro's abduction. Despite the belated demand for an exchange of prisoners, Moro's letters were suggesting such a solution from the very start of his captivity. In fact, that is the recurring theme in all of his efforts to communicate with the outside world.

There have been differences of opinion among commentators regarding the principal goal behind Moro's abduction. Whereas it may not be possible to list BR aims in their order of priority, these aims are nevertheless obvious. Targeting Moro fully coincided with the BR intent "to strike at the heart of the State." To the BR, Moro symbolized not only the state but also the relative-majority Christian Democratic Party that for over 30 years constituted the foremost representative of the Italian political system. Moreover, Moro had been instrumental in putting together a broad coalition that, despite its contradictions, included for the first time since 1947 Italy's official Communists, who were viewed by the BR as revisionists. Foremost appears to have been the BR's aim to obtain from the state recognition as combatants and as political equals. In this they failed, but they were marginally successful in bringing abut a split between those hard-line political forces, most notably Christian Democrats and Communists, and those who were open to negotiations, most notably the Socialists.

In the ultimate analysis, however, the operational aspects of the Moro abduction are what constitute the truly remarkable aspect of this bloody episode. The sophistication that went into the seizure itself has already been described. In addition, the BR managed to checkmate the state for 55 days and, despite a massive manhunt by the police forces, they carried out a series of complementary actions in cities widely apart: two murders in Turin and Milan, respectively, and six woundings unevenly distributed from Rome to Turin and from Milan to Genoa. Equally demanding were the procedures followed for the clandestine delivery of the nine communiques (at times multiple copies in different cities simultaneously) and Moro's letters, only a few of which were attached to the communiques themselves. Besides telephone contact, it is believed that the BR may have established privileged channels with the Moro family, who only too naturally favored negotiations.

On May 9, following the state's refusal to bend to BR demands, Moro was put in the trunk of a stolen Renault R-4 and "executed" with a submachine gun and a pistol. The car with the body, covered by a blanket, was symbolically left on the Via Caetani, halfway between the DC and Communist Party headquarters. According to the autopsy, Moro was not subjected to physical mistreatment during captivity.

Some commentators still debate whether Moro could have been saved or whether the BR intended from the start to eliminate him. But what is perhaps most disconcerting at this late stage is the fact that all reconstructions of the Moro affair are largely based on the testimony of two "repentant" red brigadists, Patrizio Peci and Antonio Savasta, neither of whom had an operational role in the affair, and one "disassociated" red brigadist, Valerio Morucci, who was part of the assault element but claims no knowledge of events subsequent to the transference of Moro into a van minutes after the abduction.[7]

The next kidnap victim was Supreme Court justice Giovanni D'Urso, 47, who was detailed to the Ministry of Justice as head of the Third Division of the General Directorate for Penitentiaries. This target symbolized both the judiciary and the prison system. D'Urso's abduction occurred in

Rome on December 12, 1980, at 8:30 P.M. On his way back from the ministry, D'Urso had parked his car some distance away from his residence because of parking problems and was proceeding on foot in the darkness. Suddenly seized by four men, forced into a van, and blindfolded, he eventually found himself in a tent presumably erected inside a brick structure. In his estimation, the trip to the "people's prison" lasted two hours. During his captivity, he noted three hooded men, two of whom acted as interrogators. Though blindfolded part of the time, he was never tied or chained.

His captivity lasted 33 days, in the course of which ten communiques were issued. As in Moro's abduction, all of them were typed on the same machine to assure authenticity; however, this time *Il Messaggero*, a Rome daily, was their recipient, in contrast to past practices of sending communiques to different media services.

The BR immediately disclosed their political objective in communique no. 1, that is, "the end of differentiation between inmates" and the closing of the maximum-security prison on the island of Asinara (off Sardinia). In fact, their strategic resolution of October 1980, consisting of 112 pages, had dedicated 22 of them to the prison system and stressed that "a coherent line of attack and a tight state of siege against the prison system means striking at the apex of the Ministry of Justice, at the central directorate of the prison institutions, at the chief wardens of the individual prisons, [and] at those who elaborate the most criminal and sophisticated techniques to control and annihilate the imprisoned proletariat." At this stage the BR were equating the prison system with "capitalist repression."

In contrast to Moro, who was expected to make revelations on the illusory "imperialist state of the multinationals," D'Urso was questioned on more mundane matters: specifically, the organization of, and personnel assigned to, the prison system. His chief interrogator, a criminologist who had joined the BR, possessed the appropriate background for this task. Reportedly, D'Urso provided the most minute details, including the physical appearance of the officials assigned to this sector of interest to the BR.

On December 26 the governmental authorities announced that the Asinara prison would be closed, but they stressed that this decision had been taken well before D'Urso's abduction. Two days later a terrorist-led revolt broke out in the Trani (Bari) maximum-security prison, in the course of which hostages were taken. The following day it was quelled by the Carabinieri Special Intervention Group (Gruppo Intervento Speciale). On New Year's Eve, the BR retaliated by murdering Carabinieri brigadier general Enrico Galvaligi, deputy director for the coordination of prison security, in front of his Rome apartment. Tragically, Galvaligi was one of the officials so well described by D'Urso.

Communique no. 8 of January 4, 1981, announced that D'Urso had been sentenced to death. At the same time, it left the final decision to the "comrades" held in the maximum-security prisons of Trani and Palmi (Reggio Calabria) and demanded that their verdict be published by the Italian press and be reported on television. Since media attitudes were becoming discordant with respect to the coverage of terrorist propaganda, the BR insisted on publicity and some papers did publish their communiques. In its issue of January 11, the Rome weekly *L'Espresso* printed not only the record of D'Urso's interrogation but also an interview clandestinely provided by Giovanni Senzani, the criminologist who had interrogated the magistrate. Moreover, a Radical Party–connected television station aired an appeal from D'Urso's daughter, who personally read a BR communique defining her father as an executioner.

D'Urso was released on January 15, pursuant to the "clemency" accorded by the Palmi and Trani inmates. Tied and gagged, he was abandoned in a FIAT-127 parked on Rome's Via del Portico d'Ottavia, not far from the Ministry of Justice. Throughout his trip to freedom, he had on a blindfold as well as stereo earphones. Although he wrote a letter to his superiors supporting the BR's demand to shut down the Asinara prison, there is no evidence of attempts on his part to manage his own release.[8]

Because of the long time lag between them, the Moro and D'Urso kidnappings are not likely to be considered a cluster, even though continuity may be found in the fact that both targets represented the state and, in both cases, specific political demands were made. Moreover, it is interesting to note the similarities in the language and style of the communiques issued in each case.[9] This continuity exists, despite the different personalities and approaches of the leading operatives in each instance: Mario Moretti of the BR's historic nucleus in Moro's case, and Giovanni Senzani, theoretician of the "movementist" wing, in D'Urso's case. Both men have since been captured, but neither is cooperating with the authorities.

In the history of the BR, 1981 is on record as "the year of the kidnappings." Four of them were carried out over a partially overlapping period of time in different areas of the country. This feat is all the more significant considering the setbacks suffered in 1980 following the confessions of "repentant" red brigadist Patrizio Peci, former head of the Turin column, and the "great spring offensive" by the law-enforcement agencies. Moreover, each of the targets—Ciro Cirillo, Giuseppe Taliercio, Renzo Sandrucci, and Roberto Peci—represented a different political objective as the BR were combating their war on different fronts. The only reservation about the correctness of classifying them as a coordinated cluster arises from the consideration that the Cirillo and Peci abductions were largely the result of Senzani's own initiative rather than of the BR central organs.

The abduction of Ciro Cirillo, 60, former president of the Campania region and incumbent DC councillor for urban planning and economic affairs, had two ostensible objectives: the deepening of the BR's penetration southward, and the exploitation of governmental inefficiency in relieving the damages caused in the area by the previous year's earthquake.

This commando action took place in Torre del Greco (Naples) on April 27, 1981, at 9:30 P.M. Cirillo, accompanied by a secretary and two escort members, was returning to his apartment in an armored sedan. The escort commander, who was responsible for opening the building's garage door, uncautiously left the car door unlocked. The driver, in turn, failed to wait for the garage gate to close before opening his car door after parking in the garage. Meanwhile, three members of the BR commando squad moved in. One fired a submachine gun and killed the escort commander beside the garage entrance, another fired a pistol killing the driver, and the third fired a pistol wounding the secretary. Cirillo was forced out of his now-useless armored sedan and was pushed into a van that had taken up position in front of the entrance, thus blocking it, while two BR back-up vehicles were deployed in the immediate vicinity. The assault unit had in advance sabotaged the local telephone line. Fifteen red brigadists presumably participated—all without masks—in the operation.

Cirillo was held captive for 88 days, during which twelve communiques were issued that listed several demands: distribution of empty buildings to the victims of the earthquake, removal of trailer-homes provided as emergency relief, subsidies to the local unemployed, and publication of the record of Cirillo's "trial." These communiques reflected thorough familiarity with local affairs. In support of the BR's demands, Cirillo wrote approximately twenty letters to his family and to political figures. He also addressed on tape the victims of the earthquake. The tape was distributed by the BR to a Naples and a Rome television station, together with a videocassette of the "trial." Cirillo's prison, a two-by-two-meter, soundproof, wooden structure equipped with artificial ventilation and a cot, had been mounted inside the office-residence of a female cardiologist in the municipality of Cercola near Naples. The woman's husband served the councillor his meals, prepared upstairs by the woman's parents. Senzani would visit the prison from time to time to question Cirillo.

The councillor was released on July 24, at 6:20 A.M., in an area of Naples particularly damaged by the earthquake. According to the BR, the price of his release amounted to 1.45 billion lire paid by his party and family. Cirillo subsequently declared that his family did in fact disburse this amount. The aftereffects of the Cirillo affair still entail polemics and investigations regarding the alleged mediation of local organized crime in bringing about his release and the related role of the intelligence services. Nonetheless, it appears to be an established fact that the BR demands were substantially met to their satisfaction.

While Cirillo was still in hands of his captors. Giuseppe Taliercio, 53, manager of the Montedison petrochemical plant in Marghera (Venice), was abducted on May 20, 1981, at 1:30 P.M., by four members of the Veneto column who gained access under false pretenses to his apartment in Mestre (Venice). One of them was disguised as a Finance Guard member. After overpowering and tying up the victim, his wife, and two children, the commando group searched the premises and then departed from the service entrance carrying Taliercio inside a trunk. According to "repentant" red brigadist Antonio Savasta, who was in charge of the operation, Taliercio's abduction, in addition to the symbolic significance of the target, was to serve as an "exemplary campaign" for the purpose of settling internal feuds between the "militarist" and "movementist" wings of the organization.

Taliercio was held captive for 46 days in a safe house located in Tarcento (Udine). He spent this time chained to a cot inside a tent pitched within the safe house. His reluctance to respond in detail to the interrogation resulted in beatings. No demand was ever made in exchange for his release. Communique no. 5 of June 26 announced his "death sentence" with the following explanation: "In 30 years of antiproletarian activity, he personified the role and functions of the imperialist personnel that plan and carry out [industrial] restructuring at the service of the multinationals." The "execution" took place on July 6. After a telephone call by the BR to the news agency ANSA, the body was found at 1:30 P.M. near Taliercio's plant in Marghera inside a stolen car in which the speedometer had been broken to conceal the mileage after the theft. According to the autopsy, sixteen bullets fired from two different pistols were embedded in the corpse. Moreover, Taliercio had lost ten kilograms of weight, his hair had grayed, and one tooth was missing.

The third abduction of this cluster was that of Renzo Sandrucci, 53, an executive employee of Alfa Romeo responsible for production and labor organization at the Arese (Milan) plant. He was kidnapped on June 3, 1981, at 7:30 A.M., by elements of the Milan column a few hundred meters away from his residence as he was driving to work on his habitual route. Sandrucci's sedan was boxed in by a FIAT-124 and an Opel Ascona in the immediate proximity of a parked van, from which members of the commando group wearing workers' overalls dismounted, ordered bystanders into a snack bar at gun point, overpowered Sandrucci's corporate bodyguard, who was sitting next to him, and forced Sandrucci into the FIAT-124. Seven to nine red brigadists presumably participated in this operation.

During his 51 days of captivity, Sandrucci was kept in a tent inside an apartment. As in Cirillo's case, he was assigned ideological readings before each interrogation. From his prison Sandrucci wrote several letters, including one tendering his resignation from Alfa Romeo. The BR also issued eight communiques demanding the annulment of a corporate decision to reduce the labor force. In practice, Alfa Romeo merely postponed it. Sandrucci was released on July 23 at 6:10 P.M. A telephone call to a private radio station indicated where he could be found. He had been left tied in a stolen Alfa Romeo Giulia Super (the choice of vehicle was symbolic) near the Ercole Marelli plant in Crescenzago (Milan).

The fourth and final victim of this cluster was Roberto Peci, younger brother of "repentant" red brigadist Patrizio Peci. He was kidnapped in the afternoon of June 10 in San Benedetto del Tronto (Ascoli Piceno) after being lured into a trap; Peci thought he was responding to a repair call received at his electrician's shop. During 55 days of captivity, Peci was forced to write polemical letters to his brother Patrizio, and the BR issued their classical communiques. The purpose of this operation was primarily to intimidate "repentant" terrorists and secondarily to contradict Patrizio's confessions. In a complementary action, a BR commando assaulted and wounded attorney Antonio De Vita in Rome on June 19; De Vita was the court-appointed defense counsel for Patrizio Peci. Roberto was ultimately murdered on April 3 in a macabre setting. As twenty pistol and revolver rounds entered his body, the "execution" was recorded on videotape. The corpse, under a BR flag, was abandoned in an impromptu garbage dump inside some ruins on a road perpendicular to Rome's Appian Way. A poster read: "Death to traitors!" [10]

Until Taliercio's murder, the BR had held the four abductees captive contemporaneously for nearly one month. At the end of 1981, the BR embarked on another unprecedented and clamor-inducing kidnap venture: the abduction of U.S. Army brigadier general James L. Dozier, deputy chief of staff for logistics and administration of NATO's Land Forces Southern Europe with headquarters in Verona. Dozier became the first American victim of Italian domestic terrorism. Prior BR condemnations of American "imperialism" in theoretical tracts had already evidenced their hostility toward the United States. Moreover, a strategic resolution of February 1978, disseminated as an attachment to BR communique no. 4 issued during Moro's captivity, defined NATO as "the political-military organism to which imperialism entrusts the guiding role in relation to both the defense against the 'external enemy' and the annihilation of the 'internal enemy.'" [11]

On December 17 at approximately 5 P.M., two red brigadists disguised as plumbers looking for a leak gained easy access to Dozier's apartment along Verona's Adige River. The general and his wife were quickly overpowered. Joined by two more members of the commando, the "plumbers" tied and gagged the American couple, searched the premises for documents of interest, placed the general in a trunk, and vacated the premises taking him along. The alarm was given four hours later when neighbors responded to Mrs. Dozier's noisy efforts to untie herself.

Dozier's abduction had been decided several months in advance by the BR's strategic directorate, and the operation had been entrusted to the Veneto column, headed by now-"repentant" red brigadist Antonio Savasta, who was until his capture a member of the national executive committee. He subsequently reconstructed the abduction for the police and the judiciary.

The operational details were worked out in Milan at a meeting of the executive committee two months before the event. Eighteen million lire were budgeted for the kidnapping and eight terrorists participated in the operation. After his seizure, Dozier was loaded aboard a rented FIAT-238 van, transferred en route into a purchased FIAT-Ritmo, and taken to an apartment in Padua, where the same tent used for Taliercio had been set up with a cot inside. Dozier was kept hand-chained to the cot and with earphones over his ears. He was allowed to exercise in place, was regularly fed, and was even given the opportunity to bathe. His five "jailers," three men and two women, wore ski masks inside the safe house. Dozier was interrogated seven times at long intervals by Savasta himself, always in Italian but with the aid of a dictionary. Questioning on military matters turned out to be shallow. No forceful methods to elicit responses were used.

During Dozier's 42 days of captivity, the BR issued five communiques, to the third of which they appended a transcript of the general's interrogation. The BR clearly indicated that through Dozier they were putting American "imperialism" on trial. In their communiques, they reiterated that the "imperialist state of the multinationals" is nurtured in Italy by NATO structures imposed by the United States on Western Europe. Moreover, Dozier was made to appear as the de facto commander of NATO's land forces rather than just the senior U.S. staff officer.

A nearly concurrent abduction was attempted in Rome on January 6, 1982, when a BR commando squad failed to seize Deputy Police Commissioner Nicola Simone in his apartment; Simone was wounded but managed to repel the attackers by firing his revolver. In the BR responsibility claim for his wounding, it is stated: "War on NATO! War on preventive counterrevolution! Attack the men and structures of the preventive counterrevolution in order to disarticulate the imperialist war plan and to build the transition toward communism!" Their language ties this action to the one against Dozier.

On January 28, 1982, at 11:30 A.M., ten members of the State Police Central Operative Nucleus for Security—a SWAT-type unit—broke into the Padua safe house, captured Dozier's "jailers," including Savasta, and recovered the general unharmed wearing a sweatsuit similar to those of his captors and a long beard. The identification of the hideout was made possible by investigations in circles peripheral to the BR.

Dozier's abduction is attributable not only to the ideological and political considerations outlined above, but also to the fact that he was the most accessible of the ranking U.S. military officers in Italy, as the BR inquest disclosed. Savasta has stated that to avoid the risk of a shootout with Dozier's Carabinieri driver—the only visible security measure—it was decided to seize the general in his unguarded residence.[12]

Dozier's liberation by the State Police and Savasta's cooperation with the governmental authorities marked a substantive decline in the effectiveness and operational rhythm of the BR onslaught. The BR have since been unable to field spectacular operations, particularly in the form of abductions. Their most recent kidnapping—indeed a modest one—took place in Naples on July 19, 1982. They abducted hospital x-ray technician Giovanni La Greca for the pragmatic purpose of assisting commando members wounded by the police while escaping after their deadly attack on Deputy Police Commissioner Antonio Ammaturo and his driver a few days earlier in the same city. La Greca was released on July 24.

The other known practitioners of the kidnapping craft on the Marxist-Leninist side of the terrorist spectrum are the October XXII Circle, the NAP, the Communist Combat Units (UCC), and elements connected to Workers' Autonomy (AUTOP).

The October XXII Circle is in fact the initiator of terrorist abductions in Italy, although in its short life this formation carried out only one such action, a pragmatic one to boot. On October 5, 1970, at 11:30 P.M., three masked militants kidnapped nineteen-year-old student Sergio Gadolla by his garage door; Gadolla's wealthy Genoa-based family quickly paid a ransom of 200 million lire. The young man was released six days later along a country road near Rezoaglio (Genoa). The group did not issue a responsibility claim and its paternity was established only after a number of arrests in connection with other crimes. Gadolla had been held captive in a tent in a mountainous area, a technique frequently used by common criminals. In this connection, it might be noted that Circle membership included common criminals as well as idealists. The proceeds from the Gadolla abduction were used for paramilitary training.

The NAP have been responsible for three abductions and thus rank second behind the BR. The first two were to finance the organization; the third was for ideological purposes. On July 25, 1974, at 2:30 P.M., the NAP kidnapped in Naples student Antonio Gargiulo, son of a local medical doctor, and released him on the same day after a payment of 70 million lire.

The victim reportedly never left the abduction vehicle. On December 18 of the same year, at 6:30 A.M., they kidnapped Naples liquor producer Giuseppe Moccia, who was forced out of his car at gunpoint when he stopped in response to a fake road sign. His release occurred four days later, at 7:45 P.M., after a disbursement of 1 billion lire. Neither kidnapping was claimed. The proceeds from the first ransom were used to strengthen the NAP Naples network and those from the second to expand the network to Rome and other areas. In various ways these first two abductions constitute a cluster.

In the afternoon hours of May 6, 1975, the NAP kidnapped under uncertain circumstances Supreme Court justice Giuseppe Di Gennaro, who had been detailed to the Ministry of Justice to oversee prisoner rehabilitation programs. This time a responsibility claim was issued and Di Gennaro was subjected to questioning regarding the internal functioning of the penitentiaries, a matter of institutional interest to this prison-oriented terrorist formation. Di Gennaro was released in Rome on May 11, at 10:30 P.M., in exchange for the transfer of three riotous NAP inmates from the Viterbo prison to penitentiaries of their choice.

The UCC injected an element of novelty into Italian political kidnappings. Their sole consummated action in this sector entailed the abduction of Rome meat dealer Giuseppe Ambrosio, 53, on June 14, 1976, at 5:30 A.M. In exchange for his release, they demanded the distribution of 7,100 kilograms of meat at below-market price in the "proletarian" neighborhoods of Rome. Ambrosio was freed by the Carabinieri the following day before distribution could take place. The UCC, whose membership included ideological militants and common criminals, had mostly planned abortive kidnappings of purely criminal nature. In fact, elaborate facilities to hold kidnap victims were discovered by the Carabinieri in a UCC hideout in Vescovio (Rieti).

The remaining abduction attributable to the terrorist left again combines political and criminal elements. On April 14, 1975, 26-year-old engineer Carlo Saronio was kidnapped in Milan. Though planned by Carlo Fioroni, a friend of the victim, to finance AUTOP, the mechanics of this abduction were left to common criminal Carlo Casirati. Saronio's family paid a ransom of 470 million lire, but the victim never returned. He had died the same night of the kidnapping because of improper gagging, even before the ransom was demanded. Saronio's body was recovered in the suburbs of Milan in November 1978.[13]

In contrast with leftist abductions, the two rightist ones on record represent exclusively revenue-raising ventures. On November 22, 1973, at 7 P.M., four militants of the Revolutionary Action Movement kidnapped 28-year-old industrialist and race-car driver Aldo Cannavale in front of his

Milan residence. A ransom of 350 million lire was paid and the victim was released on December 4. Only subsequent investigations disclosed the political matrix of this operation, which was not followed by a responsibility claim. The other abduction was commissioned by rightist elements and carried out by hired common criminals. The victim was 39-year-old landowner Luigi Mariano. Kidnapped on July 23, 1975, at 7:50 A.M. in front of his home in Gallipoli (Lecce), he was released on September 9 following a ransom payment of 280 million lire.[14] The nature of these two kidnappings and their negligible number constitute yet another indication of the lack of operational sophistication peculiar to the terrorist right.

Kidnappings and Common Crime

A commonly held view regards Sardinian banditry as the initiator of kidnappings for ransom in Italy. These bandits, notably from the Barbagia area, are indeed among the oldest practitioners. Parliamentary committee hearings on criminality on the island established that the first recorded kidnapping dates back to 1477. Other evidence discloses that the Saracene raiders from the Arabic world had already introduced this practice in Sicily in more remote times. Nevertheless, it may accurately be held that the origins of Italy's contemporary kidnap industry are traceable to the Sardinian shepherd/criminal milieu of the early 1960s. By 1967, out of thirteen abductions countrywide, twelve had been perpetrated in Sardinia. The following year, eleven out of fourteen were likewise carried out on the island.[15]

With the start of the 1970s, as the annual number of abductions in Sardinia itself dropped in most cases to half or less of the 1967–1968 level, kidnappings for extortion began to proliferate throughout the national territory. By March 1978 the industrial region of Lombardy, which had experienced only one such incident for the first time in 1963, had reached a total of 76 abductions.[16] The spread of this type of crime is partially attributable to the changing nature and territorial expansion of the classical criminal organizations that formerly had a regional sphere of action: Sicilian mafia, Calabrian 'ndrangheta, and Neapolitan camorra, whose origins and development will be traced in Chapter 5. Likewise, Sardinian bandits established appendages on the mainland following the emigration of a large number of islanders. The significance of this is shown by the aggregate abduction figures for six major regions—three southern and three northern—from 1972 through January 1984: 146 in Lombardy, 81 in Calabria, 56 in Latium, 37 in Piedmont, 23 in Campania, and 18 in Sicily. The needle clearly reflects a northward shift.[17]

The operational patterns that emerge from the study of kidnappings for extortion appear to follow the practices of Sardinian bandits, as summarized below:[18]

1. Selection of the victim in relation to the financial ability to pay the demanded ransom.
2. Study of the victim's habits in order to determine the most suitable time and place for the abduction.
3. Preparation of the initial facility in which to hide the victim immediately after seizure.
4. Setting up the premises (cavern, gorge, hut, tent, or other property) where the victim will be hidden in the subsequent stages of captivity until settlement of the ransom.
5. Choice of routes, means of transportation, and meeting places with intermediaries.

According to the parliamentary findings, Sardinian kidnappers associate and subsequently disband upon accomplishment of their criminal venture. This is in keeping with the comparatively loose structure of Sardinian banditry. Somewhat more stable appears to be the task force—or, at least, its upper echelons—organized by crime syndicates for this purpose. However, in the interest of security, rigid compartmentalization separates the various operatives. Thus, criminals performing their respective roles as surveillants, snatchers, jailers, telephone operators, mail carriers, and collectors are not likely to be familiar with one another. A coordinator reports to the planner(s).[19] It is estimated that ten to fifteen operatives are involved in each kidnapping. As opposed to political abductions, whose perpetrators generally belong to age groups in their twenties and thirties, common-crime kidnappers are often older. In some cases, certain phases of the abduction are assigned to different criminal organizations that specialize in particular functions.

Victims are most frequently seized on the street in the proximity of their residence or office, preferably during hours of limited visibility, by masked men. In contrast, terrorists are usually disguised. Whereas to date political extremists have seized only adult males, common criminals have indiscriminately abducted men, women, and children. To these profit-minded criminals the abductees are of value only so long as they are alive. Unlike terrorists, they are not seeking publicity for a "cause" and consequently are not interested in murders and woundings as an alternative show of strength, should the seizure phase fail.

Captivity can vary from a few days to several months, and it can be extremely harsh largely on account of exposure to the elements and/or detention in primitive and dirty facilities. There have also been cases where the victims were sexually abused. Moreover, in at least two instances, an ear of the victim was amputated and sent to the relatives to reinforce the ransom demand. Pressures on the victim and family generally include threats of future harm even to other relatives. Normally the abductee is released shortly after payment of the ransom; only occasionally is a supplementary one demanded. However, in a notable number of exceptions, the victim is either killed or disappears, despite ransom payment, presumably because he or she saw too much. Statistics collected from various press sources show that 28 corpses were recovered between January 1970 and June 1982. In 1985, out of seventeen kidnappings, only one victim was murdered.[20]

Kidnappings for extortion—610 between 1960 and mid-1986—are generally the work of specialized syndicates, elements from the same milieu that occasionally diversify their criminal pursuits, or unaffiliated or ad hoc bands seeking unlawful financial profits. This last category is considered the most dangerous because of the lack of expertise on the part of its components.

Prior to the emergence of the kidnap industry in the early 1960s, abductions carried out by the traditional crime organizations—mafia, camorra, and 'ndrangheta—were most often intended as instruments to obtain compliance with criminal demands in no way related to the acquisition of a ransom payment. Since then, abductions for ransom in Sicily have been the work of the *corleonesi,* one of the mafia "families," but their number has not been significant. However, mafia elements operating in and out of Rome have also been responsible for this type of crime on the peninsula. The Calabrian 'ndrangheta has perpetrated abductions for ransom on a systematic basis since 1974, primarily for the purpose of financing other activities. This development coincided with the geographical expansion of the various 'ndrangheta elements outside of their traditional boundaries. Consequently, a number of kidnappings perpetrated in the regions of Lombardy, Piedmont, and Latium are traceable to the 'ndrangheta matrix. Sardinian elements—usually members of transplanted banditry from the island—have likewise exploited their expertise in this field, particularly in the regions of Tuscany and Latium. In conjunction with these developments, several convicted criminals from the South were legally forced to take up residence in the North as a security measure. Ironically, these elements joined forces with local crime, to which they contributed their specialized criminal experience.

A reliable estimate sets at 300 billion lire the aggregate ransom money obtained from kidnappings between January 1965 and January 1984, only 10 percent of which has been recovered by law-enforcement agencies.[21] Ransoms have kept up with the pace of inflation. It is estimated that 180–

200 billion lire were extorted between 1980 and 1984.[22] The payer of a ransom is frequently forced to take long trips with several stops at intermediate check points before being allowed to deliver the pertinent sum. Postponements in making contact with the collector or, more precisely, with the "drop area" are likely to happen if the kidnappers suspect a trap.

Once collected, the ransom money is "laundered" in Italy or abroad. If the services of a specialist are required, his fee can be as high as 30 percent of the ransom. Standard laundering channels include compliant banks, financial firms, and casinos. Alternatives include deposits in several different accounts with different banks or use of bearer passbooks, cashier's checks to the order of real or fictitious individuals, and postal money orders. Recent legislation has complicated most of these procedures by requiring depositor's identification for sums in excess of twenty million lire.[23]

The largest amount of the ransom money goes to the crime syndicate or to the freelance organizers, as applicable. The coordinator generally receives a percentage, whereas those who perform the "manual work" are most often paid a flat fee.

In the discussion above of political abductions, mention was made of the links with common-crime elements entertained by the BR, the October XXII Circle, the NAP, the UCC, AUTOP, and the neo-Fascist terrorist right. With respect to the UCC, it might be added that its common-crime component maintained an operational connection with elements of the Calabrian 'ndrangheta. Though unquestionably noteworthy, these links appear to be, at least as of mid-1986, occasional rather than systematic.

Nevertheless, the existence of such links is disconcerting. No less so are the traces of incipient political goals or, at the least, efforts to give their ventures ideological justification by substantially criminal formations that practice kidnappings for ransom. Two cases are to the point. The Sardinian Armed Movement, which in conjunction with its criminal actions—including seven abductions for ransom—calls for Sardinian independence, has threatened (in politically couched language) and assaulted former criminals that cooperate with the authorities. During the night of July 28, 1984, in Nuoro, the group abducted journalist Michele Tatti of *Unione Sarda*, who was held long enough to "interview" the band's reputed leader, Antonino Mele. The interview turned out to be a monologue.[24] The other case coincides with the abduction for ransom of a member of the Bulgari family, renowned Roman jewelers, in December 1983. The group assumed the name Attacking Communists (Comunisti d'Attacco).[25]

On the positive side for law and order, there have been no political abductions since 1982, and annual statistics show that kidnappings for extortion purposes have been on the decline since 1983.

CHAPTER FIVE

Organized Crime

A laborious study published in 1985 by the Center for Social Studies and Investments (CENSIS) of Rome endeavors to quantify the effect of unlawful activity on the economy in terms of "business [that is, monetary] turnover" and "work force."[1] CENSIS estimates that the yearly turnover ranges from 100 trillion to 137 trillion lire and the relative work force encompasses 785 thousand to one million "operators." Considered in these estimates are eleven sectors of unlawful activity:

1. Manufacture and trade of drugs. Turnover: 25–35 trillion lire. Operators: 20,000–30,000. Ninety percent of the turnover is deemed to constitute pure profit. The work force is roughly subdivided as follows: 1,000 "bosses" 3,000–6,000 "technicians"; and 10,000–20,000 "pushers." Moreover, Italy's over 200,000 drug addicts often operate as pushers to finance their own needs.

2. Clandestine manufacture and trade of arms. Turnover: 4–5 trillion lire. Operators: 50,000. The turnover is significant, particularly when compared to that of the legitimate arms industry, which amounts to approximately 4 trillion lire.

3. Clandestine manufacture and trade of art works. Turnover: 1–2 trillion lire. Operators: 5,000–10,000. Much of this activity is for foreign markets.

4. Exploitation of prostitution. Turnover: 5 trillion lire. Operators: 50,000. Prostitutes themselves are believed to range from 350,000 to 400,000.

5. Clandestine gambling. Turnover: 3–7 trillion lire. Operators: 10,000.

6. Extortion and blackmail. Turnover: 15–20 trillion lire. Operators: 75,000–150,000. This activity is increasing in large urban cen-

ters and frequently takes the form of "protection money" demanded of commercial establishments such as stores, bars, restaurants, and entertainment facilities.

7. Thefts, robberies, and receiving stolen property. Turnover: 20 trillion lire. Operators: 400,000. Included in these estimates is an army of petty thieves ranging from 250,000 to 300,000 individuals responsible for thefts in the aggregate of 1–2 trillion lire. A minimal amount of the total stolen property is recovered and only 10 percent of these criminals are arrested and convicted.

8. Smuggling. Turnover: 2–3 trillion lire. Operators: 25,000–50,000. Many criminal careers begin in this sector, which also serves as a training stage for more sophisticated crimes.

9. Illicit foreign currency trade. Turnover: 5–10 trillion lire. Operators: No estimate given.

10. Illicit commissions for services legally due. Turnover: 8–12.5 trillion lire. Operators: 50,000–100,000.

11. Other unlawful activities such as forgeries, fraud, and exploiting people of unsound mind. Turnover: 12.5–17.5 trillion lire. Operators: 100,000–150,000.

It follows that roughly one out of every twenty Italian citizens or residents of working age is involved in some unlawful activity of economic nature.

Two other surveys, both published by the weekly *L'Espresso* in 1985, address charges of misconduct against councillors at the local levels of government and against members of the judiciary.[2] In 1984, for example, 269 councillors from all of Italy's twenty regions were indicted and/or convicted of unlawful activities. Statistics are particularly high for Sicily (50), Campania (35), and Calabria (22), all of which have long-standing organized crime traditions, and for Liguria (32), Piedmont (19), and Lombardy (16), which constitute the industrial triangle of the North. The parties enjoying nationwide representation were affected roughly in proportion to their political weight and patronage potential: Christian Democrats (77), Socialists (71), Communists (30), Social Democrats (18), Republicans (9), Liberals (3), and Italian Social Movement (1). Between January 1980 and February 1985, approximately 100 magistrates were investigated and/or subjected to disciplinary action by the Superior Council of the Judiciary.

Structures and Dynamics
of Crime Syndicates

In postindustrial Italian society, organized crime has played the most incisive role in the sphere of unlawful practices, particularly those of an economic nature. Although social deviance in individuals and in minor groups still persists, crime syndicates have extended their penetration into, or control over, most sectors of criminality. Consequently, their structures and dynamics have steadily become more sophisticated and, indeed, more dangerous for the orderly functioning of democratic society. Lesser criminal organizations are frequently absorbed by, or are turning into appendages of, the powerful crime syndicates whose material and geographical sphere of action has expanded in geometric dimensions.

In this evolutionary context, the term "mafia" and its adjectival derivatives, which were originally used to describe Sicilian organized crime, have acquired a broader geographical application. More important, they are now indicative of a particular criminal mentality or mind-set, *mentalità mafiosa*, that encompasses four principal elements: the intent to violate the law, the expectation to do so with impunity, simultaneous patronage and favoritism, and a sense of security deriving from the conviction of enjoying the protection of the powerful. This reality readily emerges from the analysis of the principal criminal organizations and their modi operandi in postindustrial society.

Sicilian organized crime itself has never used the term mafia.[3] Much of what is known about the internal structure and dynamics of Sicilian mafia is the result of the confessions of former member Tommaso Buscetta, who calls the organization "Cosa Nostra."[4] The basic organizational cell, called the "family" (*famiglia*), is a territorial unit with criminal control over a portion or the entirety of an urban area from which it draws its full name—for example, the Corleone family. Members of a family are "men of honor" (*uomini di onore*) or "soldiers" (*soldati*) organized in subgroups of ten, each headed by a "leader of ten" (*capo decina*). The head of a family, called the "representative" (*rappresentante*), is elected and in turn appoints a "deputy" (*vice-capo*) and one or more "advisers" (*consiglieri*).

The activity of the families is coordinated by a collegiate board, called the "commission" (*commissione*) or "dome" (*cupola*), consisting of the "district chiefs" (*capi mandamento*)—that is, the representatives of three or more families territorially contiguous. As a rule subject to exceptions, a district chief is also the head of a family. The commission itself is chaired by one of the district chiefs, originally called the "secretary" (*segretario*), but, of late, simply "chief" (*capo*). Whenever contingent events foreclose the election of a family representative, a "regent" (*regente*) is appointed by the commission. The jurisdiction of the commission roughly corresponds to the territory of a Sicilian province. According to Buscetta, whose association with the mafia began in the early 1950s, the organization functions in seven out of nine provinces, Messina and Siracusa being the exceptions. There are, therefore, seven commissions. The one responsible for the Palermo province has traditionally exercised a sort of supremacy over the other commissions. In recent times a new body, called the "interprovincial" (*interprovinciale*), was set up to regulate mafia affairs in a plurality of provinces.

There are no written rules or membership lists for the organization. Rather, all information is transmitted by word of mouth. Prerequisites for membership include courage and cruelty, "transparent" family background, and an absence of family ties with law-enforcement personnel. Cruelty is a requirement insofar as a candidate is tested through the performance of a bloody criminal act. Initiation entails a ritual oath—"May my flesh burn as this holy picture if I do not remain faithful to my oath"—pronounced in front of three men of honor while holding the burning picture of a saint until it completely burns in the oathtaker's bare hands. The picture is first stained with his blood from a punctured finger. Man-of-honor status ends only at death or by expulsion, but the latter does not extinguish secrecy obligations.

Knowledge of mafia affairs by the men of honor themselves is strictly based on need-to-know and hierarchical status. Secrecy, even about personal membership, is an iron rule whose violation is punishable by death. Truthfulness among men of honor is mandatory, but curiosity must never be displayed. When matters pertaining to two or more families are discussed, the presence of a third man of honor, as a witness, is deemed advisable. In order to preclude the possibility of infiltration, introductions between two men of honor are arranged, whenever necessary, by a third member who knows them both. Passage from one family to another, which at one time was strictly forbidden, now takes place.

Arrest or confinement does not dissolve mafia ties, but if a family head is imprisoned, organizational decisions are made by his deputy, to whom he can provide nonbinding advice through clandestine channels set up by the organization. An imprisoned member's needs and those of his immediate relatives are taken care of by the organization. Under no circumstances may a man of honor resort to the police or the judiciary for personal matters, other than reporting the theft of a motor vehicle. This one exception is a security measure in the event that a common criminal should use the stolen vehicle for his own unlawful purposes.

Many of the same criminal traits are discernable in the Calabrian 'ndrangheta and the Neapolitan camorra. Both organizations have membership prerequisites, initiation rituals, security rules, and confederate bonds comparable to those of the Sicilian mafia.

The structure of the 'ndrangheta has been reconstructed thanks to the seizure of its written codes, which reflect the traditional absence of a unitary or rigidly homogeneous organization. It is, rather, a federation of over 120 individual clans (*cosche*), each operating over a specific territory. The largest concentration of clans, over 90, is in the province of Reggio Calabria, as opposed to over twenty in Catanzaro and fewer than ten in Cosenza. Each clan has rules that do not substantially differ from those of its counterparts. Although reverential mention is often made of an overlord, "holiest mother" (*mammasantissima*), this figure is not believed to exist. Each clan is headed by a "boss" (*capo bastone*), assisted by an "accountant" (*contabile*). Full-fledged members are known as *camorristi* and are specifically referred to as *camorristi di sgarro* or *camorristi di sanque,* depending on whether they are responsible for crimes against property or against persons. Camorristi take turns as "master of the day" (*maestro di giornata*) in the supervision of the clan's sphere of influence. A recruit is called *picciotto* and a candidate is a "youth of honor" (*giovane di onore*).

The camorra, part of whose terminology is similar to that of the 'ndrangheta, originated in Naples and expanded to the rest of the region of Campania. Internal rules were subsequently committed to writing. Neapolitan, or Campanian, camorra consists of various clans with territorial jurisdiction. However, two principal groups have emerged in recent times: the New Organized Camorra (Nuova Camorra Organizzata) and the New Family (Nuova Famiglia). The New Organized Camorra has a pyramidal structure whose apex imparts directives to a number of area bosses. Prison inmate Raffaele Cutolo, referred to as "The Word" (*Il Verbo*), is the supreme head. The New Family, in contrast, is more akin to a "federation" of approximately ten clans, and it more faithfully reflects the camorra tradition.[5]

All three organizations—mafia, 'ndrangheta, and camorra—display a similar development that parallels societal, economic, and industrial modernization. A rapid historical overview is beneficial for a better appreciation of the *mentalità mafiosa* and its pervasive influence.

In the nineteenth century these criminal associations had already embarked on a parasitical course by providing private protection to the landed gentry and even to commoners against nonaffiliated criminals, as well as against a variety of actual or perceived dangers and abuses. In a social climate imbued with such values as obsessive commitment to personal and family honor, they were able to create for themselves an aura of chivalry, despite the fact that from their genesis these organizations resorted to unlawfulness, violence, and ruthlessness. Because of indirect advantages for law and order or mere political expediency, such a "policing" and pseudo-judicial role was frequently tolerated or encouraged by the authorities in both preunification and postunification Italy.

From debatable private police functions, these criminal organizations went on to impose their "protection" through intimidatory practices and to make their services available to patrons who could either financially afford them or reciprocate in tangible as well as intangible ways. Here lies the traditional link, under the *quid pro quo* formula, between a mafia-type organization and those in a position of economic, administrative, or political power. It also explains the comforting feeling of a mafioso that he is "untouchable."

Although the *mentalità mafiosa* has substantially remained unchanged over the years, the aspirations and techniques of mafia-type crime have evolved with the times. As late as the 1960s, the classic mafia-type organization still existed, although it was largely circumscribed to local provincial levels. The respective clan leaders, who continued to enjoy widespread prestige, were readily identifiable but relatively "untouchable" because of the wall of silence and sufficiently high-placed patrons that surrounded them. Notably, mafia activity encompassed the outwardly lawful collection of certain local duties, on a commission basis, and the unlawful collection of protection money; control over specific sectors of agricultural and livestock production, water supply and distribution, and market places; and the settlement of a number of local controversies and disputes. Collusion between the mafia and public figures resulted in the channeling of electoral votes toward certain candidates, the preferential granting of administrative licenses and public-works contracts to mafia figures, and, not least, widespread impunity for mafia crimes.

The multifaceted role of mafia-type organizations in the 1970s and 1980s is far more complex than that of previous decades. These organizations have become criminal consorteries and entrepreneurial entities at the same time. Their proceeds from unlawful activities are laundered and reinvested in legitimate businesses that give work, in many cases, to unsuspecting individuals or to individuals who lack criminal affiliation.

A portion of the investment capital derives from the more traditional mafia-type endeavors. Among other kinds of malfeasance, the Sicilian mafia is active in smuggling foreign-processed tobacco and in the clandestine weapons trade; the Calabrian 'ndrangheta in illicit mediation and supply affecting agriculture, forestry, trade, manufacturing, and transportation, in addition to blackmail and armed robbery; and the Neapolitan camorra in racketeering and smuggling. All of them, as noted in Chapter 4, are practitioners of kidnappings for extortion. To these proceeds for reinvestment should be added large funds that have been appropriated by the central government for development of the South, but that work their way into criminal coffers. The development projects themselves, underhandedly assigned to organized crime representatives, are frequently subcontracted to other firms under conditions dictated by the crime syndicates themselves.

The most substantial capital for clean reinvestment, however, is the profit from drug trafficking, a booming activity for organized crime since the early 1970s. It has been facilitated by a long-standing smuggling experience with other merchandise and by Italy's central location along the Mediterranean transportation routes from East to West. Although Italian territory had served for decades as a transit area for opium, morphine, and heroin, Italian international primacy in the drug trade, particularly heroin, came about in large measure with the disruption of the Corsican or French "connection" in the early 1970s. At that point, the Sicilian mafia began to manage the entire cycle: importation, processing, refinement, transshipment, distribution, and sale. Conversion laboratories became fully operational on the island in the mid-1970s. A significant amount of the heroin that reaches the East Coast of the United States—60–80 percent—is shipped, processed, and/or brokered through Italy, principally Sicily. The Neapolitan camorra has similarly penetrated the cocaine market, which was formerly the preserve of South American suppliers.

Laundered proceeds from criminal ventures that go into otherwise legitimate businesses re-emerge in the form of goods and services in the commercial, industrial, and tertiary sectors of the economy. For laundering purposes, the crime syndicates can rely on banks and other credit institutions that they are able to control or manipulate. Obviously, these methods of entrepreneurship frustrate the rules of competition. Mafia-type organizations have access to immediate liquidity—the fruit of their crimes—unburdened by passive bank interests. At the same time, they do not concern themselves with paying taxes and other duties on the original capital acquired from criminal ventures. Moreover, they overcome a variety of business formalities and controls in the conduct of "legitimate" economic activities because of their preferential relationship with local administrators and other political figures. Not least, the use of intimidation toward competitors, where other underworld methods are not available or effective, often affords these organizations a near or total monopoly status. All of this clearly damages the free-market system.[6]

The transformation of organized crime has occurred simultaneously with the passage of society from a substantially rural/agricultural setting to an urban/industrial one. This has led, from a functional standpoint, to the formation of a three-tiered criminal system. The first tier comprises operators active in practically all of the eleven sectors of unlawful activity discussed above. These operators are concerned with the acquisition of capital in their specific sector of criminal expertise. Included in this operational segment are killers and thugs who are obviously responsible for violent actions but who are not necessarily full-time personnel. Because of their peculiar personality, mediocre intellect, and unreliability as to confidentiality, they are often hired as needed or even temporarily brought in from abroad for the job.

The second tier is concerned with the placement of unlawful capital into domestic and international credit/financial institutions for laundering purposes. The services of intermediaries are frequently used, but the principal operators are those criminals who actually manage the pertinent laundering channels. This is where macroscopic collusion begins to take place between organized crime and political/administrative/financial circles. Unsuspected operators are colorfully referred to as "snake heads" (*teste di serpente*). The environment as a whole is called white-collar mafia.

The third tier of the system is the "entrepreneurial" one. Those who operate at this level make investment decisions, find dummy heads, set up a variety of seemingly clean entities—including nonprofit ones—to conduct business operations, and entertain necessary or desirable relations with the authorities. The municipal administrators are most vulnerable to their overtures and are generally manipulated through representatives of the various political parties.[7]

Naturally enough, the traditional mafia-type families and clans have had to modify their internal structures in order to participate effectively in this modernized and more demanding system. Whereas at one time it was sufficient for a local boss to surround himself with fifteen to twenty followers on a more or less permanent basis, he now needs as many as 70 to 80 adult male subordinates and a rather large biological family of his own, preferably related by marriage to other biological families within the system.

This complex organized-crime system is reliant, in turn, on a vast support network in order to function smoothly. The criminal organizations constitute the core, while their various tangible and intangible support elements may be graphically represented by concentric circles that stand for active support, auxiliary support, legal support, and support issuing from opportunists, from the *mentalità mafiosa*, and from the indifferent. The numerical strength of individuals bound by actual mafia-type ties roughly falls within the following estimates: Sicily, 15,000; Calabria, 5,000; Campania, 10,000; the northern industrial triangle, 10,000; Sardinia, 1,000; and elsewhere, 5,000. By way of an overall estimate, it is calculated that between 35,000 and 46,000 persons participate in the system[8]

Active support is provided by those who are directly connected to a mafia-type organization or sustain its actions indirectly and receive compensation for their services. Auxiliary support stems from common criminals at the periphery of organized crime. In practice, these individuals constitute a reservoir. Legal support is provided by members of the learned professions who make their technical services available. Such professionals, even when full-fledged members of a crime syndicate, are not required to undergo the typical tests of worthiness demanded of less educated criminals.

Opportunists are those individuals who do not intend to join a criminal organization but expect to derive certain material benefits from it. In mafia parlance, they are *gli amici degli amici,* the friends' friends. The spillover effect of the *mentalità mafiosa* on society likewise constitutes a form of support. Finally, those who are indifferent facilitate the aims of crime syndicates; their lack of civic mindedness, which translates into unwillingness to cooperate with the authorities, creates a fertile ground for mafia-type structures and endeavors.[9]

The influence of three-tiered organized crime on society is sadly dramatized by a recent event. In January 1986 about 500 employees dismissed by a Palermo public-works firm—which was going out of business following the sentencing of its managing director—staged a demonstration to protest against their plight. In the course of the demonstration in downtown Palermo, they raised posters that read: "We want the mafia" and "Mafia gives us work—No mafia, no work." The demonstration coincided with the opening of the most important antimafia trial to date, which was aimed at shaking the mafia at its foundations.

The transformation of organized crime has been characterized by other developments as well. Most obvious is the geographical expansion of traditional spheres of operations. Domestically, the Sicilian mafia, Calabrian 'ndrangheta, and Neapolitan camorra, in addition to giving birth to joint ventures involving several families or clans, have also spread their tentacles to central and northern Italy. Typical examples of joint ventures include the cooperation between the New Organized Camorra and the principal 'ndrangheta clans and between mafia families of western Sicily and the New Family. Moreover, significant testimony concerning the drive northward is authoritatively provided by the chief prosecutor of Rome:

Latium and Rome in particular have become the epicenter of the mafia, camorra, and 'ndrangheta, which operate in the most disparate and lucrative sectors ranging from drugs to kidnappings and from racketeering to laundering of dirty money. An agreement has been reached among these criminal organizations, pursuant to which the field of unlawful activity is parceled also with respect to territory. The move of mafia and camorra clans to Latium is facilitated by the presence of the Fiumicino airport, which is a mandatory passage way for drug traffic, a sector in which they are particularly active because of the substantial unlawful profit issuing therefrom.[10]

In a subsequent report, the chief prosecutor stated that they "also avail themselves of the support of local crime." [11]

With respect to the domestic linkages of organized crime, an observation regarding Sardinian banditry (*banditismo sardo*) is in order at this point. Sardinian criminals tend to organize themselves into bands that are deeply influenced by Sardinia's rural, mountainous, and pastoral environment and by the individualistic personality of its inhabitants. The traditional rapport between this natural setting and local crime has only partially changed. In fact, the theft of livestock and kidnappings for ransom continue to characterize Sardinian banditry, although more sophisticated criminal dynamics of recent years have given way to the investment of laundered money into such economic sectors as the island's tourist industry. Because of these environmental factors, there appears to be limited intercourse between Sardinian banditry and organized crime. However, the presence on the island of prisons and penitentiary-related work colonies populated by hundreds of mafia and camorra inmates could generate linkages with the Sardinian bandits.

International links, as the smuggling and drug-trafficking activities imply, are strongly corroborated by judicial findings. The courts have established that the Sicilian mafia entertains contacts with counterpart organizations in the United States, Canada, Venezuela, Brazil, Thailand, and the Middle East; the Calabrian 'ndrangheta with counterparts in the United States, Canada, and Australia; and the Neapolitan camorra with counterparts in the United States. Links with the Americas and Australia have been facilitated by blood ties resulting from Italian immigration.

With respect to the Sicilian-U.S. mafia connection, it is worth referring once again to Buscetta's confessions. To his knowledge, "Sicilian Cosa Nostra and Cosa Nostra in the United States are two separate organizations that stay in contact only in relation to mutual interests in the traffic of certain drugs." [12] In 1985 Giovanni Falcone, one of Palermo's leading investigating judges, stated:

> Cosa Nostra used to be an affiliation of Sicilian mafia . . . Today, it is made up entirely of people born and raised in America, reared in a less backward subculture. Sicilian *mafiosi* are no longer of right members of Cosa Nostra as in the past. Before admission, they must prove themselves. This is demonstrated by the so-called pizza connection, the great trial conducted in New York by prosecutor Rudolph Giuliani. [13]

Another development concerns the disquieting rhythm of violence reached by organized crime. In 1984, 156 murders were perpetrated by the mafia, 137 by the camorra, and 48 by the 'ndrangheta; in 1985, there were 123 murders by the mafia, 121 by the camorra, and 78 by the 'ndrangheta.[14] Even more ominous is the unprecedented onslaught against select human targets as a direct challenge to the authority of the state. Most significant are the pertinent trends in Sicily. As such, they deserve particular attention.

The first incidents that reflect the mafia's violent refusal to be investigated and prosecuted were recorded in the early 1970s. In September 1970, journalist Mauro De Mauro of Palermo's *L'Ora,* who had authored a series of articles on the mafia, was forced into his own car and driven away never to be seen again. One year later, in September 1971, Palermo prosecutor Pietro Scaglione was murdered in an ambush. After a quiet spell of some years, Carabinieri lieutenant colonel Giuseppe Russo was killed in August 1977 and mafia boss Giuseppe De Cristina, who had made some revelations to the Carabinieri regarding the Corleone family, was silenced forever in May 1978. But a truly clamorous crescendo began in 1979, in the course of which journalist Mario Francese, Christian Democratic regional secretary Michele Reina, Public Security (now called State Police) Palermo investigative-branch chief Boris Giuliano, and member of Parliament Cesare Terranova of the Independent Left were murdered.

In January 1980 it was the turn of regional president Piersanti Mattarella, a Christian Democrat opposed to political collusion with the mafia. Captain Emanuele Basile, commander of the Monreale Carabinieri company, who was pursuing Giuliano's unfinished investigation, was murdered the following May. Also in 1980, Palermo prosecutor Gaetano Costa and Castelvetrano mayor Vito Lipari were killed. A respite of twenty months followed.

Then, in April 1982, PCI member of Parliament Pio La Torre, who like his late colleague Terranova had served on the parliamentary antimafia committee, was brutally eliminated. On September 3, retired Carabinieri general Carlo Alberto Dalla Chiesa, who had been sent to Sicily as prefect of Palermo to resume the antimafia battle he had waged twice before on the island during his long law-enforcement career, was murdered together with his young wife and a State Police agent who followed the prefect's car as an escort. Dalla Chiesa had been in Palermo only 100 days filling his new position and was already conducting an aggressive investigation into the heart of the mafia empire.[15]

Murders of select public officials resumed in 1983. Trapani assistant state attorney Giacomo Ciaccio Montalto was killed in January; Carabinieri captain Mario D'Aleo, the late Basile's successor, in June; Palermo investigating judge Rocco Chinnici in July; and State Police agent Calogero Zucchetto, assigned to the Palermo investigative branch, in November. Another journalist, Giuseppe Fava, was murdered in Catania in early 1984 as he was investigating Palermo-Catania mafia links. Two ranking members of the State Police Palermo investigative branch were killed in that city in 1985: Giuseppe Montana, head of the fugitives section, in July, and Antonio Cassarà, chief of the branch itself, in August.

These once-unheard-of attacks against key public officials regarded by organized crime as a threat to its survival have been accompanied by the degeneration of what at one time constituted a "code of honor," albeit a specifically criminal one. Until Italian organized crime emerged as an "entrepreneurial" entity, there was an unwritten rule to the effect that women, children, and those who were not the intended and direct target of a criminal venture would be spared all violence. Attacks were consequently planned so as to avoid the useless shedding of blood.

This is no longer so. An example is the murder of Mrs. Dalla Chiesa with her husband. Less clamor-inducing but equally significant examples include actions such as the murder of La Torre's driver together with his employer and the physical elimination of relatives of former members of the criminal fold that turn state's evidence. Moreover, as noted in Chapter 4, women and children are now kidnap targets. This degeneration has disgusted even some "old timers," including Buscetta, whose confessions he alleges to be motivated by this sense of repugnance. According to Buscetta, "those [mafiosi] of today are disgusting people who have nothing in common with the old Cosa Nostra. They are bloodthirsty, unreliable, and honorless people that kill without any purpose. They have no right to exist." [16]

This criminal milieu's new generation, which now sets the rules, is motivated more by practical than by other considerations. In fact, the sense of power that was at one time the misguided driving force behind the *mentalità mafiosa* has been matched and even supplanted by pure economic greed.

Although Italian organized crime looks increasingly like a huge corporate body, the foregoing discussion of its structures and dynamics should not engender the idea that it has become an absolute monolith. Indeed, it is more appropriate to speak in terms of crime syndicates having notable direct and indirect ties with one another; moreover, it is worth noting that a large number of the statistics reported above on mafia-type murders include the casualties of gang wars as well as internal power struggles. Paradoxically, however, what at times appear to be gang wars are actually operations aimed at achieving a tighter cohesion among families or clans. [17]

Organized Crime and Politics

The collusion between organized crime and political circles has old roots, particularly in southern Italy. The tolerance of preunification and postunification governments toward the private police role of mafia-type organizations has already been discussed. Other precedents and links are no less significant.

In 1860, when Giuseppe Garibaldi's volunteer forces took over Sicily and other areas of the South from the Kingdom of Naples in the pursuit of Italian unification under the Kingdom of Piedmont and Sardinia, there was collaboration on the part of the Sicilian mafia, which secretely hoped to reap its own fruits from the fall of the Bourbon-Sicily regime. On his part, Francis II of Bourbon, the last ruler of the Kingdom of Naples, also called Kingdom of the Two Sicilies, financed brigand paramilitary formations in Campania, Lucania (now Basilicata), and Calabria. In so doing, his initial goal was to resist the Piedmontese. After his defeat and proclamation of the Kingdom of Italy in 1861, the deposed monarch, who by this time had taken refuge in the vanishing remnants of the Papal State, continued to finance and entertain links with 'ndrangheta and camorra clans in the futile hope of bringing about the restoration of his former kingdom. These irregular forces subsequently lost their complementary "legitimist" role and went back to criminal ventures exclusively as a manner of living.[18]

The government of the young Kingdom of Italy repeatedly deployed its military forces to combat the fiefs of organized crime in what still largely remained a rural setting. Collusion at the local levels and, at times, at the central level of government were sufficiently serious to be harshly denounced from the floor of Parliament as early as 1875.[19] Stronger measures against mafia-type organizations, particularly in Sicily, were adopted by the Fascist regime, but not even its repressive apparatus could totally eradicate such a solidly entrenched sociological phenomenon.[20] In fact, the Allied landing in Sicily and subsequent military operations on the island during World War II were facilitated by resorting to mafia influence arranged through Italo-American criminal channels. Ironically, merits gained from resisting Fascism enabled a number of mafia bosses to become part of local municipal administrations, positions they exploited in the pursuit of criminal designs.[21]

Notwithstanding past as well as current linkages between political/governmental circles and organized crime, the latter does not entertain a political ideology, nor is there evidence of a specific political preference on its part. What readily emerges, instead, is the need of these mafia-type organizations to ride or manipulate the political establishment in order to achieve their criminal/economic objectives. So long as this can be accomplished, little does it matter to organized crime whether one party or another or even a coalition of parties is in office at a given time and place. Obviously, a dictatorial regime that eliminates the ballot and consequently forecloses organized crime's possibility to influence elections in favor of its candidates or patrons would not suit mafia-type organizations. Their long-term survival hinges on the systematic exploitation of democracy, on the one hand, and of societal malfunctions, including unemployment and bureaucratic inefficiency, on the other.

The pragmatic linkages between organized crime and the political domain—the latter intended in its broadest connotation, ranging from the various public administrations to the circles that contribute to societal dynamics—have led observers to speak in terms of a combined "politico-mafia lobby." In this connection, a frequently used metaphor is "the third level," an expression that is reminiscent of the three-tier criminal system described above. According to Palermo assistant prosecutor Guido Lo Forte, "The third level is not a well-delineated mafia-type supercommission, but a mobile structure, an ensemble of centers of power that entertain a relationship with mafia-type organisms and stipulate agreements on specific matters." [22]

Concern over the links between organized crime and politics has increased in recent years. A major contributing factor was the discovery of a highly exclusive Masonic lodge, Propaganda 2 (P2), that secretly brought together members of Parliament, ministers, top-ranking officials of the public administration, magistrates, financiers, and, indeed, individuals indicted or convicted of economic malfeasance. Although administrative, judicial, and parliamentary findings to date are neither univocal nor definitive, this matter is worth considering, with due caution, within the context of this chapter. [23]

On March 18, 1981, pursuant to a warrant issued to ascertain suspected connections between the fraudulent bankruptcy of the late international financier Michele Sindona, a Sicilian, and the activities of entrepreneur Licio Gelli of Arezzo, Tuscany, the business premises and luxurious residence of the latter were searched by the Finance Guard. Copious documentation was confiscated, including a list—ostensibly partial—of 953 names of politicians, public servants, businessmen, and professionals affiliated with the P2 lodge, headed by Gelli. Other compromising documents reflected political-military espionage on Gelli's part, thus leading to the issuance of an arrest warrant. Gelli fled but was arrested in Geneva, Switzerland, in September 1982; however, he managed to escape in August of the following year. Meanwhile, he was also indicted for conspiracy, fraud, slander, corruption, and extortion. [24] The lodge itself was forcibly dissolved in January 1982 on the grounds of violating a constitutional provision that bars secret associations. [25]

Gelli's background is equivocal. A Fascist and a volunteer in the Spanish Civil War during Mussolini's regime, he served both the Nazis and the communist partisans during the latter portion of World War II. As late as

1952 he still entertained links with the PCI, and a 1950 Italian intelligence investigation shows that he was also suspected of being a Soviet agent. However, since the mid-1950s his political preference seems to have steered a conservative course. His postwar business career is likewise varied. From a smuggler of cigarettes, he moved on to operate as a book dealer, a typewriter salesman, a mattress manufacturer, and a highly successful clothing industrialist. Throughout his business career he did not limit himself to useful contacts with Italy's political parties and influential circles, but also worked his way into the top echelons of foreign establishments. The list includes Romania, Argentina (on whose behalf he enjoyed honorary diplomatic status in Italy), Spain, and Libya. His business success owes much to these high-level public relations. His record in the Masonry is also that of a rising star. A member of negligible importance from 1963 to 1967, he became secretary to an authoritative "brother" during the remaining portion of the decade, was appointed organizational secretary of the P2 lodge in 1971, and has been the P2's powerful leader since 1976. This, too, furthered his personal ambitions. The blatantly unsuccessful mark in Gelli's career has been his failure to achieve any academic distinction or even a title.[26]

Investigations—official and otherwise—into the P2 lodge have stressed the pervasive and exploitative role played by Gelli. At the same time, considerable attention has been devoted to the P2's political aims. In fact, among the internal papers pertaining to the lodge, one is entitled "Plan for Democratic Rebirth."[27] Under close scrutiny, however, this plan is more concerned with the individual and class interests of the members of the lodge than it is a blueprint for the transformation of Italy's democratic system into an authoritarian one, as many have argued.

Gelli himself, who is unquestionably an able operator, has never displayed comparable intellectual aptitudes. His writings are a clear indication of this. (The Plan for Democratic Rebirth was authored by someone with a more solid educational background.) At the same time, Gelli's record would negate specific political ideals. Judgments expressed by former Masonic "brothers" supposedly well acquainted with him ring as follows: "That fellow is a pragmatist without ideals of any kind. His greatest joy, his greatest satisfaction, would have entailed bringing about peace—pardon my irreverence—between the Pope and [the late PCI secretary-general] Berlinguer. Gelli is a man without ideals. With hindsight I realized that he has never desired a strong government. In a strong government, mediators have no role."[28] Or, more concisely, Gelli is "a person open to any market."[29]

The Masonic connection as a means for organized crime, or elements thereof, to pursue profitable alliances apparently does not end with Gelli's P2. As late as March 1986 another lodge surfaced in Palermo. Its members include seemingly respectable public servants and professionals as well as mafia bosses.[30]

Organized Crime and Terrorism

Mafia-type organizations operate outside of the law and against the law to achieve a specifically economic objective. Structures and dynamics have adapted to changing times, but their ultimate goal is as recognizable as ever: the illicit accumulation of wealth. Indeed, parasitical exploitation, political corruption, and, not least, terrorism are part of their tactics, but even as practitioners of violence mafia-type organizations do not qualify as terrorist formations within the conventional meaning of the term discussed in Chapter 3. To the operator of organized crime, politics are instrumental. To the political terrorist, they are his reason for being.

Nevertheless, linkages between organized crime and terrorist formations have been corroborated by recent evidence. More than once the prime minister has attributed to organized crime, in his semiannual intelligence report to the Parliament, a destabilizing role comparable to that of political terrorism.[31] In addition, in March 1980 the interior minister had already pointed out on the floor of Parliament that "mafia-type criminality is adopting operational procedures peculiar to terrorist activities: from this it might be inferred that collusion takes place between mafia-type circles and subversive groups through the exchange of operational experience and low-level operatives."[32] In fact, the attacks perpetrated by organized crime against public officials since the late 1970s do reflect the ambush and hit-and-run patterns so well mastered by terrorist formations.

Students of political terrorism and organized crime have noted that connections between the two presuppose either tactical or strategic considerations. Tactics are based on pure utilitarianism, whereas strategies set out to weaken the structures of the state.[33] Unfortunately, in the 1970s and early 1980s the battle against political terrorism absorbed the best efforts of the police forces to the detriment of the equally important battle against the new tactics of organized crime and its expansion into the drug trade. Above and beyond economic profit, mafia-type organizations and lesser criminal aggregations served their own interests by providing political terrorists with material tools for the achievement of objectives that are of no ideological significance to organized crime. Pragmatic considerations have likewise brought about cooperation between terrorists and gangsters in the prisons.[34]

Moreover, new evidence of disconcerting linkages at the operational level may emerge from ongoing investigations. Several leads deserve attention. "Repentant" red brigadist Antonio Chiocchi has testified that camorra boss Raffaele Cutolo approached the BR in 1981 to request the liberation of Christian Democratic regional councillor Ciro Cirillo, who was being held captive by the BR. According to another "repentant" red brigadist, Roberto Buzzati, contacts between his organization and Cutolo's clan actually took place earlier and entailed a projected mass escape from the Ascoli Piceno maximum-security prison.[35] It remains to be established whether, besides the BR, the camorra was also a recipient of ransom money paid for Cirillo's liberation.

More disquieting investigative leads address the matter of operational links between organized crime and the terrorist right. Seven arrest warrants were issued in January 1986 against mafia and camorra bosses and neo-Fascist extremists in relation to the December 23, 1984, bombing of the Naples–Milan express train that caused fifteen deaths and 131 injuries. Moreover, 130 arrests carried out by the Carabinieri in February 1986 and followed by searches and seizures reportedly prove that organized crime has supplied principally neo-Fascist terrorists—but also leftist ones—with weapons and hideouts since 1980. Several criminal gangs appear to be involved, as opposed to a single mafia-type organization. Some of the weapons seized by the Carabinieri in these criminal circles may have been used in felonies perpetrated by neo-Fascist extremists either alone or together with common criminals. Finally, recent reports corroborate older ones regarding the involvement of rightist extremists, including Stefano Delle Chiaie of National Vanguard (AN), in the drug traffic for self-financing and/or destabilization purposes.[36]

Qualified observers have also expressed concern over potential hostile patron-state support for organized crime as a form of surrogate warfare wherein the objectives are similar to those of terrorism, since organized crime has the capability to disrupt the mechanics of society. Those who subscribe to this theory point to the twin political objectives behind the flow of drugs toward the West: the weakening of the new generations and the increase of capital in the hands of criminal groups that are de facto enemies of the rule of law.[37]

CHAPTER SIX

The Pacifist Movement and Subversive Agitation

Any objective analysis of Italy's post–World War II record, including recent developments, should reflect the absence of military trends, or even single incidents, that could constitute a threat to peace. However, current media and popular perceptions are indicative not only of concern and preoccupation over the outbreak of war, but also of specific displeasure with Italian defense policies. Little importance seems to be attributed to the fact that Italy is pursuing a policy of collective deterrence coupled with peacekeeping in adjacent areas.

The decision, in particular, to deploy the cruise missiles in Comiso has been accompanied by cries of alarm even in newspapers and periodicals lacking political-party affiliation, as evidenced by articles bearing such titles as "Italy: H Hour," "The Last Man," "Science Questions Itself on Nuclear Apocalypse," "Before the World Blows Up," "How to Live with the Bomb," "NATO: A Cascade of Missiles," and "Nuclear Attack on Comiso: In Eleven Seconds a Radioactive Desert." Public opinion polls disclose similar perceptions. A survey of these polls provides an indicator of popular attitudes not only about the nuclear armaments issue, but also about war in general, patriotism, Italian participation in NATO, and related matters.

As one small but telling example, in 1980 39 citizens—including the Christian Democratic defense minister, members of Parliament, officer candidates, private military academy cadets, draftees, fire-fighters, intellectuals, and common workers—were asked: "Would you die for the Fatherland?" There were sixteen negative responses, thirteen affirmative (but in most cases qualified) responses, and ten blatantly evasive ones. The defense minister, the head of the conservative Italian Social Movement, two cadets, and a car attendant unqualifiedly indicated their readiness. The officer candidates, the draftees, the firefighters, and nearly all of the intellectuals flatly expressed their refusal.[1]

Much broader polls were conducted in subsequent years. For example, according to a December 1981 poll, 73.3 percent of all respondents were afraid that a war could involve Italy, as opposed to 60 percent in the spring of the same year; 36.1 percent favored continued Italian participation in NATO, but with less dependence on the United States; 16.1 percent favored withdrawal from NATO and neutrality; 65 percent were against the installation of the cruise missiles in Comiso, but 33.9 percent of these objectors felt that as an ally Italy could not refuse.[2] An October 1983 poll showed that 58.1 percent of all interviewees disagreed with the installation of the missiles in Comiso; 18.7 percent were favorable on condition that the missiles be kept under Italian control; and 40 percent, as opposed to 40.4 percent holding the opposite view, did not think that Italy's international role would acquire greater importance.[3] A concurrent poll reflected that 35 percent of the respondents would not deploy nuclear weapons regardless of what the Soviet Union does, and 47 percent considered the use of nuclear weapons an immoral act regardless of the circumstances.[4]

Italian international peacekeeping efforts have likewise been greeted by sarcastic and hostile media titles such as "We, the Vigilantes of the Mediterranean," "Nostalgia for Africa," "To Die for Beirut," "From Hell in Lebanon," "Deported to Lebanon," and "Shall We Die for Reagan?" An opinion poll held in November 1983 reported that 56.9 percent of all respondents favored Italian withdrawal from the multinational force in Beirut, while 39.8 percent indicated their apprehension that the civil war in Lebanon would escalate into a world conflict.[5]

Upon close scrutiny, however, actual militancy for peace—no matter what significance is given to the word peace—is conducted neither by the nonpartisan press nor by public opinion. Rather, it is the preserve, to varying degrees, of political or politicized forces that find in the media and in public opinion a fertile ground for their own purposes.

Pacifist Organizations and Objectives

A variety of adjectives have been used to identify or categorize the sundry organizations active in the Italian pacifist movement. The term "institutional" has been submitted to characterize political-party and labor-union affiliated or supported groups; "noninstitutional" characterizes independent formations; and "anti-institutional" has been used as a catch-all term for subversive bands that exploit pacifism for revolutionary purposes, as opposed to political or ethical aims.

More simply put, Italy's peace movement may be viewed as consisting of two principal components inspired by Marxist/radical and Christian/progressive ideologies, respectively. However, within each of these components there are marked differences not only with respect to the goals to be achieved, but also as to the pacifist approach itself. Each component draws additional support from unaffiliated elements (groups and individuals) that believe in the pacifist cause and express their pacifist commitment through the activities organized by the parties and entities that are part of those components. Supportive nonaffiliated elements include conscientious objectors, antimilitarists, libertarians, anti–nuclear energy activists, intellectuals, and idealists.

On the Marxist/radical side of the pacifist spectrum, the principal organizations are the Italian Communist Party (PCI), the Democratic Proletarian Unity Party (PDUP), Proletarian Democracy (DP), the Radical Party (PR), the League for Unilateral Disarmament (Lega per il Disarmo Unilaterale; LDU), Struggle for Peace (Lotta per la Pace), the Revolutionary Communist League–Fourth International, sundry affiliations of all of the foregoing, anarchist groups, and the politically violent and terrorist-prone Workers' Autonomy (AUTOP). On the Christian/progressive side of the spectrum, the principal groups are the Christian Associations of Italian Workers (ACLI), Pax Christi, the International Reconciliation Movement (Movimento Internazionale di Riconciliazione; MIR), Christians for Socialism, and Christians for Dissent. The organizations and groups that make up the Christian/progressive component of the pacifist movement are frequently motivated by religious and/or ethical values intermingled with leftist earthly objectives. Their policies generally favor cooperation with Marxist-oriented parties and formations in the interest of humanitarian goals.

The PCI

Most significant in the overall deployment of the pacifist forces is the role played by the PCI, whose organizational capability and capillary structures constitute in essence the backbone of the pacifist movement. The official position of the PCI is perhaps best illustrated by quoting one of its most propagandized statements issued during the campaign for the parliamentary elections of June 26, 1983, which took place as preparations were underway at Comiso to host the cruise missiles:

> Do you prefer the rearmament race, with its attendant and ever-increasing danger of war, or the gradual reduction of armaments and the resumption of detente? It is a well known fact that Italian policy has opted for rearmament. Our government, chaired by the Christian Democratic Party and supported by a five-party coalition, was the first one in Europe to say yes to the Euromissiles and, in 1983, it appropriated twelve thousand billion lire for armaments. But do you really want Italy to become an atomic target? Or do you agree with us in wanting: First, the interruption of the works at the Comiso base. Second, even if an agreement is not reached in Geneva within 1983, the

continuation of negotiations without installing the missiles. Third, simultaneously with an adequate reduction of the missiles in the USSR, the non-installation of the American missiles in Western Europe. Fourth, the dynamic commitment, with a genuine will toward a freeze of all nuclear armaments in the world, to commence a real reduction. This is because there are neither good bombs nor bad bombs: they are all terrible. On June 26 you can vote for a rearmament policy or for a peace policy. If you want peace, vote PCI. And remember: he who does not vote is silent. And he who is silent consents to rearmament.[6]

Inherent in the PCI's statement is its ostensible lack of concern over the fact that acceptance of such a platform for peace would place the West in a position of weakness at the negotiating table with the Soviet Union, whose SS-20 missiles have already been deployed in Europe. In this connection, three considerations are not easily dismissable: the long history of bonds between the PCI and the USSR; an almost perfect record of alignment over foreign policy issues; and the continuing presence of Sovietphiles in the PCI, despite the party's efforts of recent years to project a pro-Western orientation.

A member of the Communist International (Comintern) and then of the Communist Information Bureau (Cominform) until their dissolution, the PCI of the late 1940s and the 1950s made no secret as to its allegiance. A few examples suffice. On March 6, 1951, Defense Minister Randolfo Pacciardi asked from the floor of the Chamber of Deputies: "What would you do in case of a Soviet aggression? Would you defend the Fatherland?"; the Communist M.P.'s responded by shouting in unison: "No!"[7] Indeed, PCI posters in the Cold War years frequently depicted the Italian flag under or alongside the Soviet one, and standard party slogans entailed such rhetoric as: "In the name of Stalin and under the guidance of [then–PCI secretary-general] Togliatti, we carry forward the flag of peace, liberty, national independence, and socialism." The USSR's appreciation for these sentiments is reflected in the 1961–1962 diary of the late Colonel Oleg Penkovskiy of Soviet military intelligence (GRU), who wrote: "There is a large Communist Party in Italy. Instructors at the academy advise our officers that 'our Italian friends' can be of great service in operations."[8]

In the course of the 1960s and 1970s, as the PCI consistently expanded from a party of cadres to a party enjoying heterogeneous mass support, its fidelity to the Soviet Union conversely became less solid. Nevertheless, reference to "fraternal" ties continued to be part of official party statements; the PCI assumed an ever-increasing role as privileged middleman (and indeed commission agent) in import-export relations between Italy and the USSR;[9] and top PCI exponents often met with their counterparts in the

Soviet Union. As late as November 14, 1979, Giancarlo Pajetta of the PCI's Directorate officially expounded:

> We regard the USSR as a country essential to a new balance and to any possibility of progress in the world. We celebrated the October Revolution as a historic turning point in a harsh, troubled process marked by the victory in the antifascist war and the liberation of the colonies. This is still an incomplete, but irreversible process. A break in, or refusal of, dialogue would not only constitute a denial of our tradition and an inconsistency with our desire to transform society; it would, we believe, damage the workers' and liberation movement and would constitute a grave occurrence in our country's politics.[10]

The position of the PCI on foreign policy matters has nearly always paralleled that of the Soviet Union. When at variance with the USSR, it has been characterized by ambiguity. Again, a few examples are to the point.

Marshall Plan assistance as well as Italian participation in the European Economic Community (EEC) and in NATO met the vehement opposition of the PCI, which subsequently did modify its stance toward both the EEC and NATO. Yet the PCI's acceptance of NATO in particular is suspiciously sudden and ambiguous. Although as late as 1974 PCI militants still used the slogan "Italy out of NATO, NATO out of Italy," during the 1976 parliamentary campaign PCI secretary-general Enrico Berlinguer presented a platform nonpreclusive of Italy's North Atlantic defense commitments. In accepting NATO, the PCI stressed detente rather than defense; it refused even to entertain the hypothesis of military aggression by the Warsaw Pact against a NATO country.[11]

Other manifestations of the common USSR-PCI foreign-policy stance do not directly relate to the Italian scene. These include PCI opposition to U.S. involvement in the Korean War, support for the North Vietnamese and Viet Cong throughout the duration of the U.S. military commitment in Southeast Asia, condemnation of Israel during the 1973 war, condemnation of the Israeli rescue mission in Uganda in 1976, opposition to U.S. deployment of the neutron bomb in Europe, rejection of the Olympic boycott and condemnation of the U.S. rescue attempt in Iran in 1980, and unrelenting support for Soviet policies in the Third World, especially regarding so-called national liberation movements.

With respect to the pacifist issue in particular, Soviet-PCI alignment is evidenced not only by the PCI's opposition to the deployment of the cruise and Pershing II missiles in Western Europe—the so-called Euromissiles—but also by its opposition to the peacekeeping operations in Lebanon and to the minesweeping operations in the Red Sea.

Until the recent events in Poland, USSR-PCI divergence of opinion was substantially limited to the Soviet military intervention in Czechoslovakia in 1968 and in Afghanistan in 1979. However, PCI dissent merely took the form of verbal condemnation, in contrast to 145,000 demonstrations against the United States organized or supported by that party during the Vietnam War years.

Moreover, two 1981 polls of the party's rank and file reflected that 35 percent justified Soviet intervention in Czechoslovakia and 30 percent justified Soviet intervention in Afghanistan.[12] In 1980 Secretary-General Berlinguer himself had in fact toned down his party's condemnation of Soviet action in Afghanistan by stating: "Afghan autonomy must be guaranteed and at the same time the USSR's concern for her security must be borne in mind."[13]

PCI-USSR relations reached a low ebb in the aftermath of the Polish crisis. On December 15, 1981, Berlinguer stated: "A phase is closing. The propulsive thrust that had its origin in the October Revolution has exhausted itself. The capacity for renewal of the societies of Eastern Europe has exhausted itself."[14]

Although the issuance of this statement has come to be widely interpreted as constituting a "wrench" (Ital. *strappo*) away from the Soviet Union, it by no means reflects a complete break with that country. The USSR and the PCI continue to exchange delegations, the PCI continues its middleman role in the import-export business with the USSR. On a symbolic level, for example, the national headquarters of the PCI paid tribute to Leonid Brezhnev's demise in November 1982 by displaying the flag at half mast. Whereas it is true that at the Central Committee level Armando Cossutta alone objected to the "wrench" statement and only two other members of that central body abstained from voting, the presence of Sovietphiles in the party is not altogether negligible.

The strength of these Sovietphiles is not that of the past, but they do hold positions of influence in the party's financial structures (import-export and cooperatives), in the party's organizational structures at the provincial level, and in the party's tourism and cultural structures. (Out of 22 major tours and cruises organized by the party for 1983, eleven were to the USSR and satellite countries, four to Cuba, and one to Guinea-Bissau.[15] In addition, pro-Soviet sentiments are solidly entrenched among the rank and file. A poll held in 1981 reflected that approximately 40 percent of the PCI's militants continued to attribute ideological importance to the USSR. Although only 6 percent of the those polled considered the Soviet Union "an example to be imitated," 32.3 percent regarded it as "a country that counterbalances imperialism and assists those nations that struggle for liberation."[16] Moreover, the results of a poll conducted at approximately the same time indicated that 79 percent of the rank and file viewed the USSR as "a socialist country."[17] Another poll of December 1982 reflected that 40.7 percent of the militants consider the October Revolution as a point of reference and that 51.6 percent regard the United States as the country that most threatens peace.[18]

With respect to Berlinguer's "wrench" statement, PCI provincial congresses held in early 1983 provide particularly instructive insights. Whereas in most cases opposition to the statement did not exceed 15 percent of the vote, in some notable instances opposition was high: 25 percent in Aosta, Lucca, Pistoia, Macerata, Potenza, and Agrigento provinces; 26 percent in Belluno; 27 percent in Pescara; 30 percent in Trieste and Avellino; 40 percent in Massa-Carrara; and 65 percent in Isérnia. Of comparable significance is the concomitant vote of the provincial congresses on Italy's participation in NATO. In many cases the opposition vote reached 30 percent and above: 30 percent in Brescia and Turin; 35 percent in Trieste, Massa-Carrara, Imperia, and Brindisi; 38 percent in Caserta and Catanzaro; 40 percent in Florence; 47 percent in Bari; 49 percent in Salerno and Cosenza; 51 percent in Reggio Calabria; 52 percent in Lucca; 55 percent in Chieti; and 65 percent in Viterbo.[19] The party line does not therefore always take precedence over ingrained values.

Moreover, even after the "wrench" statement, PCI foreign-policy views continue to be in tune with Moscow's. In April 1983, Berlinguer criticized President Reagan's defense policies and stated that it is "indeed comprehensible that the Soviet Union should worry." In July the PCI's Secretariat asked the Italian government to disassociate itself from U.S. policies in Nicaragua. In September PCI Central Committee member Gerardo Chiaromonte, in commenting on the Soviet downing of the South Korean commercial airliner, said: "It would be pure folly to think that the authorities of the Soviet Union ordered to shoot down that plane."[20]

In light of the foregoing, it remains open to debate whether the commitment of the PCI is to peace itself or whether its peace platform is tainted by vestiges of pro-Sovietism.

The PDUP and DP

More strongly opposed to Italian defense policies are the small Marxist parties to the left of the PCI—namely, the PDUP—which has now largely been absorbed by the PCI—and DP. Both of these parties unambiguously advocate unilateral disarmament and withdrawal from NATO, and both parties, though officially opposed to a world balance entailing superpower bipolarity, are especially critical of U.S. "imperialism."

In the course of a November 1983 parliamentary debate on the deployment of the cruise missiles in Comiso and Italian participation in the multinational peacekeeping force in Lebanon, Luciana Castellina of the

PDUP expressed her party's position in the following terms: "Europe would be more secure if it took care of its own security in political terms by guaranteeing her independence through a policy of nonalignment, by finding in the relationship with the peoples of the Third World the strength of her own autonomy and of their autonomy."[21] In stating that the current nuclear balance actually tips in favor of the United States, Castellina also alleged: "It is sufficient to look at the map to realize that the Soviet Union is totally surrounded . . . by an American military belt, which includes even the presence of troops: the most recent of which are those that arrived in Lebanon accompanied by a fleet that constitutes the largest American naval concentration in the Mediterranean since the end of World War II."[22] During the same debate, similar views were voiced by Franco Russo of DP: "The Atlantic choice was a choice of subordination to American imperialism, [it was] the recognition of the hegemony of the United States in the world, to which [the United States] dictated the rules of international coexistence and [imposed] internal regimes upon the various countries . . . Reagan's present offensive aims at realigning all of Europe along the lines of blind Atlanticism so that it will accept all decisions made at this time by Washington, the capital of the empire."[23]

The PR

Unilateral disarmament is also advocated by the PR, which for several years has been conducting libertarian battles not only against nuclear weapons but also against the defense budget and military service itself. In fact, even before the Italian armed forces were assigned the greater visibility role described above, this party acted as the flag bearer of antimilitarism. Favorite PR targets include military discipline regulations, real estate used for military purposes, the Codes of Military Justice, and military courts. This party relies heavily on youthful tendencies to oppose the draft system[24] and has been instrumental in the birth and growth of conscientious objection in Italy. The League of Conscientious Objectors (Lega Obiettori di Coscienza; LOC) is an affiliate of the PR with an estimated strength of approximately 600 members.[25]

The LDU and Struggle for Peace

Other organizations of note within the Marxist/radical component of the pacifist movement are the LDU and Struggle for Peace. The LDU was founded in 1977 by novelist Carlo Cassola, who stated during an interview: "Naturally the League is not the only pacifist organization. Many have preceded us, such as the Nonviolent Movement and the anarchists, who have always been antimilitarists. In the workers' movement, instead, there have been large defections, such as the Communists and Socialists, who, by their nefarious actions at the Constituent Assembly, gave us an armed democracy. The Communists have now reversed their position." [26] In contrast, Struggle for Peace was founded by retired air force general Nino Pasti, who was elected to Parliament as an independent on the PCI ticket in 1976 and in 1979. His organization is an affiliate of the Soviet-run World Peace Council.

The Pacifist Movement: Structure and Activities

The parties, organizations, and groups present in the Italian pacifist movement are, in the vast majority of cases, entities whose platform or articles of association include (among other ideological, political, economic, or religious goals) a stance—whatever its underlying motivation—on the interrelated issues of peace, defense, and armaments. Only the smallest groups of the movement militate exclusively for peace.

There is no exact Italian equivalent of the German Greens. The aggregate 1.7 percent returns obtained for the first time by ecological/green candidates at the 1985 municipal, provincial, and regional elections has turned out to be negligible not only numerically but also in political terms. Nor is the Italian pacifist movement backed either officially or in practice by the Papacy or by the Italian hierarchy of the Catholic Church, in contrast to the encouragement and material support pacifist groups receive from Protestant Churches in Holland and elsewhere. Both Pope John Paul II and the Italian Conference of Bishops have repeatedly spoken in favor of peace, but neither has patronized the Italian peace movement. Support from Catholic ecclesiastical circles occurs at the level of individual prelates or groups without official sanction.

It follows that Italian pacifist activism constitutes a movement rather than a tight organization. Because of its looseness, it must rely on cooperation among groups whose ultimate aims are not homogeneous. This characteristic constitutes a simultaneous source of strength and weakness: each organization or group preserves the autonomy of its own proposals, views, and initiatives but lacks, with the exception of the PCI, the potential for mass action.

To counterbalance its organizational weakness, the Italian pacifist movement has given itself a structure consisting of a national coordination committee, a regional coordination committee in each of Italy's twenty regions, and hundreds of local committees at the municipal level. While this loose structure enables the movement to plan and carry out a variety, though not the entirety, of pacifist demonstrations through joint efforts, it falls short of providing satisfactory and sufficient facilities and sources of financing.

This problem is solved to a large extent by relying on the capillary structure of the PCI—the Italian Communist Youth Federation, the Italian General Confederation of Labor, PCI-run or PCI relative-majority municipalities (in 1983, 384 were PCI-run and 1,579 had a PCI relative majority)[27]—and, above all else, on the Italian Recreational and Cultural Association (Associazione Ricreativa e Culturale Italiana; ARCI). The ARCI's president is a Communist and the majority of its 1.3 million members are also PCI members or sympathizers. Moreover, the ARCI has at its disposal 14,000 clubs throughout the country and an affiliate known as the Environmental League (Lega Ambiente), consisting of 20,000 members.[28] However, reliance on PCI structures in practice reduces the autonomy of the pacifist organizations.[29]

Pacifist manifestations in Italy take on various forms of expression, the majority of which are adopted from the experience of the German Greens and adroitly adapted to the Italian scene.

Marches and Rallies

The basic and intrinsically dynamic form of Italian pacifist expression is the march followed by a rally. This type of activity offers substantial advantages. First, it readily affords broad exposure to the cause by the sheer visibility of its participants. Most marches are limited to a single municipality; however, if the municipality is a large one, the marchers converge on the final rallying point from several routes. In other cases, the march starts in one city, crosses others along the route, and terminates in a distant one. A second advantage is derived from the fact that the participants, with their signs, chants, and slogans, can pass in front of several buildings or facilities of political significance, such as governmental and party offices, military structures, and embassies. Third, the march can be efficaciously planned as part of a program of interrelated pacifist initiatives. A fourth substantial advantage is the comparatively greater ease with which the march can be programmed by various parties and/or organizations that do not share identical platforms. In fact, once the planning and organizational phases are completed, each marching group generally maintains its assigned place on the route and thus retains a notable degree of at least formal autonomy. Last but not least, peace marches attract many individuals or groups that have no affiliation with the organizers, thus giving the pacifist cause a projection of universality.

Peace marches are not new to the Italian scene. Their usefulness as a propaganda instrument was discovered as far back as the 1950s by the so-called Partisans for Peace, Moscow-oriented communists whose protest was directed exclusively against U.S. armaments and "imperialism." The late Aldo Capitini, founder of the Nonviolent Movement (Movimento Nonviolento), was also among Italy's first marchers for peace and the first organizer, in 1960, of a march to Assisi, the medieval town that gave birth to St. Francis, patron of peace and of the poor.

Within the current wave of Italian pacifist militancy, marches were used as a fundamental tool in 1981, as exemplified by the march from Perugia to Assisi in September, the march/rally in Comiso in October, and, in particular, the march/rally of October 24 in Rome, which, according to press estimates, attracted approximately 500,000 demonstrators. Among ancillary techniques, the 1981 marches marked the resurgence of the collectively chanted political slogan, often entailing vulgar language.[30] Such slogans reflect the various "peace" themes as well as their frequent anti-American or anti-Western slant.

Since 1981, marches and rallies or modified forms thereof have come to constitute a monthly event, at least at the local level, and they now correspond to a standard typology. Many participants carry signs, posters, streamers, or puppets representative of the evils of war, military service, or certain political regimes; a number of demonstrators wear representative costumes or masks; all of them chant slogans of various inspirations. Although the United States and the Italian parliamentary and governmental majority coalition (Christian Democrats, Socialists, Republicans, Social Democrats, and Liberals) continue to be the principal objects of denunciation, there has been an increase in the use of a more neutral slogan: "From Sicily to Scandinavia: No to NATO and to the Warsaw Pact." In the course of these actions, the demonstrators frequently fake a nuclear holocaust by collectively dropping to the ground at a prearranged signal and lying still and silent for seconds or even minutes. Integral aspects of peace demonstrations are concluding speeches, projection of films, displays of pictures, or a combination thereof. Participation most often includes representatives from foreign countries.

A few demonstrations that fall within the march/rally pattern are worth focusing on because of their particular articulation. The most elaborate of these was the peace march that started in Milan on November 27, 1982, and ended in Comiso on December 18 of the same year. This event combined a number of overlapping techniques. The proposal for the march was formally announced by eleven intellectuals and artists whose appeal began with the words: "Peace is in danger, peace is possible, peace is necessary." The rest of the text parallels the official position of the PCI on the peace/balance-of-forces issue. It was repeated a few days later by additional signatories, including private organizations and municipal councils.[31] In the days that followed the appeal prior to the beginning of the march, more individuals and groups wrote to the press to proclaim their participation and support, while "friends-of-the-march" committees were being set up throughout the country. Moreover, a group of Italian and foreign demonstrators in Comiso announced a hunger strike in conjunction with, and in support of, the march.

It is estimated that fifteen to twenty thousand persons actively participated in the starting phase of the march up to Milan's city limits, but only five marchers of the initial group reportedly made it to Comiso, 1,600 kilometers down the peninsula and across the channel into Sicily. Moreover, when the procession passed through cities and townships, especially PCI-run or PCI-relative-majority ones such as Bologna, Florence, and Rome, the ranks of the marchers swelled once again from less than one hundred to several thousand participants. In Rome, for example, the communist mayor of that city led the marchers. They were likewise feted and joined not only by local party groups of the left (PCI, PDUP, and DP), but also by delegations of the Greek Communist Party, Palestinian and Iranian students, members of the Evangelical Church, homosexual militants, and sundry other groups. On the morning of their departure for the next halting point, a Catholic solemn High Mass was celebrated by way of farewell in the Ara Coeli Church by Franciscan priests. In Comiso the marchers were greeted by 5,000 demonstrators bused in from various Sicilian municipalities and by foreign delegations.

In conjunction with the Milan/Comiso peace march, fifteen senators of the Independent Left (that is, "independent" candidates elected on the PCI party ticket) introduced a bill to make it possible for a popular referendum, having the force of law, to decide on the deployment of the missiles in Comiso.

Within the general march pattern, other notable actions were conducted in 1983. On April 9 several thousand demonstrators of different political affiliations marched in front of the headquarters of the U.S. Army Southern European Task Force in Vicenza. *Pace e Guerra* (Peace and war), a now-defunct publication connected with PDUP, reported that among the demonstrators were the Nicaraguan Consul to Italy, the representative of the Salvadoran Farabundo Martí Front, and American pacifist Ed Grace.[32] On May 21 a motorcade organized by the ACLI left Palermo, Sicily, for Geneva, Switzerland, symbolically to take the peace appeal to the negotiations table itself. A secondary aim was to collect en route signatures on a petition for the abrogation of Italian military secrecy laws regarding the arms trade. On June 5 approximately 300 LDU militants, dressed up as ragged soldiers, attempted to stage an unauthorized "countermilitary" parade. One of their intentions was to protest the decision of the government to hold a military parade in Rome to commemorate the proclamation of the Republic. Formerly an annual practice, this custom had been discontinued eight years earlier. On October 10 a march was conducted in Assisi with PCI secretary-general Berlinguer in the lead. In preparation for the event, Berlinguer had dined with the Franciscan Fathers in the local monastery. The desired symbolism of Marxist/Catholic unity of intent with respect to peace also constituted a political success for the PCI.

On October 22, as part of worldwide demonstrations, Italian pacifists marched once again through the streets of Rome. This demonstration, which attracted approximately 500,000 participants, was anticipated by several smaller ones in the days immediately preceding it. The PR boycotted the action, alleging that it did "not accept communist hegemony over the movement." [33] PR activists attempted, instead, to stage a demonstration in Prague. Catholic participation, on the other hand, was highly visible. It included Franciscan friars and nuns. However, Vatican Radio praised those who stayed away because they were "distrustful of all possible pollution." [34] Also notable was the presence of Italian Protestants, who constitute a very small percentage of the overall population. Throughout the demonstration, slogans with references to the Warsaw Pact were immediately and more loudly followed by such slogans as "From Sicily to Lombardy, one shout: Americans go away!" The last noteworthy march of the year entailed an unusual technique: a single-file demonstration on the sidewalks of Rome organized by the small parties of the left in December.

Possibly because the first group of Euromissiles was deployed in Comiso early in 1984 despite all organized protest, pacifist marches in 1984 and 1985 did not keep up the rhythm of previous years. Nevertheless, some of them deserve attention. In 1984 and again in 1985, fruitless attempts were made to "counteract" the reinstituted military parade on Republic Day. A more successful three-event action was organized on June 3, 1984, in the Vicenza municipality and province by the Veneto region committees for peace and disarmament with the support of the PCI and other organizations. The first event encompassed a demonstration in front of a military installation in Longare labeled by the militants as a "nuclear storage site" and the concomitant blocking of its gates by specially trained "affinity groups." The next event entailed a "human chain," reportedly made up of 10,000 participants, from Longare to Vicenza. The final event was a gathering, followed by a feast, in Vicenza proper. In the leaflets distributed to announce the initiative, the organizers stressed three objectives: a referendum against the cruise missiles in Comiso in order to ban all nuclear weapons, refusal to pay taxes for military expenditures, and denuclearization of Italy and Europe.

In 1985 two demonstrations in particular attracted attention. The first, organized by several women's groups, took place in Rome's artistic Piazza Navona on May 25. After converging on the square, the organizers set up a show open to public participation. A reconstructed "Berlin Wall" could be crossed both ways, messages attached to balloons could be "sent" eastward, and stacks of cardboard boxes bearing the words "NATO" and "Warsaw Pact" could be knocked down—all for the modest sum of 100 lire (approximately five cents in U.S. currency). Finally, two women dressed in U.S. and Soviet military uniforms, respectively, threw away their fake weapons and embraced each other. The second demonstration was the traditional Perugia-Assisi march, which took place on October 6 and attracted between 30,000 and 40,000 participants, including for the first time an official Christian Democratic regional representative. Also present was PCI secretary-general Allessandro Natta, who replaced Berlinguer. As opposed to two years earlier, this time the Perugia-Assisi peace march attracted various political forces usually distrustful of PCI initiatives.

Denuclearized Municipalities

Although marches constitute the most visible aspect of pacifist activism, pacifist militancy does not exhaust itself in marching endeavors. The pacifist movement can count on "denuclearized municipalities" such as Bologna in Emilia-Romagna, Leghorn in Tuscany, and Vittoria in Sicily; these are PCI-run or PCI relative-majority townships, where the local municipal council is able to pass symbolic resolutions—nonbinding on the central government—to the effect that nuclear armaments are unwanted in the municipality. In addition to the statement of principle inherent to these resolutions and its attendant propaganda value, these municipal governments provide support and logistical structures for pacifist activists, including headquarters for the various coordination committees, mailing addresses having an ostensible character of officiality, and premises for conferences, exhibits, films, and the like.[35] Moreover, the "denuclearized municipalities" project the image of an antinuclear network through their joint conferences and exchanges of delegations.

Education

Another nationwide pacifist technique entails conferences and seminars. Whereas the approach and, most frequently, the names given to the discussion topics reflect a preestablished partisan position, the subject matter is sufficiently technical and interrelated. For example, in April and May 1983 a Naples peace committee organized a series of seminars to discuss "The Arms of the Apocalypse," "Use and Trade of Weapons," "War Industry and Productive Reconversion," and "Civil-Nuclear and War-Nuclear: Is Science Neutral?"

The most articulate initiative along these lines took place in Perugia, where a "Summer University for Peace" was organized in July 1983, "under the patronage of the Region of Umbria, the Province of Perugia, the Munic-

ipality of Perugia, and the University for Foreigners" and "in cooperation
with the Umbria Committee for Peace, the Environmental League of the
ARCI, and the Disarmament Archive," as advertised by an announcement
in the press in large characters.[36] In the words of Maurizio Lallerorni of the
Umbria Committee for Peace (which, incidentally, is headquartered in the
governmental offices of the Umbria region): "Now, after the strong re-
emergence of pacifist movements, there is a need to deepen knowledge;
there is a need for more information and less agitation. This time we do not
want to say 'no' to something, but we want to understand better"[37] The
Summer University for Peace was conducted with the participation of university professors, intellectuals, and pacifist exponents from Italy and
abroad. Its curriculum included lectures on the international arms trade;
North-South development and resources; environmental defense in industrial society; new ecological and pacifist movements; peace/war information
and the role of mass media; and sources of "alternative" knowledge.

In conjunction with the activities of the Summer University, the province of Perugia resolved to establish a permanent documentation center on
peace and disarmament to be managed by the ARCI. Selection of the ARCI
was not accidental, since it is endowed with a suitable budget largely derived from its multifaceted role in the entertainment field.

Publications

Both outdoor and indoor pacifist activities are accompanied by writings
published by the groups themselves or elsewhere in the press. Perhaps the
most notorious and elaborate effort of this nature was a book-size publication put out in 1983 by the PR and the Radical Parliamentary Group
through their Research Institute for Disarmament, Development, and Peace.
Polemically titled "What the Russians Already Know and the Italians Must
Not Know," this publication lists in geographical detail NATO, U.S., and
Italian military installations on the peninsula and furnishes a pertinent
map.[38] According to the authors, these military forces and facilities render
Italy a target for devastation and, because of their cost, foreclose the pos-
sibility of developing needed civilian structures and services.

More frequent coverage of the pacifist scene from a partisan standpoint
is made possible by the official press organs of the parties involved in the
pacifist movement and by publications of the pacifist formations themselves. For example, the PCI's *L'Unità* has not only devoted a lot of space
to pacifist issues and demonstrations, but it has also published articles submitted by pacifist activists who are not party members. The same can be
said about *Il Manifesto*, which is close to DP. For its part, the PR's *Notizie
Radicali* (Radical news) is a forum for all sorts of antimilitarist topics and
information.[39] Among the pacifist organizations in the strict sense, the Non-

violent Movement is particularly prolific; its publishing house prints various monographs on the philosophic and pragmatic aspects of nonviolence
and a monthly, *Azione Nonviolenta* (Nonviolent action), which is reportedly subscribed to by 4,000 readers.[40]

This type of written propaganda is supplemented by letters to the press.
A survey of those published in 1983 by dailies having national circulation
reflects appeals for the withdrawal of the Italian contingent in Lebanon by
the PCI's female members of Parliament, by a group of 140 farm workers,
by individual parents and groups of parents whose sons were serving in the
army in Italy or in Lebanon, and by pacifist activists who suggested ways
and means to avoid serving in Lebanon; complaints against the "useless"
and "repressive" nature of military service by groups of draftees; declarations of support for sundry peace initiatives, including one issued by a
group of 129 prison inmates on the occasion of the October 22 peace march
in Rome; and proposals from Sardinian conscientious objectors suggesting
that the actions against the cruise missiles in Sicily be extended to include
U.S. military installations in Sardinia.

Polemics over fatal accidents in the performance of military service have
led to the formation of an organization referred to as the "National Assistance Association to the Victims of the Armed Forces and to the Families of
the Fallen"; this group is presided over by former naval officer Falco Ac-
came, who, after having served as a Socialist member of Parliament, left the
PSI and ran as a DP candidate for Rome's City Hall. The association prepared a white book reporting 237 ascertained deaths since 1951, but alleging that many more took place.[41] In fact, the press tends to give wide coverage to such accidents, whether or not directly attributable to military
causes; likewise, the media frequently cover incidents involving near colli-
sions between military and commercial aircraft. The defense minister com-
mented that out of 126 deaths among draftees in 1984, only 33 were directly related to military service.[42]

Referendums

Since the bill introduced in Parliament by the senators of the Independent Left for a popular referendum on the deployment of the cruise missiles
will take time to undergo the required constitutional process (not to mention the uncertainty of its successful conclusion), the pacifists have resorted
to unofficial and nonbinding referendums along the lines of public opinion
polls as a form of moral suasion.[43] One of these referendums parallels the
legislative initiative of the Independent Left, another addresses armaments
in general, and still others are aimed at local issues such as nuclear energy
plants or firing ranges.

Most recently, increasing attention has been devoted by pacifism-oriented organizations to the Italian arms trade, to the point of organizing a referendum on the trade laws in this field. Among the primary sponsors are exponents of the ACLI, Pax Christi, Scientists for Disarmament Union (Unione Scienziati per il Disarmo), Independent Left, PR, and DP. Italy is normally ranked as the fourth largest arms producer in the world, and 93 percent of its arms exports are reportedly destined to Third World countries.[44] Less critical reports concur with the 93 percent figure, but place Italy as sixth in the arms field (which roughly coincides with Italy's seventh place as an industrial power) and stress the economic fact that this trade accounts for 3 percent of Italian exports.[45]

Comiso

The techniques and actions outlined above are indicative of pacifist dynamics at the national level, but the fulcrum of pacifist agitation remains Comiso itself. Ever since the preparatory works for the renovation of Vincenzo Magliocco Military Airport began in 1981 to host the cruise missiles, pacifist activists largely from out of town have established a permanent or rotating presence in Comiso. They have also relied heavily on the neighboring municipality of Vittoria, whose municipal executive committee is composed entirely of PCI councillors, and other supportive elements on the island. In fact, until recently Comiso's municipal council was headed by unsympathetic socialist mayor Salvatore Catalano and the PCI was not represented in the municipal majority coalition.

The area in front of the gates of the installation immediately became a preferred site for protests. Standard demonstrations entail gatherings of activists from Italy and abroad, who shout the word peace in several languages, throw flowers over the fences of the installation, sit in prayer or meditate Buddhist style, or celebrate the Catholic rite of the Way of the Cross using the installation gates as the last station. For its part, the township of Vittoria has refused to allow the American basketball team from the missile base to play in the local basketball tournament and has agreed to host a convention of the "denuclearized municipalities." Sympathy demonstrations have been staged elsewhere on the island, such as projection of the film "The Day After" in a church in Zafferana (Catania), a protest of clergymen of the dioceses of Noto against the consecration of a church inside the Comiso missile site, and the organization of a "human chain" of 10,000 pacifists extending from Catania to Sigonella, where the cruise missiles were reportedly stored in a U.S. military installation pending deployment to Comiso. Participants in this last event included ACLI and CGIL members.

Because of the presence of the missile site in Comiso, other local pacifist initiatives are more incisive. Pacifist propaganda frequently raises the specter of crime. Pacifist militant Giacomo Cagnes, a former communist mayor of Comiso, stated during a March 1984 interview that "the base in Comiso means drugs, mafia, [and] corruption of morality."[46] In May 1982 the PCI assistant regional secretary for Sicily, Luigi Colajanni, had made the following comment on the mafia murder of his political boss, Pio La Torre: "They killed him because of his peace policy, because of his firm opposition to the new missile base in Comiso."[47] Other political figures, including PCI, PDUP, and DP members of Parliament, are frequently present during demonstrations in front of the four gates of the missile site. These demonstrations often entail "sit-ins" aimed at blocking military transit. Finally, four tracts of land have been purchased by pacifist groups to set up permanent or seasonal camps in proximity to the installation.

Ownership of these lands affords the pacifist militants substantive advantages. Ironically, they can be compared to military barracks where pacifists who reside in Comiso on an indefinite basis sleep, eat, and take care of most other personal needs. At the same time, they are sites for conferences, seminars, organizational meetings, preparation of signs and other propaganda material, and hostels for transient militants. Most important, they are permanent bases for direct agitation against the missile site and training grounds for various forms of "passive resistance" and "civil disobedience."

The four tracts of land have been named Green Vineyard (Vigna Verde), the Cobweb (La Ragnatela), International Meeting Against Cruise (IMAC), and Green Swan (Cigno Verde). Green Vineyard is patronized by such groups as the LOC, LDU, MIR, Nonviolent Movement, and Pax Christi. This camp stands for antimilitarism and nonviolence and advocates unilateral disarmament. The Cobweb, which entertains close ties with the British pacifist camp at Greenham Common, is a female-run operation with objectives similar to those of the Green Vineyard but occasionally characterized by the presence of extremists. IMAC is patronized by heterogeneous groups principally of leftist orientation, including anarchists and AUTOP militants. IMAC's position is frequently expressed in anti-U.S. and anti-NATO terms (that is, "anti-imperialism") and endeavors to link pacifism to Third World causes and to the "revolutionary struggle." Green Swan attracts those parliamentary forces opposed to the current governmental coalition, and its principal aim is the pragmatic exploitation in political terms of the pacifist movement.[48]

Although these pacifist camps possess different characteristics and are endowed with different facilities, they all extend over several thousand square meters. Former mayor Catalano indicated that three of them were sold to the pacifists for 37 million, 12 million, and 35 million lire, respectively.[49] According to the pacifists, the required funds came from private subscriptions and donations.

Also present and quite active in Comiso is the Unitary Committee for Disarmament and Peace (Comitato Unitario per il Disarmo e la Pace), which rents office space in town. Headed by Giacomo Cagnes, the CUDIP draws its inspiration from the PCI and Third World causes. Cagnes has categorized the CUDIP as "autonomous from the parties, but not against the parties." [50] The CUDIP enjoys the largest number of domestic and international contacts of all pacifist groups, and it maintains close ties with the Green Swan camp. [51]

Unlawful Acts and Violence

Notwithstanding the laudable humanitarian inspiration of many pacifist activists and sympathizers, this type of militancy is not immune from degenerative phenomena and exploitation. Examples of justification and encouragement of unlawful practices in the name of peace are certainly not wanting.

In a December 1982 interview, the famous Italian writer and pacifist Alberto Moravia advocated the "transformation of pacifism into a large political movement, that is, a force capable of influencing, blackmailing governments." In response to a query about how to accomplish this, he replied: "With all legal means and, if governments will use force to oppose pacifism, with illegal ones." [52] Also in 1982, member of Parliament Giancarla Codrignani—who was elected as an independent candidate on the PCI ticket—addressed the modernized theater nuclear force issue in the following terms: "The government must clearly understand that if it wishes to have the cruise missiles, it must call in the army." [53] In the course of the same year, Roland Vogt, a leader of the German Greens visiting Comiso, stated: "We are now aware that the decisive battle for peace is being waged here in Comiso . . . We wish to defend ourselves, but with peaceful means, passive ones: for example, with sabotage actions." [54]

In addition to the pacifist technique of using road blocks, "civil disobedience" and "passive resistance" entail various other unlawful actions. One of them, called "fiscal objection," is the refusal to pay a percentage of personal income tax equal to the defense-spending percentage of the national budget. As of November 1983 there were 1,649 cases of fiscal objection, as opposed to 419 recorded during the previous year, when this practice was initiated. By October 1985 the figure had risen to 2,564 cases. According to press accounts, three members of Parliament—Gianluigi Melega and Roberto Cicciomessere of the PR and Mario Capanna of DP—as well as Bishop Luigi Bettazzi of Ivrea, the president of Pax Christi, are active fiscal objectors. Other organizations that advocate this method of protest are the LDU, MIR, LOC, and Nonviolent Movement. The amount withheld from tax payments is reportedly donated to the peace camps in Comiso, to Amnesty International, and to Third World aid organizations.[55]

A parallel initiative by Catholic elements (who evidently choose to disregard the fact that Catholic doctrine does not prohibit military service) is aimed at organizing disobedience and sabotage within the armed forces by draftees as a twin to conscientious objection.[56] This initiative is reminiscent of the Proletarians in Uniform (Proletari in Divisa) of the early 1970s—that is, Marxist-Leninist agitators within the military establishment who drew their inspiration from Ongoing Struggle. In those days the PID and another short-lived organization called Democratic Noncommissioned Officers (Sottufficiali Democratici) were substantially the only groups that paralleled the antimilitarist action of the Radicals.

Along the ecological/pacifist lines, additional types of unlawful behavior are part of the record. Rare birds on display in public parks have been liberated by activists, and at least three groups on the Interior Ministry's subversive formations list—Green Brigades (Brigate Verdi), Popular Ecological Groups (Gruppi Ecologici Popolari), and Ecological Action Nucleus "Robin Hood" (Nucleo d'Azione Ecologica Robin Hood)—have claimed responsibility for such actions as damaging property.

Moreover, during pacifist marches and demonstrations, participating AUTOP militants resort to illegal forms of agitation generally ranging from disturbance of the peace to acts of vandalism. AUTOP-connected elements have also set off, within the time frame of planned pacifist actions, incendiary devices against targets such as military vehicles and a botanical research center connected with the U.S. embassy.[57] AUTOP members have likewise been present in the CUDIP of Comiso, as confirmed by Cagnes himself.[58] These practitioners of violence were responsible for the November 1983 aggression in Comiso against a policeman who attempted to stop a pacifist from spray-painting slogans on a police car, while still others were slashing police car tires. A few months earlier, in August, young "pacifists" had sprayed on police vehicles the words: "We will kill you all."[59] Swift police intervention in cases such as these, as well as on the occasion of road blocks, has been severely reprimanded by the PCI, PDUP, and DP. These parties did not display analogous solidarity when policemen were injured by rioting "pacifists."

Another unlawful pacifist technique repeatedly utilized in Comiso entails clandestine entrance into the missile site for the purpose of drawing sketches of the installation. In 1983 alone, at least ten persons were arrested on espionage-related charges. But the most representative raid took place during the night between Good Friday and Holy Saturday of 1984, when two women from the Cobweb camp penetrated the protective fence and spray-painted slogans on the installation's water tower and 23 military vehicles.[60] Another significant incident was reported in January 1985: a detailed map of the installation was found in a Comiso post office together with a letter addressed to the *New Statesman* of London.[61]

Anarchist groups whose approach does not ultimately differ from that of AUTOP have likewise decided to exploit pacifist and antimilitarist issues. In early 1985, members of the Italian Anarchist Federation (Federazione Anarchica Italiana) formulated a platform encompassing civil and military insubordination, draft resistance and conscientious objection, desertion, damage to military property, increase of fiscal objection and utilization of pertinent funds to support deserters and jailed objectors, and sabotage actions against military-production industries. In order to achieve those goals, these members envisaged the intensification of contacts with kindred organizations, including AUTOP, and a "counterinformation" program based on private radio stations, writings on military installation walls and military vehicles, and distribution of leaflets inside and outside military barracks. In the summer of 1985 the Anarchist Committee for Antimilitarist Initiatives (Comitato Anarchico di Iniziative Antimilitariste) was founded. Like the Radicals in earlier years, the anarchists count on the antimilitarist sentiment among the youth of draft age. Draft protesters are estimated to exceed 18,000 individuals.[62]

Most ominously, the pacifist movement has also attracted the attention of the Italian terrorist milieu. Early in the 1980s, the Red Brigades (BR) referred to the installation of missile bases on the national territory as an act of war and declared their intention to participate in the mass movement for disarmament.[63] It is not irrelevant that BR member Francesco Varanese, who was arrested in May 1982, had requested to be exempted from military service as a "conscientious objector."[64] Then, in Rome on February 15, 1984, a BR commando murdered U.S. diplomat Leamon R. Hunt, director-general of the Multinational Force and Observers. The responsibility claim included the following exhortations: "The imperialist forces out of Lebanon! Italy out of NATO! No to the missiles in Comiso!"

Since 1983 BR interest in the pacifist issue has been increasing. In *Politica e Rivoluzione* (Politics and revolution), a book authored by unrepentant imprisoned brigadists, "the movements against war, the deployment of the missiles and nuclear (energy), and even the ecology (movements)" are defined as "an ensemble of proletarian antagonism." The authors therefore propose "liaison between combatant initiative and these mass movements."[65] Moreover, all BR writings in recent years include anti-NATO and anti-Euromissiles exhortations, even when they address unrelated topics.

BR appeals do not appear to have fallen on deaf ears. Besides the BR's own militancy, at least two serious actions of terrorist nature were perpetrated by other formations. On September 10, 1983, a group called New

Armed Partisans for Communism (Nuovi Partigiani Armati per il Comunismo) damaged with explosives a national television transmitter in Trent, causing a blackout. A leaflet dropped off at the site of the incident stated that the action was taken "against the disinformation of national radio-television, against those who prepare war and the armaments race . . . against dismissals and unemployment." [66] On July 27, 1984, a group called Communists Struggling Against Imperialism and Armaments (Comunisti Combattenti Contro l'Imperialismo e gli Armamenti) bombed the Rome residence of Leonetto De Leon, editor of *Notizie NATO* (NATO news). His wife and son were injured.

It is difficult to estimate the numerical strength of full-time infiltrators within the pacifist movement; there are thousands of AUTOP extremists and hundreds of anarchists available for the exploitation of pacifist initiatives. In September 1984, Italy's prime minister had told the parliamentary oversight committee on intelligence that 70 terrorists were active in the antinuclear, antimilitarist, pacifist organizations. [67] Moreover, the semi-annual intelligence reports submitted by the prime minister to the two chambers of Parliament since 1983 have repeatedly voiced concern over the potential degeneration of pacifism. [68] These reports are a sanitized version of the ones prepared by the intelligence and security services. Worse yet, however, as will be seen in the discussion of hostile foreign-intelligence operations in Italy, there is evidence of linkages between the Italian pacifist movement and foreign provocateurs.

CHAPTER SEVEN

Transnational Hostility and Links to Domestic Terrorism

The Italian peninsula constitutes a lucrative as well as a vulnerable target for hostile foreign operations. Italy's geostrategic position in the Mediterranean, its politico-military role in NATO's southern flank, and its significance as the world's seventh most industrialized nation contribute to the lucrative nature of the target. Likewise, endemic politico-ideological strife, socioeconomic conflict, governmental instability, and the presence of a subversive and revolution-oriented milieu contribute to Italy's vulnerability.

The designs of hostile foreign powers usually translate into two general types of clandestine operations: those directed against the Republic of Italy and the minuscule but otherwise influential State of the Vatican City,[1] and those meant to exploit Italian territory in the pursuit of objectives not directly related or even totally unrelated to Italy. The spectrum of clandestine operations conducted in Italy includes espionage, recruitment of agents, infiltration, funding of dissidents, disinformation, promotion of subversion and terrorism, and surrogate warfare. The most significant actors are the Soviet Union, its satellite and client states, and Third World national and subnational organizations with interests in the Mediterranean basin.

The very nature of clandestine operations across international boundaries makes their detection particularly difficult. But even when they are detected by the Italian authorities, political, economic, and/or security considerations pertaining to the maintenance of viable foreign relations frequently lead to downplaying hostile actions and thus to limited and unsystematic public disclosure.

Soviet and East European Clandestine Operations

The most recurrent media coverage of Communist Bloc clandestine operations addresses the matter of classical espionage.[2] The Soviet Union and its satellites have in fact repeatedly sought access to elements of Italian military, political, and industrial information that are subject to governmental security controls or to other restrictions on dissemination. These elements of information are, of course, frequently interrelated. Typical espionage targets directly engaged by the Soviet intelligence services—the KGB and GRU—include Italian and NATO military offices and installations,[3] the Ministry of Foreign Affairs,[4] and sensitive industrial concerns.[5] Similar espionage operations have been undertaken by satellite intelligence services, especially those of Czechoslovakia, Hungary, and East Germany.[6] Bulgarian involvement in such operations appears to be more recent.

In some cases, the Soviets and the Czechs in particular succeeded in setting up espionage rings headed by Italian nationals who in turn reported to a Communist Bloc "case officer."[7] All espionage operations that used Italian nationals, regardless of personal role, have shown repetitive practices: bribery of public officials, enlisting private citizens of mercenary orientation, exploitation of individuals conditioned by a state of necessity, blackmail, and utilization of persons committed to the communist cause. Co-optation of Italians has occurred principally in Italy but also abroad.

Espionage has been accompanied by recruitment, infiltration, and influence operations. This is how, in the early 1960s, the late Colonel Oleg Penkovskiy of the GRU described the Italian operational environment:

Our experts in Italy . . . give our officers detailed information about where to plant agents and how to organize contacts in Rome . . . There are many foreigners there and the Romans themselves get along well with foreigners, seeing in them a source of income. Therefore we can operate inconspicuously. The Italians are extremely talkative. That helps us, too . . . There is a large Communist Party in Italy . . . 'our Italian friends' can be of great service in operations.[8]

Moreover, Penkovskiy lists the Italian Communist Party (PCI) among "'fifth columns' that support our work."[9]

The importance of this "support" is elaborated on in Penkovskiy's commentary:

There was a period at the end of Stalin's reign when the Central Committee CPSU issued an order restricting the active use of Communists in intelligence work . . . Experience later showed that it was much more difficult to work without the help of the Communists. So Khrushchev and the Central Committee put out a directive to the KGB and GRU to activate recruitment of Communist Party members for intelligence work. In 1956 and 1957 we again began to recruit Communists in the West. We would use them as spotters and agents and, through them, spread misinformation and propaganda. Contact was re-established with former agents . . . Because the communist parties in the West are able to exist openly, they have the opportunity to organize conspiratorial activities in their respective countries in support of Soviet intelligence work. Many of the leaders of these communist parties move in the highest circles of their governments.[10]

The setting described in Penkovskiy's narration clearly coincides with a long-lasting political era—late 1940s and 1950s—when the PCI's alignment with the Soviet Bloc was unequivocal. The Italian Communists would refer to Radio Prague, which still broadcasts propaganda in Italian, as "our radio." It was also in Prague that the archives of the PCI were kept at least until Stalin's death.[11] But perhaps most symptomatic is the autobiographical account of his feelings toward the Soviet Union provided by Silverio Corvisieri, a former PCI member of Parliament who has been in and out of the party:

The Italian Communist Party seemed to me a giant with one thousand eyes and one thousand arms, but with a single brain and a will of iron . . . And behind the party I would always see the immense 'Socialist camp led by the Soviet Union, the country of the October Revolution, Lenin's country.' The USSR was above any challenge: at the Olympics of 1960, which in fact took place in Rome, each time that the flag with the hammer and sickle would go up the flagpole my heart would beat hard and some times I could not hold back my tears [of joy].[12]

Corvisieri's sentiments of that period were indeed the reflection of his party's state of mind, frequently expressed in rather pedantic terms highly reminiscent of intellectual affectation.[13]

As noted in Chapter 6, since the mid-1960s the PCI has modified the political image it wishes to project. Nevertheless, the KGB has maintained close contact with the ostensibly minor, albeit influential, rigidly pro-Soviet wing still present in the Italian party. Moreover, notwithstanding the party's new course, Soviet subsidies to the PCI's official daily, *L'Unità*, were reportedly raised from $800,000 in 1967 to $2.5 million in 1976 at the height of the "Eurocommunist" period. Cash delivery methods have included diplomatic courier from Russia to the Soviet Embassy and thence to PCI representatives, direct cash transfers to PCI officials visiting Moscow, use of party couriers and intermediaries, and transfers through bank accounts of East European trade companies and Italian import-export firms.[14]

Journalistic findings of this nature are corroborated by the revelations of Communist Bloc defectors. For example, former Czech intelligence officer Frantisek August, who defected in 1969, testified before a U.S. Senate panel that:

> Every Communist Party has within its organizational structure a committee
> . . . concerned . . . with preventing the penetration of police agents . . . [Its]
> members are recruited by KGB agents and . . . then operate, under the guise
> of the committee, almost entirely on behalf of the KGB, in the interest of the
> Soviet Union. They conduct this activity without the knowledge of the mem-
> bers of the central committee and of the secretary general [of their respective
> parties]. Thereby the KGB insures political control of the communist parties.[15]

Italian police investigations also uncovered devious procedures whereby
PCI militants were consensually expelled from the party in order to facilitate their infiltration and espionage operations in various sectors of Italian
society on behalf of the Communist Bloc. A particularly intriguing case
took place in the late 1940s, when a mixed group of common criminals and
"former" PCI militants operated under the direction of a stateless Armenian
resident of Italy, Colust Megherian, who was an avowed admirer of the
USSR and Stalin as well as a reputed Soviet agent. Megherian himself had
been "expelled" from the PCI. The police ultimately arrested 48 members
of Megherian's network, which is credited, inter alia, with having infiltrated
Italy's parachute unit and two conservative political parties.[16]

Communist Bloc reliance on, and utilization of, Italian "comrades" is
a time-honored practice that can be readily seen from a number of cases in
the public domain. This practice, which straddles the entire spectrum of
clandestine operations, not only predates Penkovskiy's testimony but has
also proven its effectiveness thereafter, as evidenced by the sequence of a
variety of cases recorded since the end of World War II.

Declassified Interior Ministry records indicate that prior to Yugoslavia's break from the Soviet fold in 1948, PCI members received training in
that country's paramilitary camps under the guise of "work brigades." Recruitment centers, operated by local PCI leaders, were set up in Bari, Udine,
Milan, and other Italian cities. Ranking Italian Communists Luigi Longo
and Corrado De Vita were responsible for coordinating recruitment and
communications. Two Yugoslav liaison agents were posted in Trieste,
whereas overall operational control was exercised from Milan by a Soviet
Red Army colonel. It is interesting to note that several "trainees" moved
on from Yugoslavia to Greece to fight under guerrilla leader Marcos Be-
feiades.[17]

Other Interior Ministry records pointed out that Viktor Pavlov, who
was associated with the Soviet Embassy in Rome, was the Cominform's
officer responsible for the paramilitary readiness of the PCI's clandestine
apparat during the period 1948–1950.[18] It should be noted that U.S. National Security Council estimates of the early 1950s assessed the PCI's covert paramilitary force as consisting of over 100,000 armed men.[19] As late
as 1963, the USSR still arranged for the arming of Italian Sovietphiles

through Austrian Communist Party channels, according to a high ranking Czech military officer, General Jan Sejna, who defected to the West in 1968.[20]

Over the years, Czechoslovakia too has played an incisive role as a Soviet proxy. In the late 1940s and early 1950s, Czech territory served as a safe haven for Italian Communist fugitives, namely, members of the partisan underground of World War II and of the postwar Red Strike Force who were wanted by the Italian authorities for political and common crimes perpetrated in connection with the unsuccessful attempts to set up an Italian Soviet republic. Particularly notorious among the few hundred fugitives are Red Strike Force members Giulio Paggio, Natale Burato, and Paolo Finardi,[21] as well as partisan Francesco Moranino, who was later pardoned by the president of the Republic of Italy and elected to the Senate on the PCI ticket in 1968. Several of these fugitives have since remained in Czechoslovakia.

Besides safe haven, Czechoslovakia has provided training to Italy's Communists. Senator Eugenio Reale, himself a former Communist who headed the PCI's administrative secretariat, exposed the existence of Czech training camps that had been organized as early as the 1950s and partially manned by Communist fugitives from Italy.[22] Others of these fugitives, including Moranino, performed propaganda-related functions as staff members of Radio Prague's Italian-language broadcast. In addition, an Italian intelligence report—which was partially quoted in parliamentary records and referred to as having been prepared "subsequent to September 1979"— states that "according to multiple sources, at least 2,000 Italians have attended courses for extremist activists in Czechoslovakia and other countries from 1948 to date. Of these, 600 names are known to SISMI [the Service for Military Intelligence and Security]."[23] Another source that claims familiarity with the intelligence report has identified the "other countries" as being the USSR, Cuba, and Albania.[24]

Links between Czechoslovakia and the PCI have likewise facilitated the infiltration of Soviet "illegals" abroad—that is, Soviet or Communist Bloc nationals who infiltrate Western countries under a false identity. Frantisek August formally testified that several PCI members were brought over to his former country in 1965 on instructions from the Soviet Union so that the KGB could provide its "illegals" with a new identity by using the Italian passports.[25]

Included in the more recent record of Communist Bloc covert endeavors are several instances of Russian reliance on the PCI's pro-Soviet wing, some of whose members have experienced an uneasy relationship with the party. Within this milieu, the Soviet Union has established receptive channels for disinformation and influence operations. The role played by retired air force general Nino Pasti is notorious. Pasti, who was twice elected to the Senate (in 1976 and again in 1979) as an independent on the PCI ticket and who served with NATO's headquarters staff, has repeatedly alleged that the military balance favors NATO, while stressing that the military posture of the Warsaw Pact is purely defense oriented.[26] Among other disinformation-spreading techniques, Pasti was interviewed about the NATO-Warsaw Pact balance by *Komsomolskaya Pravda*, the official organ of the Soviet Communist Youth League; this interview, published on November 3, 1980, was then picked up by *Corriere della Sera* of Milan, Italy's most circulated daily, and by Italian radio. Pasti also heads Struggle for Peace, a "pacifist" anti-NATO organization affiliated with the Soviet-run World Peace Council.

Other Soviet-aligned centers and structures in Italy are Aurora, a publishing house founded in late 1978; *Interstampa*, a periodical revamped in 1982; and the Lenin Institute, incorporated in 1982.[27] Additional Italian publishers that specialize in pro-Soviet works are Nicola Teti of Milan and Roberto Napoleone of Rome. Napoleone, whose résumé includes editorship of *Interstampa*, was expelled from the PCI in October 1982, only to be readmitted in November 1984.[28]

Clandestine recruitment and exploitation of the PCI by the Communist Bloc do not exclude similar practices toward less orthodox communists or even noncommunists. For example, the now-defunct Italian Socialist Party for Proletarian Unity was so heavily financed by Moscow from its very birth, in 1964, that it came to the point of losing all political autonomy.[29] Close links also exist between the Soviet Union and Struggle Slate (Lista di Lotta), another minor party founded by Nino Pasti in 1983 when the PCI failed to sponsor him as a senatorial candidate for a third term. Struggle Slate's 52 candidates for the 1983 parliamentary elections were not old nostalgic Stalinists; in fact, nineteen were in their twenties and eighteen in their thirties.[30]

Czech intelligence agents, too, according to defectors' accounts, have infiltrated Italian political parties—both parliamentary parties of "bourgeois" orientation (that is, noncommunist) and extraparliamentary communist ones to the left of the PCI. Depending on the sensitivity of their activities, operatives would report to headquarters through alternate channels; they might report to colleagues assigned under diplomatic cover to the Czech Embassy in Rome, use nondiplomatic-status cut-outs (that is, individuals who serve as clandestine links) in Italy, or even travel personally to Prague with a stopover in Vienna. When travel was involved, an Italian passport would be used during the first portion of the trip and then a Czech one. Operations of this nature were carried out by the Czechs at least until 1968.[31]

Like political parties, the Italian labor movement has also been targeted for infiltration and collateral espionage purposes. In the 1970s the Soviets set their sights on Italian labor unions even down to the provincial level, as evidenced by programmatic documentation drawn up by the Central Council of Soviet Labor Unions. Moscow's plans called for the periodic exchange of delegations to discuss "scientific and technological progress." Closer relations with the Italian labor unions at all echelons were also to be enhanced by jointly sponsoring the "pairing" of Italian and Soviet cities: Venice-Tallinn, Carrara-Erivan, Palermo-Tiflis, Bologna-Kharkov, Genoa-Odessa, Florence-Kiev, Rimini-Sochi, Milan-Leningrad, Ferrara-Krasnodar, Turin-Volgograd, Leghorn-Novosibirsk, Modena–Alma-Ata, and Reggio Calabria–Sukhumi. Given the industrial, commercial, maritime, and/or strategic significance of these Italian cities, one can easily surmise what the Soviets mean by "scientific and technological progress." Moreover, in their plans and estimates they expressed concern over the absence of direct contact with local labor organizations in the Italian cities of Trento, Venice, Udine, Trieste, Ancona, Pescara, Bari, Catania (Sicily), and Cagliari (Sardinia). The first four are located in the area that borders Eastern Europe, the next three are port cities along Italy's Adriatic (eastern) coast, and the last two are of military relevance on their respective Mediterranean islands.[32]

The Vatican also falls within the scope of Communist Bloc clandestine operations on the Italian peninsula. A network was already in place in 1952, when it became known that the Reverend Alighiero Tondi was a Soviet agent under the cover of a professorship at the Gregorian Academy in Rome.[33] In 1975 press accounts disclosed that two former Czech priests, Jaroslav Vojetch and Frantisek Krusik, had spied on military facilities and surveilled Czech emigres during their enrollment at the Collegio Nepomuceno, the Vatican's Czech institute in Rome. After their return to Czechoslovakia, the two authored a book entitled *The Vatican at the Crossroads,* in which they "expose" the Vatican's anticommunist role. These unmasked operations presumably constitute just the tip of the iceberg, since several East European defectors have stressed the attention devoted to the Vatican and to the Catholic Church in general by the USSR and its satellites.

According to former Czech intelligence officer Ladislav Bittman, who defected in 1968, Hungarian intelligence was the most active satellite service in penetrating Catholic circles abroad at least until 1956.[34] Joseph Frolik, another Czech intelligence officer who defected in 1969, testified that Radio Vatican and the Czech emigres who work for it attract considerable Czech surveillance.[35] Yet another defector who served with Polish intelligence until 1967 indicated that the near totality of that service's effort to collect information in Italy is aimed at the Vatican and the Catholic Church.[36]

The Spread of Disinformation

Of particular importance among Communist Bloc clandestine practices in Italy are those intended to undermine NATO and Western solidarity. These operations frequently entail the spread of disinformation. Known cases, such as the ones summarized below, reflect the direct as well as the instrumental targeting of Italy within the global Western context.

After the May 25, 1970, meeting of the NATO foreign ministers held in Rome, the Soviets forged a press release announcing that "the weakness of democracy" and "the lack of political stability" in Italy had led the Allies to recommend the transfer of U.S. troops from the Federal Republic of Germany to northern Italy in order to offset PCI strength. The forged document was received by a doctrinaire socialist member of Parliament, Riccardo Lombardi, who brought it to the attention of the Foreign Affairs Committee of the Chamber of Deputies. A protest against "U.S. interference in Italian domestic affairs" was immediately raised in the columns of the PCI's *L'Unità*. The forged document was ultimately denounced as such by the Italian Ministry of Foreign Affairs and by NATO.[37]

In the immediate aftermath of the 1978 abduction in Rome of Christian Democratic Party president Aldo Moro by the Red Brigades (BR), Radio Moscow aired a number of broadcasts insinuating that this crime was attributable to "reactionary forces." In its turn, the French Communist Party daily, *L'Humanité,* echoed Moscow by directly blaming "secret services whose activity is connected with the NATO military base in Naples." This and other *L'Humanité* reports that specifically named the CIA were then quoted by Radio Moscow. As Radio Moscow and *L'Humanité* were feeding each other "information," the Soviet news agency Novosti collated for international distribution foreign press articles that addressed the same theme as well as one report that alluded to negative comments made against Moro by then–U.S. ambassador to Rome Richard Gardner. This type of induced press coverage caused the resurfacing of another forgery made earlier in the decade: U.S. Army Field Manual FM 30-31 B, "which purports to contain guidance to U.S. military security services regarding measures for influencing the internal affairs of friendly countries where U.S. armed forces are stationed and which are confronted by internal security threats from leftist and Communist forces."[38] Among other noncommunist periodicals, the "connection" between the Field Manual and Moro's abduction was made by Spain's *El Pais* and Italy's *Europeo*. The emerging theme suggests that the United States had arranged for the kidnapping and subsequent murder of Moro to preempt his efforts to seal a "historic compromise" between his party and the PCI, which would have led to the latter's participation in the Council of Ministers; in other words, this was allegedly an example of U.S. clandestine and violent interference in Italian internal affairs.

Another notable forgery was consummated in 1979. A letter dated March 29 and purporting to be issued by the U.S. defense attaché in Rome was mailed to a number of dailies in Naples. The letter, which denied that the deaths of a number of local children and other environmental hazards had been caused by U.S. and NATO chemical and biological weapons stored in the area, implicitly confirmed their storage at a time when left-wing pressures were mounting for the removal of U.S. installations from Italy.[39]

On January 15 of the following year, Radio Prague alleged that Italian prime minister Francesco Cossiga was on his way to Washington "in order to receive United States directives with regard to foreign policy." The ensuing protest delivered to the Czech government by Italy's ambassador to Prague referred to the "periodical regularity" with which Radio Prague had made "negative and unfounded remarks on Italian affairs during the last months."[40]

In January 1982 Czech emigre Jiri Pelikan, who fled his country in 1968 and subsequently became an Italian citizen as well as a member of the European Parliament on the Italian Socialist Party (PSI) ticket, filed a criminal complaint with Rome's police headquarters stating that:

> some letters written on my letterhead and bearing my signature have been addressed to Proletarian Line [Linea Proletaria], Communist Platform [Programma Comunista], and the Italian Social Movement. They are clearly provocative letters I never wrote, that is, forgeries. I immediately realized that the Prague secret services are responsible, also because a similar operation was recently conducted in various European countries against Czech emigres. Moreover, during the same period, Radio Prague aired a weekly program, 'Dialogues from the Other Side,' against Czech emigres. The ongoing broadcast is based on excerpts of bugged telephone conversations from the Paris office of *Temoignage*, one of the periodicals published by the Czech emigres. I personally heard excerpts of my own conversations, artfully manipulated, with the editor of the journal, Pavel Tigrid. A trial will shortly commence in Prague against intellectuals charged with conspiracy . . . Radio Prague's campaign is aimed at convincing public opinion that Czech intellectuals are conspirators against the regime. In my case, the aim of [Gustáv] Husák's agents is to discredit a European parliamentarian and to . . . place the blame on neo-Fascist circles.[41]

Although Radio Prague is a frequent medium for propaganda and disinformation campaigns directed at Italy, it is by no means unique. Over the years, similar broadcasts in the Italian language have also been aired from Moscow, Sofia, Bucharest, Warsaw, and Budapest. Italians employed abroad, particularly in West Germany where there is a large community of

Italian workers, constitute the specific target of a portion of these radio programs. Others are aimed at Italian ham-radio operators. Communist Bloc Italian-broadcast schedules have been so devised as not to compete with one another and to reach the largest possible audience during key listening hours of the workday and holidays. Typical program titles include "In Italy Today" and "Voice of the Italian Emigre."

At times, propaganda and disinformation endeavors have been accompanied by operations that resort to violence. In a deposition before a U.S. Senate panel, as well as in his subsequent autobiographical work, the former Czech officer Joseph Frolik stated that Czech intelligence surreptitiously supported violent Germanic separatist aspirations in the South Tyrol in the early 1960s. Czech agents actually conducted a number of dynamite attacks against power lines in that German-speaking area under Italian sovereignty. The ultimate objective was the fomentation of discord between Italy and bordering Austria and, indirectly, between Italy and West Germany, a NATO partner.[42]

The Bulgarian Connection

As indicated above, the clandestine role of Bulgaria's secret services in Italy appears to be recent. Although two seemingly isolated incidents had already occurred in 1962 and 1972, systematic Bulgarian involvement did not surface until the start of the 1980s.[43] The multifaceted "Bulgarian connection" is likely to remain a matter of heated debate, since it encompasses issues that defy conclusive settlement in a court of law. Included under this heading are the indictment of two Italian labor union officials on espionage and subversion charges; Bulgarian involvement in the assassination attempt against Pope John Paul II, whose continuing links to his native Poland conflict with Soviet interests; a suspected plot to murder Polish labor union leader Lech Walesa while in Rome; and illicit marketing of weapons. All four deserve further scrutiny.

The first incident involved Luigi Scricciolo and his wife, Paola Elia, who were employed by the Italian Union of Labor (UIL) when arrested in February 1982. During prior militancy in the ranks of Proletarian Democracy (DP) from 1977 to 1979, Scricciolo had accepted clandestine Bulgarian funding for his party in exchange for political and military information. After resigning from DP and joining the UIL, Scricciolo was blackmailed into continuing his collaboration with the Bulgarians, who threatened to disclose his past association with them. Although Scricciolo and Elia are now accusing each other of responsibility for the more serious offenses, it would appear that they operated in unison. Their sensitive work in the UIL's international relations office was of particular interest to Bulgarian intelligence since it included close contacts with Poland's Solidarity. Pending conclusion of the judicial proceedings, the couple's services to Bulgaria appear to have included information on Italian affairs, reports on U.S. labor matters, and incipient arrangements to deploy a network of Italian students in the United States who would be charged with the task of collecting political and technical data.[44] Three Bulgarian diplomats identified by Scricciolo as his points of contact were withdrawn by their government before expulsion could take place.[45] It had also been intended that Scricciolo would serve as a link between the BR and Bulgarian intelligence.

The second incident was the abortive murder attempt against Pope John Paul II in Saint Peter's Square on May 13, 1981, by Turkish gunman Mehmet Ali Agca. Agca was captured that same day and, shortly thereafter, convicted and sentenced to life imprisonment. Not until a year after the assassination attempt did Agca begin to cooperate with the Italian authorities; this cooperation led to the indictment of four additional Turks, whose alleged roles had been those of instigation and logistical support, and three Bulgarians, who had allegedly planned and organized the operation. Of the three Bulgarians, two were assigned to the embassy in Rome and one to Balkan Air at Rome's Leonardo Da Vinci International Airport in Fiumicino. The two diplomats were transferred before the expulsion procedure could take place, but the Balkan Air representative was arrested in November 1982.[46] Agca's testimony, coupled with his identification of persons, objects, and places, was corroborated by circumstantial evidence, including his highly suspect 50-day sojourn in Bulgaria in July and August 1980 and spasmatic travel in and out of Italy, and by parallel police and judicial investigations. However, when the conspiracy case finally came up for trial, Agca's behavior became erratic and bizarre to the point of his claiming to be Jesus Christ, even though psychiatric examiners in Turkey—where he had been previously jailed for other crimes—and psychiatric observers in Italy consider him to be legally sane. The motivation behind Agca's court behavior remains a matter of conjecture, but the trial did result in the acquittal of the Bulgarians on the basis of "lack of evidence," an official Italian judicial formula intended to leave room for doubt. The Balkan Air agent has since been repatriated. Meanwhile, another judicial/police investigation is in progress regarding pertinent criminal issues raised by the prosecutor during the trial that were not fully examined at the time.[47] It is worth noting that the trial was preceded and accompanied by propaganda against the findings of the prosecution. Books and press accounts have alleged that evidence was fabricated and that Italian and U.S. intelligence "coached" Agca. One such book, authored by French attorney Christian Roulette, was published by known Communist Roberto Napoleone.[48]

The third instance of the so-called Bulgarian connection to a terrorist act was also unsuccessful. According to Agca's testimony, contingency plans had been made to assassinate Lech Walesa of Poland's Solidarity during his January 14–19, 1981, visit to Rome hosted by Italy's major labor unions, including the UIL. That time frame coincides with one of Agca's sojourns in Rome prior to the papal assassination attempt. Moreover, Agca displayed familiarity with Walesa's Roman itinerary, and he identified as one of the plotters Bulgarian diplomat Ivan Tomov Dontchev, whose name also appears in Scricciolo's confessions.

The fourth incident, or series of incidents, involved the illicit marketing of weapons. With respect to a judicial investigation initiated in Trent in 1982, Italy's minister of defense Lelio Lagorio stated before the Parliament that "counterespionage has ascertained that . . . an important structure is provided by Kintex, a Bulgarian state-owned import-export company whose presence has been noted in all significant traffic in this field." [49] He specifically cited the case of a lot of Beretta 7.65 millimeter semiautomatic pistols that had been manufactured in Italy and sold to Bulgaria but were subject to a no-transfer-to-third-parties international trade clause. These weapons subsequently reached Turkish terrorists. [50]

It would be virtually impossible to quantify the Communist Bloc nationals that operate in Italy on behalf of their respective intelligence services. In his two books, which address only Soviet operations abroad, John Barron has identified 145 KGB and GRU operatives who worked in Italy under cover at different times from 1945 until the end of December 1982. [51] Also difficult to come by in the public record are reliable statistics regarding the number of such foreign nationals arrested, convicted, expelled, and/or barred from re-entering Italy. A reconstruction from research works and media accounts indicates that the Italian authorities have identified and taken action against at least 72 Communist Bloc nationals involved in intelligence operations from the end of World War II through the first quarter of 1986. Included in this number are forty-four Soviets, nine Bulgarians, nine Hungarians, six Czechs, two Romanians, one East German, and one Pole. Six Yugoslav and two Albanian agents can be added to the list, since their countries are governed by Communist regimes albeit no longer part of the Soviet fold. [52]

In this context it is also relevant to note the large number of Communist Bloc personnel assigned to their respective embassies in Rome with diplomat credentials: USSR, forty-seven; Czechoslovakia, nineteen; Poland, seventeen; Hungary, sixteen; Bulgaria, fourteen; East Germany, thirteen; and Romania, thirteen. [53] These figures are considered out of proportion with legitimate needs of the Communist Bloc in Italy.

Third World Clandestine Operations

Of more recent vintage are the clandestine operations conducted in Italy with increasing frequency and sophistication by Third World national and subnational groups in the pursuit of a variety of objectives related to domestic or regional interests of their own. Consequently, Italian territory has become a transit area or even an alternate battleground for feuding elements totally extraneous to Italy. The most notorious of these groups usually have roots in the Middle East and Northern Africa. Actors and victims include Armenians, Palestinians, Israelis, Egyptians, Iraqis, Jordanians, Iranians, and, not least of all, Libyans. Listed in Appendix 5 are significant episodes of transnational violence that dramatically reflect this development. However, not all of these clandestine operations were necessarily violent.

From mid-1977 through late 1981, Armenian terrorist groups presumably headquartered in Lebanon were also active in Milan and Rome; they had possible linkages to members of the Italian-Armenian communities there as well as in Venice. They targeted Turkish diplomats with firearms and planted explosive devices at centrally located offices of the Turkish and other non-Italian airlines and tourist agencies. A recurrent technique was the detonation of two-phase bombs at short intervals. Their stated aim in Italy parallels their operations elsewhere in the world: the liberation of Armenia from Turkey, vengeance for the "Armenian genocide," and retaliation against the property of countries whose police authorities arrested "Armenian freedom fighters." Bystanders have frequently been hurt in the process. Major incidents, as well as the organizational names under which responsibility was claimed, are listed in Appendix 5.

Also recorded in Appendix 5 are incidents traceable to the Palestinian issue and to a variety of broader conflicts inherent in Middle Eastern politics and power struggles. Some of these acts are clearly the work of the more classical Palestinian organizations, whose nationalist aspirations are frequently accompanied by additional political goals; examples of such groups are the Popular Front for the Liberation of Palestine, the Popular Front for the Liberation of Palestine–General Command, and the Black September and Black June organizations. Others, such as the Abu Nidal network, which uses several different names in Italy and elsewhere, seem to operate within the context of intra-Arab feuds as well. Still other actions and groups are the reflection of Iraqi-Iranian clashes away from the home front or of feuds involving the Iranian pro-Khomeini and anti-Khomeini clans that reside in Italy. The spillover of Middle Eastern issues into Italian territory has also given way to clandestine and violent operations on the part of the Egyptian and Israeli intelligence services.[54]

Italian countermeasures against these forms of surrogate warfare or even against the "mere" transit of firearms and explosives intended for other destinations have resulted in threats against Italy. These threats have been made by the Lebanese Armed Revolutionary Faction (LARF) and Islamic Jihad, among others, in order to obtain the release of some of their militants arrested in Italy. For example, on August 6, 1984, the frontier police at Villa Opicina (Trieste) arrested LARF member Abdallah Al-Mansur, who had entered Italy from Yugoslavia with over seven kilograms of Czech explosives. The following December another LARF member, Josephine Abdo Sarkis, was arrested at Rome's International Airport on similar charges. Both have been convicted and are serving prison terms in Italy. Also at the end of 1984 the Italian authorities, in cooperation with those of Switzerland, had uncovered a plot to bomb the U.S. Embassy in Rome by Islamic extremists from Lebanon. Two out of six defendants were convicted. On November 27, 1985, a Jordanian national by the name of Omar Saadat Salem Abdel Fattah, who claims to be a captain in the Palestine Liberation Organization, was arrested in Castelnuovo (Verona) while in possession of weapons and explosives. Convicted the following month, he personally threatened Italy with retaliation by his "fellow commandos," without even waiting for the standard terrorist organizational admonition against the Italian government.

No less disruptive of Italian and, oftentimes, regional tranquility are the clandestine operations undertaken by Libyan elements on behalf of, or against, Moammar Qadhafi's dictatorial regime. In fact, almost all of the incidents listed under the Libyan heading in Appendix 5 address internecine disputes. Most recurrent are the attacks by Qadhafi's hit squads against Libyan residents of Italy who refuse to repatriate with their financial assets or to collaborate abroad with the colonel's regime; these are complemented by attacks against active dissidents or disillusioned erstwhile supporters. Less frequent cases encompass conspiratorial designs and violent actions attributable to Libyan anti-Qadhafi militants, some of whom operate under the name Al Forkan (Vulcan). Both sides largely rely on firearms as a means of persuasion. Other hostile actions listed in Appendix 5 are directed against the United States and other countries branded by Qadhafi as his enemies.

The Libyan connection, however, in its overt and covert manifestations, stretches beyond factional feuding and transnational actions against third-party states. Qadhafi's policy toward the Italian peninsula is unquestionably multifaceted, as it ranges from economic and cultural penetration to the direct use of threats and violence.

In October 1970, only a few days after providing assurances to the contrary to Foreign Affairs minister Aldo Moro, Qadhafi expelled 20,000 Italian residents from Libya and confiscated all their possessions.[55] Despite this initial hostile gesture, Italian-Libyan economic relations have generally prospered. Italy is Libya's foremost economic partner: 25 percent of Libyan imports come from Italy, which, in turn, relies on Libyan oil exports for 15 percent of its needs. Both countries have consistently invested heavily in each other's economic sectors. Libyan capital is present in approximately 100 Italian firms. Libya also has extensive real estate holdings on the islands of Sicily and Pantelleria. The accumulation of these holdings in Pantelleria has been interpreted by some observers as having strategic and military purposes. Libyan investments are not necessarily overt, since they frequently take place through "dummy" corporations. Moreover, ownership of television and radio stations, such as Teleradio Sicilia International and Voce Sarda, is aimed at cultural penetration and propaganda. Influence is likewise exercised through the network organized in Sicily by Catanian attorney Michele Papa and, nationwide, by the Italian-Arabic Friendship Society. The pro-Libyan lobby reportedly includes political and parliamentary figures such as Emo Egoli, Enrico Manca, and Michele Achilli.[56]

Similarly, Libyan virulence against Italy has taken on different forms. Most recurrent are the demands for damages caused by Italy's occupation of its former colony, harassment of Italian fishing boats in international waters, praise for and declarations of solidarity with Italian terrorist groups, demonstrations against and unwarranted arrests of Italian contract workers in Libya (not to be confused with the settlers expelled in 1970), and repeated threats of military action against Italian/NATO military installations, particularly after U.S.-Libyan clashes such as those in September 1981 and March 1986. Some incidents have been even more serious. In September 1973 two Libyan jet fighters strafed an Italian navy corvette. In August 1980 two Libyan warships forced an Italian oil-drilling rig—"Saipem II"—in the employ of Texaco and Malta to cease its prospecting activities in non-Libyan waters. On April 15, 1986, immediately after the U.S. retaliatory air raids on Libya, Qadhafi's forces fired two scud missiles that narrowly missed the tiny Italian island of Lampedusa in the Sicilian archipelago, which hosts a U.S. Coast Guard installation.[57]

This last incident finally led to a substantive crackdown on the part of the Italian government, as evidenced by the expulsion of at least 30 Libyan citizens from Italy, including diplomatic and nondiplomatic-status personnel, during April and May 1986. The large number of expulsions is indicative of the human assets available to Libya for covert purposes in Italy.

With respect to overall clandestine activities planned or perpetrated in Italy by Third World national and subnational organizations, most disquieting is the presence on Italian territory of aliens who are not duly registered with the police authorities. Official Interior Ministry statistics indicate that 800,000 foreigners live in Italy without authorization. Unofficial estimates cite much higher figures.[58] The potential exploitability of these individuals, whose economic condition is generally precarious when they have not been specifically infiltrated for covert purposes, is reflected by the large percentage involved in crimes. In an aggregate prison population of approximately 40,000 inmates, 10 percent is made up of aliens.[59]

Third World nationals who enter Italy for hostile or otherwise unlawful purposes frequently use genuine or counterfeit Moroccan and Tunisian passports, which do not require consular visas. Stocks of these passports are frequently available for distribution by terrorism-supporting countries such as Libya, which is believed to have done so most recently to facilitate the December 27, 1985, attack against the El Al (Israeli airlines) counter at Rome's International Airport.[60] Libya's misuse of diplomatic facilities and aliens on Italian territory has subsequently been paralleled by Khomeini's Iran.[61]

International Linkages
with Domestic Terrorism

Italy's terrorist formations of the left and the right have consistently entertained ideological, logistical, and, less frequently, operational linkages with foreign counterparts. On the one hand, the leftist formations, whose international connections are multiple, substantially express their ideological commitment to "proletarian internationalism." On the other, rightist groups appear to be influenced primarily by pragmatic considerations. Examples abound.

Since the early stages of their history, the BR have been in contact with Germany's Red Army Faction for purposes of mutual assistance with respect to safe haven, logistics, and operational experience.[62] The BR, who often imitated their counterparts, eventually surpassed their German mentors. The Hans Schleyer kidnapping clearly served as a blueprint for the Aldo Moro abduction, but by the time the BR snatched General Dozier, their sophistication outdistanced all Red Army Faction targetings of U.S. personnel and installations.

Similarly, Front Line (PL) and its surviving affiliation, the Organized Comrades for Proletarian Liberation (COLP), interacted with France's Direct Action (Action Directe; AD). In March 1980, PL members Enrico Bianco, Oriana Marchionni, Franco Pinna, and Pierluigi Amadori were arrested in Toulon, France, for participation in an armed "proletarian expropriation" organized by AD. Joint operations have since multiplied. The

COLP's Gloria Argano has been indicted for her complicity in the murder of two Parisian policemen by AD during a May 1983 gunfire engagement. Moreover, Argano is accused of involvement in two AD robberies perpetrated in the French capital in July of the same year. Another participant in one of these robberies was COLP member Vincenzo Spanò. On October 15, 1983, Ciro Rizzato, also a COLP member, was killed in Paris during a bank robbery planned by AD, which subsequently named one of its "combat units" after this fallen comrade. However, Spanò was arrested on February 22, 1984, in a Parisian AD hideout where the police confiscated firearms and explosives.[63]

Less notorious groups of the Italian terrorist left have likewise practiced "proletarian internationalism." In the summer of 1978, militants of the Communist Combat Formations joined PL members in a training session on the use of weapons and explosives and falsification of documents organized by the Basque Fatherland and Liberty near the French-Spanish border.[64] No less extensive are the international connections of the anarco-communist Revolutionary Action (AR). Chilean national Aldo Ernesto Marin Pinones, who spent over a year in Cuba before taking up "political asylum" in Italy, accidentally blew himself up in Turin in August 1977 while campaigning in AR's ranks. In April 1979 his roommate, Juan Teofilo Paillacar Soto, a fellow national with a similar background, resisted arrest in Rome brandishing a .44-magnum revolver. Also in 1979, AR members Rocco Martino and Carmela Pane were arrested in Parma in the company of German nationals Rudolf Piroch and Johanna Hartwig while transporting explosives.[65]

Moreover, press accounts have reported Italian participation at international coordination meetings attended by delegates of a variety of terrorist organizations of the left. One such meeting was held in 1981 in Oporto, Portugal, to discuss the consequences of Spain's entry in the European Economic Community. Present were representatives of PL/COLP, AD, Spain's First of October Anti-Fascist Resistance Group, and Portugal's April 25 Popular Forces. Another meeting, held in late 1984 in the Spanish Basque country to study "a unified offensive strategy against imperialism and militarism," was attended by unspecified Basque, Corsican, Irish, German, French, Belgian, and Italian elements. Both meetings coincided with periods during which ostensibly coordinated waves of terrorist attacks were plaguing the West European democracies as well as U.S. personnel and property that supported NATO.[66]

On the rightist side of the Italian terrorist spectrum, neo-Fascist groups have entertained connections with kindred formations in Spain and Portugal, prior to the democratization of those countries' political regimes in the mid-1970s, and, more generally, with affinity groups in Great Britain,

France, Lebanon, and South America. Moreover, the South Tyrolean separatists, whose aspirations for independence are intermingled with rightist sentiments, have traditionally relied on Austrian and West German extremists as their foreign points of contact.

The obvious difficulties to be encountered in monitoring the international connections of Italian terrorist groups become even greater when serious attempts are made to assess the nature and extent of foreign patron-state support for Italian domestic terrorism. What at times appears to be a matter of group-to-group linkages actually entails indirect patron-state support for purposes of destabilization. Players include the East European Communist Bloc, Cuba, Nicaragua, Libya, and subnational Palestinian organizations. Although none of them can realistically be attributed the role of a puppeteer who pulls the strings of Italian terrorism—which is a phenomenon far too complex, widespread, and autochthonous to be fully manipulated—they all share varying degrees of responsibility for its nourishment. In fact, patron-state support takes the form of safe haven, training, funding, logistics, and, possibly, guidance.

As noted earlier in this chapter, the USSR and its East European satellites have a long-standing tradition of supporting Italian subversive and revolutionary groups of communist inspiration. Testimonial as well as circumstantial evidence show that similar support has been provided by the Communist Bloc to contemporary Italian terrorism since its outburst in the late 1960s and early 1970s.

Official documents attest to the presence of Italian terrorists in Czechoslovakia during suspect times and under suspect circumstances in the early to mid-1970s when terrorism was beginning to take hold on Italian society. Between 1970 and 1972 millionaire publisher and would-be revolutionary Giangiacomo Feltrinelli made several trips to Czechoslovakia, usually using his own passport but sometimes a counterfeit one under the name of Giancarlo Scotti. During a 1971 trip he took along Augusto Viel of the October XXII Circle who was wanted by the Italian police for murder and armed robbery, a circumstance that could not have escaped the Czech authorities. Alberto Franceschini and Fabrizio Pelli of the so-called historic nucleus of the BR also sojourned in Czechoslovakia in 1973 and 1974 despite their fugitive status. Pelli, like Francesco Morannino and others before him, found employment with Radio Prague and the newspaper *Rude Pravo;* Franceschini worked in Lidice. Other Italian terrorists of the left who have enjoyed hospitality in Czechoslovakia and whose presence there has been officially ascertained are the late Roberto Capone of the FCC, who murdered state attorney Fedele Calvosa in November 1978, and his accomplices Nicola Valentino and Rosaria Biondi.[67]

In addition to these officially recorded cases, journalistic sources have reported travel to Czechoslovakia by Renato Curcio, the reputed principal founder of the BR; Alvaro Lojacono, a major exponent of the Autonomy-oriented Via dei Volsci Collective of Rome; Roberto Mander, whose militancy included contacts with anarchist and ultraleftist groups; and other extremists such as Guido Bianchini, Luciano Ferrari Bravo, and Sergio Semino.[68] Another historic-nucleus member of the BR, Prospero Gallinari, reportedly visited Bulgaria as a delegate of the PCI's youth organization when he still maintained that affiliation.[69]

The presence of Italian terrorists in Czechoslovakia and other East European communist regimes coincides with reports of training camps and other facilities set up in those countries in conjunction with the spread of the terrorist phenomenon. Press reports have repeatedly cited the existence of training facilities in such Czech locations as Doupov (near Karlovy Vary), Bochov, Brno, Malackj, Bratislava, Česká Lípa, Lidice, and Leda. Some of these reports were confirmed in the course of a parliamentary debate by retired army general Vito Miceli, who headed Italian intelligence (then called SID) from 1970 to 1974 and is now a member of the Chamber of Deputies.[70] The media have also made reference to ideological and practical training provided to unnamed Italians at the Komsomol Institute of Moscow until 1975 and near the East German town of Dresden at unspecified times.[71]

Among the sources that address clandestine funding of Italian terrorist formations is a particularly significant governmental finding that concerns a 1978 subsidy of 70 million lire given to the Milan branch of Workers' Autonomy (AUTOP) by the commercial agent in Italy of Czech motor company Skoda. Designated recipients of that money were AUTOP activists Nanni Balestrini and Jaroslaw Novak. The latter is the Italian-born son of Giovanni Novak, who migrated in 1926 from Czechoslovakia to Italy, became an Italian citizen, and operated a commercial firm, but who returned to Czechoslovakia after the 1948 communist coup and subsequently resurfaced in Italy as a Czech diplomatic courier. Moreover, Skoda's commercial agent in Italy, Pietro De Stefani, became unexplainably wealthy after he took over the Skoda dealership.[72]

A potential indicator of direct Communist Bloc involvement in domestic Italian terrorism is the recommendation made by SID on May 29, 1972, and reiterated in 1973, to expel 22 Soviet citizens, nearly all of whom enjoyed diplomatic status.[73] These foreign nationals were deemed to be hostile intelligence agents responsible for espionage and subversion, including links with Feltrinelli and groups of the extreme left.[74] SID's recommendation was rejected by the government presumably because of political considerations. Excerpts from what appears to be SID's memorandum to the government disclose that the following Soviet clandestine activities had or were taking place: ". . . liaison for the support of, and joint action with, the PCI and extraparliamentary movements of the extreme left; special operational liaison with Feltrinelli's subversive organization and, subsequently, with the Red Brigades . . . [and] training of activists in Cuba and Moscow."[75] The memorandum also states that at least until 1971 the training received in Moscow included instructions on firearms, explosives, and guerrilla warfare.

It is notable that half of the 22 proposed expellees had been feverishly involved in highly suspect activities in the 24-hour period following Feltrinelli's accidental death during the night of February 15, 1972, when he attempted to blow up a power pylon near Milan. Upon hearing of Feltrinelli's demise, one of the two Soviet diplomats who were attending a political party congress in Milan immediately called his embassy in Rome to announce his emergency return from Milan. Despite his late evening arrival, five other staff members were summoned to the embassy, including the defense attaché. After midnight, five embassy vehicles transported over twenty staff members to various areas and embassy security was increased. At 2 A.M. the defense attaché received a ciphered telephone call. At 4 P.M. another meeting was held at the embassy, this time with the participation of Soviet personnel assigned to Milan and Genoa with consular and commercial credentials.[76]

This episode acquires added significance in the light of two precedents. As early as the early 1950s Feltrinelli had been spying on behalf of Czechoslovakia, according to the former Classified Matters Office of the Ministry of the Interior.[77] Moreover, until his own death, Feltrinelli was in contact with the late Pietro Secchia, the PCI's legendary pro-Soviet hardliner.[78] These circumstances explain why Feltrinelli has frequently been regarded as a central figure in the triangular relationship between Czech safe haven/ training, Italian fugitives/instructors of the post–World War II period, and the terrorist recruits of the early 1970s.

Circumstantial evidence has also been introduced regarding possible Czech/Soviet involvement in the abduction of Aldo Moro by the BR in 1978. The hypothesis that Moro may have been held captive in the Czech Embassy was first briefly formulated by investigative journalist Mino Pecorelli, who was murdered in 1979 under still-obscure circumstances. Pecorelli's semiveiled accusations inspired a group of private citizens—all residents of the area where the abduction took place—to conduct their own inquest. They concluded that a less tortuous escape route than the one reconstructed by the police investigators was used by the captors. These area residents further hypothesized that it may in fact have led to a nearby residential complex where the Czech embassy is located. Moreover, they allege that the manager of the residential complex was unable to reach the embassy by telephone throughout the abduction period, that unusual embassy visitors were observed during the same time frame, and that, on the morning of the recovery of Moro's corpse, the vehicles of embassy guests blocked the entrances to the other units within the complex to the point of foreclosing all transit. The sum total of these activities could be an indication of Czech involvement short of co-management of the abduction. In any case, the Czech embassy reportedly aroused suspicion on the part of Rome's police superintendent Emanuele De Francesco, but a search warrant could not be obtained because of diplomatic extraterritoriality.[79] Finally, diplomat and Russian linguist Renzo Rota, who was posted as Italy's minister-counselor to Moscow from 1965 to 1972, prepared and filed with the pertinent parliamentary committee on terrorism an analysis of the BR communiques issued during Moro's captivity. Rota concluded that the ideological portion of the first communique and the entirety of the second were of Russian authorship.[80]

Press reports that Czech keys had been found in a BR safe house were subsequently declared unfounded by this parliamentary committee. However, it did establish that a brand new Soviet army jacket had been found in the residence of a red brigadist.[81]

Subtle aspects of patron-state support are specifically treated in a confidential report prepared by the Executive Committee of the Intelligence and Security Services (Comitato Esecutivo per i Servizi Informazioni e Sicurezza; CESIS) on March 31, 1983, under the title "International Implications of Italian Terrorism"; the report was subsequently declassified.[82] It states that immediately after Moro's abduction Mario Moretti, who managed the BR's international relations until his capture in April 1981, was contacted by representatives of Hyperion, "a Paris structure under the cover of a language school that was to coordinate—apparently under the direction of the Soviet KGB as stated by several repentant terrorists—the operations of various subversive groups in Europe: IRA, ETA, NAPAP, RAF."[83] After accepting Hyperion's proposal to lend international scope to the BR, Moretti was introduced to the Paris-based delegate of a Marxist minority faction of the PLO from which the BR later received two shipments of weapons, one toward the end of 1978 and another in the summer of 1979. At least one of these weapons—a Kalashnikov rifle—was given by the BR to the Sardinian separatist formation Red Barbagia.

PLO-BR agreements also called for assistance to the BR abroad, including Paris and Angola, and access to training camps in Lebanon. On their part, the BR would store part of the weapons for future PLO use and would conduct or coordinate, when requested, attacks against Israeli and Jewish targets in Italy. At the beginning of 1982, Soviet-made weapons wrapped in Arabic-language newspapers were found in a BR storage facility in Montello (Treviso). Another storage site was located in Sardinia. Moreover, when BR member Bruno Seghetti was arrested in May 1980, he was carrying an English-language note with the addresses of the Israeli ambassador and military attaché in Rome.

Still according to the CESIS report, other Italian terrorist formations of the left availed themselves of the Palestinian connection through former AUTOP militant Maurizio Folini, who was considered by a number of "repentant" terrorists to be a KGB agent. In July and August 1978, Folini had brought from Lebanon to Italy a boat-cargo of East European weapons that, though not originally intended for the Italian terrorist left, were ceded with Soviet consent. Because of his Palestinian contacts, Folini enjoyed freedom of movement in Lebanon as well as in Syria.

Another aspect of AUTOP-Palestinian linkages is evidenced by the arrest of Daniele Pifano and two other autonomists in Ortona (Chieti) on November 9, 1979. The trio was in possession of two Soviet Strela SA-7 missile launchers. After their indictment, the Popular Front for the Liberation of Palestine sent a telegram to the Italian court of jurisdiction asserting ownership of these weapons and alleging that the launchers were merely in transit over Italian territory.

The East European and Palestinian connections, both of which ostensibly intersect at the Hyperion network, shed light on the links of recent years between Italian terrorism/extremism of the left and Paris. The same CESIS report identifies Swiss-born Françoise Tuscher and Italian-born Corrado Simioni—the latter "recruited by the KGB in Paris"[84]—as two of Hyperion's principal representatives as well as promoters of the International Center for Popular Culture in Paris, which through 1982 remained the primary rendezvous point between European and Palestinian groups. Another Paris-based support network for Italian terrorist fugitives was the Unitary Collective for the Liberation of Political Prisoners. A key member of this collective, Gloria Cesari Grunbaum, who was Italian-born but a French citizen by marriage and a former Ongoing Struggle activist, is suspected, in the CESIS report, of serving as liaison between Italian and French terrorists. She has also been in contact with the International Center for Extended Space and Freedom (CINEL), a satellite of the Soviet-run World Peace Council and the pro-Soviet Henri Curiel network of Paris. At the time of his arrest, PL member Marco Donat Cattin was in Grunbaum's company.

The CESIS report also lists a variety of front organizations and other extreme circles with which AUTOP ideologue Antonio Negri has been associated in France: the CINEL, Hyperion, Autonomous Coordination, Armed Nuclei for Popular Autonomy, and the former Center for Socio-Economic Research and Investigations.

Specific information regarding the BR presence in Paris may be drawn from a combined reading of two interviews granted in 1985 by investigating judges Ferdinando Imposimato and Rosario Priore. An organizational document confiscated in January 1982 in a BR safe house refers to "an external column whose task it is to protect fugitives and to recruit new militants" and argues that successful counterterrorist operations in Italy actually strengthened this Parisian unit. Moreover, a BR "liaison office" operated in Paris from Moretti's initial travels to France in 1978 until Giovanni Senzani's capture in 1982. In order of succession, Moretti, Anna Laura Braghetti, Riccardo Dura, Maurizio Jannelli, Alvaro Lojacono, Fulvia Maglietta, and Senzani served as BR representatives in Paris.[85] Interestingly, the three Italian founders of Hyperion—Corrado Simioni, Vanni Mulinaris, and Duccio Berio—had been active in the Metropolitan Political Collective of Milan, the forerunner of the BR, and had remained in touch with Moretti despite their break with the remainder of the BR's "historic nucleus."

The organizational presence of the BR in Paris seems to have outlived the "liaison office." After the 1984 BR murder of Rome-based U.S. diplomat Leamon R. Hunt, the Lebanese Armed Revolutionary Faction, which has been particularly active in France, issued a proclamation regarding its own responsibility in this attack.[86] Moreover, BR member Giorgio Frau, who kept a list of public figures that included 1985 murder victim Ezio Tarantelli, was arrested in Paris. Not least of all, the apprehension of notorious BR member Barbara Balzerani and her companion Gianni Pelosi, who had a clean police record, in Ostia (Rome) in June 1985 was reportedly made possible by investigations conducted in Paris.

Such international structures and linkages, coupled with France's traditional policy of asylum for political dissidents and its propinquity to Italy, have certainly contributed to the flow of Italian extremists and terrorists to Paris.[87] Official figures in the public domain indicate that 117 Italian fugitives responsible for politically motivated crimes had taken up residence in France by early 1985, and 44 more had been spotted there.[88] Press sources generally cite higher estimates. Representative figures of Italian extremism/terrorism currently living in France include autonomists Antonio Negri, Oreste Scalzone, and Gian Franco Pacino, all of whom were convicted in Italy to prison sentences ranging from 28 to 36 years.

East European patron-state support for Italian terrorism in the early to mid-1970s and Soviet clandestine arrangements for the internationalization of Italian terrorism since the late 1970s through the French/Palestinian connection have been accompanied by an additional aspect of the Bulgarian covert operations in Italy. After Moretti's capture, the BR, fearing the interruption of weapon-supply channels, became interested in establishing contact with Bulgarian intelligence. This was to take place through the good offices of Luigi Scricciolo, an agent of the Bulgarians, whose cousin Loris Scricciolo was a BR militant.

According to the CESIS report, Bulgarian intelligence was in turn interested in the "interrogation" record of General Dozier, who at that time was a captive of the BR. Although the projected meeting between BR emissaries and Bulgarian secret agents does not appear to have materialized,[89] then–defense minister Lelio Lagorio reported to Parliament that Italy's current military intelligence service, SISMI, noted major anomalies as it monitored Bulgarian radio traffic "during the days of the abduction, captivity, and liberation of General Dozier." He added that "on the day of Dozier's liberation, there was a most singular transmission . . . repeated several times. Counterespionage believes that such type of transmission evidences a direct contact between (Bulgarian) intelligence headquarters and . . . a specific agent in Italy."[90]

These concrete instances of Communist Bloc support for Italian terrorism find substantiation in heterogeneous sources that address the broader spectrum of Soviet policies and operations. According to General Jan Sejna, the Kremlin's Politburo had decided in the fall of 1964 "to increase its budget in the field of terrorism and related espionage and sabotage activities by one thousand percent."[91] On his part, General Vito Miceli has indicated that one of the Western intelligence services acquired a copy of a Soviet circular of 1972 to the Warsaw Pact countries focusing on the exploitation of detente and subversive organizations in order to dominate Western Europe.[92] Finally, the CESIS report refers to a document seized from Senzani, the reputed leader of the BR "movementist" wing. It reflects Senzani's belief that the KGB was "in a position to pilot the activity of the major European and Palestinian terrorist organizations for anti-Western purposes"; according to Senzani, the KGB could "manipulate simultaneously groups of the extreme right and of the extreme left" and "had planted its agents in the militarist wing of the BR."[93]

Along with the East European Communist Bloc support for Italian terrorism, there is evidence of an early Cuban connection. Initial contacts were established by Feltrinelli, who had spent time in Cuba in the mid- and late 1960s as Fidel Castro's personal guest. In 1967 the multimillionaire publisher traveled to Bolivia to attend the trial of Regis Debray, the French revolutionary ideologue who had followed Che Guevara on his last expedition. Bolivian consul Roberto Quintanilla, who was considered responsible for Guevara's capture and death, was subsequently murdered in West Germany with a revolver owned by Feltrinelli, who, in the meantime, had become the Italian editor of Cuba's revolutionary publication *Tricontinental*. Red brigadist Renato Curcio and his late wife Mara Cagol had also spent time in Cuba, as reported in a book published by Feltrinelli's company.[94]

Later linkages with Cuba took on different forms. Several militants of the extremist Workers' Vanguard (Avanguardia Operaia) and of the Autonomy repeatedly took so-called political trips to Angola in 1977 and 1978 to confer with exponents of the Cuban-supported Popular Movement for the Liberation of Angola. In early 1979, former Workers' Power activist Achille Lollo was serving as a sergeant in the Angolan militia. At the same time, some of the Chilean exiles who had transited through Cuba found their way into the ranks of the anarco-communist AR.

In the mid-1980s it was established that extraparliamentary extremists had spent or are still spending several months in Cuba-supported and Sandinista-controlled Nicaragua. Several of them have claimed that their sojourn status in Nicaragua is related to study and development projects. According to the Italian government, however, a number of these individuals are terrorists on the run.[95]

Besides countries officially or semiofficially aligned with the USSR, Qadhafi's Libya has been a source of support for Italian terrorist formations of the left and the right, as well as for other subversive groups. Italian terrorists have reportedly attended Libyan training camps.[96] According to a number of repentant terrorists, Libya has also served as an intermediary in the acquisition of weapons. In fact, an automatic rifle sold in December 1978 by the Belgian firm Herstel to the Libyan government was found in June 1980 in a PL safe house. Moreover, Libya has played a subversive role in the Italian pacifist movement. Through his agent of influence in Sicily, Qadhafi made it clear that funding is available for pacifist demonstrations.[97] This funding is believed to be channeled to select pacifist groups through certain firms that do business with Libya. Finally, press coverage and judicial inquiries have looked into the matter of Libyan support for Sardinian separatism.[98]

The terrorist threat currently faced by Italy is posed by the actions of foreign transnational elements that have been particularly active in the mid-1980s[99] and by the efforts of indigenous groups to recover from the setbacks suffered since 1982. The latter are now particularly vulnerable to self-serving offers of assistance from patron states and their surrogates. To the patrons, whose objectives entail the destabilization of the West, it does not really matter that the terrorists' own revolutionary goals may never come to fruition.[100]

CHAPTER EIGHT

Countermeasures

Italy's response to the terrorist and subversive onslaught has been waged at the legislative, intelligence, police, and judicial levels.

Legislation

Although the Criminal Code of 1930, which is still in effect, punishes all possible crimes resulting from terrorist acts, it does not define terrorism. A first reference to terrorism was introduced by legislation enacted in the immediate aftermath of Aldo Moro's abduction by the Red Brigades (BR) in 1978. This legislation, which amended the Criminal Code by increasing the penalties for kidnappings motivated by "terrorism or subversion of the democratic order," also empowers the law-enforcement agencies to detain anyone who refuses to identify himself, and it relaxes the existing strict judicial controls over police wiretapping operations in cases of emergency.[1]

Additional legislation enacted in 1979–1980 further amended the Criminal Code to include "attempts committed for purposes of terrorism or subversion of the democratic order" and "conspiracy for purposes of terrorism or subversion of the democratic order."[2] At the same time, the penalty for all terrorism-related crimes was increased by half. Other aspects of this antiterrorism legislative packet include provisional apprehension of suspects, mandatory arrest warrants for terrorist crimes, extension of pre-trial confinement limitations, immediate search of realty or entire blocs of realty in areas where someone wanted for terrorist crimes is justifiably believed to be hiding, mandatory identification for banking transactions in excess of twenty million lire, and reduced sentences for terrorists who voluntarily mitigate the consequences of their criminal conduct and/or collaborate with police and judicial investigations.

The last of these provisions was elaborated by a 1982 law that offered varying degrees of clemency to repentant or disassociated terrorists depending on the significance of their contribution to counterterrorism efforts. The ultimate deadline to benefit from this measure was January 31, 1983.[3] Thereafter, in light of the diminished threat from indigenous terrorism, a law was passed in July 1984 reducing the pretrial confinement term and facilitating provisional release.[4] Since this law would have made possible the release of "1,300 suspected terrorists, mafiosi, murderers, kidnappers, and drug traffickers"[5] by February 2, 1985, Parliament extended to November 30 of that year pretrial confinement for individuals charged with intrinsically violent crimes. Most of the suspected terrorists released pursuant to that law are under surveillance; some, however, have disappeared or rejoined the terrorist fold.[6]

Not all antiterrorist legislation is aimed exclusively at repressive or clemency measures. In 1979 a law was passed to facilitate and enhance coordination and cooperation among Italy's three major police forces—the State Police, Carabinieri, and Finance Guard.[7] Two more laws were passed for the purpose of acquiring information of police and intelligence value with respect to common and political crime. The first of these set up the parliamentary committee to investigate the Moro affair and terrorism in Italy.[8] The second provides for a centralized data bank within the Ministry of the Interior under the supervision of the parliamentary oversight committee on intelligence and security.[9]

With respect to the intensification of transnational terrorist activity in Italy in the 1980s, bills have been introduced in Parliament to facilitate the absorption or the expulsion, as appropriate in different instances, of aliens who have entered or attempted to enter Italy clandestinely. Moreover, efforts to bring about international cooperation against terrorism have led to formal and informal bilateral agreements with several countries, including the United States, the Federal Republic of Germany, Ireland, and Egypt, to cite the most recent.

Intelligence and Police Operations

The semiannual reports of the prime minister to Parliament on the intelligence and security services consistently indicate, albeit in general terms, that these services have dedicated considerable time and assets to countering terrorism. However, their initial efforts were greatly hampered by their newness as the result of the intelligence reform. Other constraints will be dealt with below. The law-enforcement agencies have also obviously borne a notable portion of the counterterrorist effort. Both the State Police and the Carabinieri have made full use of specialized structures in the struggle against terrorism.

In 1978 the Central Bureau for General Investigations and Special Operations (Ufficio Centrale Indagini Generali e Operazioni Speciali) was established within the Ministry of the Interior in Rome; it was later renamed the Central Directorate for Crime Prevention (Direzione Centrale per la Polizia di Prevenzione).[10] Its principal purpose is to coordinate the operations of the counterterrorism branch offices organic to the State Police local headquarters in each province.[11] In the more important provinces, the branch office is termed the Division for General Investigations and Special Operations (Divisione Indagini Generali e Operazioni Speciali). In the other provinces, it is termed the Office for General Investigations and Special Operations (Ufficio Indagini Generali e Operazioni Speciali).[12]

In addition to coordinating these branch offices, the Central Directorate for Crime Prevention exercises direct operational control over the Central Operative Nucleus for Security (Nucleo Operativo Centrale Sicurezza). This nucleus, a SWAT-type unit, was deployed, for example, in the counterterrorist operation that rescued General Dozier from the BR in January 1982.

The Carabinieri instituted at the legion and group territorial echelons specialized sections concerned with political crime and terrorism. Because of their extremely capillary structure, however, the Carabinieri also rely on the entirety of their territorial organization for counterterrorist investigations and operations. Moreover, they have the capability to deploy another SWAT-type unit, the Special Intervention Group.

As an emergency measure, the Italian government resorted to a temporary and totally atypical structure in 1978–1979, which marked the peak of terrorist activity in Italy. The late Carabinieri general Carlo Alberto Dalla Chiesa, a veteran organized-crime and terrorism specialist, was placed in command of a counterterrorism task force responsible for both intelligence collection and police operations in this sensitive law-enforcement area. Included in the task force were Carabinieri, State Police, and Finance Guard personnel, thus pooling and channeling diverse police expertise and methodology. This temporary task force was not meant to replace existing counterterrorism structures within the State Police and the Carabinieri organizations but to enhance terrorism counteraction.

A survey of media reports and unclassified official records is indicative of a vast array of sources, procedures, and techniques employed by the police agencies and the intelligence and security services in combating terrorism. Sources include paid informers and social deviants who gravitate around the periphery of subversive circles. Documentation seized in raided terrorist facilities and analyses of terrorist proclamations and communiques have likewise contributed to long-range counterterrorist efforts. In several instances, moreover, identified or escaped terrorists were artfully "tailed" to seek out their points of contact. In a few known cases, marginal subversive elements have been used to indirectly infiltrate terrorist organizations.[13]

Increased knowledge of the terrorist modi operandi has reaped desirable fruits in terms of arrests, seizure of facilities, and prevention of crimes. However, the most widely publicized Italian counterterrorist measure is the utilization of confessions made by "repentant" or disassociated terrorists who decided to take advantage of the clemency legislation. These confessions, which interestingly enough reflect repentance after—never before—capture, have resulted in massive arrests and seizures of facilities and matériel, particularly in the immediate aftermath of Dozier's liberation. Conversely, repentant and disassociated terrorists have shed no light on possible behind-the-scene principals or patrons of Italian terrorism. Moreover, only rarely have confessions resulted in the disclosure of totally new information regarding terrorist structures and dynamics.

Judicial Proceedings

Allegations of torture practices on the part of Italian police toward captured terrorists in order to obtain information concerning their cohorts have been declared unfounded by the courts. However, there have been occasional cases of mistreatment.[14] Other judicial proceedings have looked into the cover-up of crimes against property perpetrated by a police-controlled political extremist so that he could acquire credibility with the BR. This co-opted operative had in fact led to the capture of red brigadists Mario Moretti and Enrico Fenzi in 1981. The Court of Assizes of Pavia inflicted a suspended sentence in April 1984 on the State Police official responsible for the operation.

In contrast to indirect infiltration, the *direct* infiltration of subversive and terrorist circles by police and intelligence elements for counteraction purposes presents both technical and policy problems. First, there is a lack of police and intelligence operatives who are educationally and culturally suited to infiltrate organizations such as the BR, which virtually constitute "a society within a society" because of their rhetoric, code of conduct, and objectives. Second, the bureaucratic process required to insure the anonymity and immunity of the would-be infiltrators is slow and inadequate. Finally, from the very enactment of the intelligence reform law, members of the parliamentary oversight committee expressed negative judgments regarding infiltration, thus discouraging operations of this nature.[15]

Nevertheless, the role of the judiciary, particularly since the late 1970s, has primarily been one of direct participation in the struggle against terrorism. In particular, prosecutors and investigating judges—both of whom belong to the judicial branch in the Italian system of government—have waged a noteworthy share of the battle. A great deal of the information available today on Italy's terrorist and subversive milieu is the result of judicial participation on the front line directing the operations of the judicial police.

This role has been especially important in countering organized crime. As noted in Chapter 5, mafia-type organizations are historically so deeply entrenched in the tissue of Italian society that not even the Fascist regime with its authoritarian and repressive apparatus was able to eradicate them. Subsequent to the fall of the Fascists, legislative measures enacted on the average every ten years have implicitly and, indeed, explicitly attempted to deal definitively with the organized-crime problem. Pertinent statutes include "Preventive Measures Against Persons Who Pose a Danger to Public Security and Morality" (Law No. 1423 of 1956), "Measures to Counter the Mafia" (Law No. 575 of 1965), and "Measures for the Safeguard of Public Order" (Law No. 152 of 1975).

The most incisive is Law No. 646 of 1982. It specifically addresses the offense of mafia-type conspiracy, as opposed to ordinary criminal conspiracy, and stresses both the intimidation element inherent to mafia-type endeavors and criminal interference with the mechanics of free competition in the economic sphere. This law further classifies as mafia-type organizations all groups that, regardless of denomination, pursue the same objectives and use the same means as those of mafia-type organizations. Law No. 646 calls for the confiscation of property when it is justifiably believed to be the fruit of unlawful actions or the product of "laundered" unlawful proceeds. The law also calls for rigid controls over public contracts and for the revenue audit of family members, co-dwellers, and business associates of mafiosi. The ostensible objective is to get to the source of unlawful accumulation of wealth by mafia-type organizations.

Law No. 726, also of 1982, instituted a high commissar for the coordination of measures against mafia-type crime. In essence, the high commissar coordinates local and national police organs concerned with combating organized crime. Powers of the office include access to the records of banking and credit institutions, in addition to all ordinary police powers. Although all police forces are committed to countering mafia-type organizations, a notable portion of the overall effort, particularly with respect to the "laundering" of unlawful proceeds and their "clean reinvestment," is incumbent upon the Finance Guard.[16] Because of the destabilizing effect of mafia-type endeavors on society, the internal intelligence and security service (SISDE) has also been tasked to contribute to this mission.[17]

Political and Technical Constraints

The political and technical factors that condition the effectiveness of the Italian law-enforcement agencies and intelligence and security services appear to be closely related. Operations against subversion, terrorism, and organized crime in general have been particularly hampered. The endemic lack of political homogeneity and governmental stability addressed in Chapter 1 has resulted in the absence of long-range policies and programs capable of eliminating environmental factors conducive to specific forms of political and nonpolitical crime, on the one hand, and in the downgrading of police, security, and intelligence efforts, on the other.

To be sure, legislation has periodically been passed to combat specific forms of crime. Nevertheless, legislative and executive measures were adopted inordinately late despite timely warnings by Italy's internal security organs. As early as December 1970, the prefect of Milan had reported to the Ministry of the Interior that there were 20,000 subversives and potential terrorists in his area of jurisdiction alone. A subsequent report drawn up in July 1972 by Milan's police superintendent listed in greater detail violent extraparliamentary organizations, their numerical composition, sources of support, and subversive aims. These reports addressed both leftist and rightist extremism. A March 1972 report by the Confidential Matters Office of the Ministry of the Interior displayed extensive knowledge regarding the origin, characteristics, and goals of the then-fledgling BR.[18] As noted in Chapter 7, even SID, the intelligence service of those years, had submitted reports to the government (in 1972 and again in 1973) on Soviet, Czech, and Cuban support for Italian subversive and terrorist circles. Unfortunately, these reports were not only ignored by the political authorities but were also violently criticized by the parliamentary left when leaked to the press.

The political climate was not ripe to heed those early warnings. In fact, the period that spans from the beginning of the decade through the Moro abduction in 1978 was marked by negative attitudes toward law enforcement. The media were primarily aligned with seemingly libertarian causes. Politicized elements of the judiciary were hostile toward the police,[19] and certain Christian Democratic politicians in Parliament and in the Council of Ministers were vying with their Communist and Socialist counterparts to display leftist attitudes and fears of rightist subversion disguised in leftist clothing.[20]

Most adversely affected by this climate were the intelligence and security services, which continue to suffer from recurrent negative publicity and internal malfunctions due in great part to external political factors. These services have been accused of involvement in virtually all major political scandals and undemocratic schemes that have afflicted the country since the 1960s. However, no judicial or administrative proceedings fully completed to date have substantiated such allegations. What has emerged, instead, is the use of service structures and assets for noninstitutional purposes by intelligence and security personnel and political figures—in other words, unethical behavior with economic overtones on the part of service personnel and exploitation of the services for partisan purposes by political figures. Curiously, while the services have come under continual attack, the politicians who issue directives to the services have not.[21]

Moreover, serious technical drawbacks are the result of the reform law of 1977, which was one of Italy's many compromise legislative enactments and which vaguely defines the responsibilities on the intelligence and security services. This has caused SISMI's and SISDE's tasks to overlap. At the same time, the complexity of the oversight and coordination structure set up by the new law reduces overall efficiency and operational speed. Likewise, the services' potential is downgraded by the statutory prohibition against permanent or even temporary employment of traditional sources of intelligence information and/or operatives: members of Parliament; regional, provincial, and municipal councillors; prosecutors and judges; clergymen; professional journalists; and individuals whose records do not guarantee fidelity to democratic and constitutional principles.[22]

Also problematic are certain Italian governmental practices with respect to the prosecution of politically motivated crimes perpetrated across international boundaries. Various media accounts allege that in the 1970s the intelligence and security services frequently returned to their land of origin Third World extremists who committed terrorist acts in Italy. The motivation behind this policy was reportedly to preserve good relations with North African and Middle Eastern nations in order to protect Italian civil aircraft from highjackings and Italian contract workers in developing nations such as Libya from retaliation. That this practice was sanctioned by the Italian political authorities is confirmed by a former high-ranking Italian intelligence officer.[23]

Although this policy appears to have been discontinued in the 1980s, as suggested by the repeated apprehension, prosecution, and imprisonment of transnational terrorists, certain "trade-offs" are still part of Italian terrorism counteraction. Following the October 1985 highjacking of the Italian cruise liner *Achille Lauro* and the consequent murder of an American passenger, the Italian government released Abu Abbas, leader of the Palestine Liberation Front and organizer of the highjacking, after the commercial airliner he was traveling on was forced to land in Sigonella, Sicily, by U.S.

Air Force combat jets. Abbas was subsequently convicted in absentia by an Italian court, but by that time he was out of reach.

In light of these constraints on law enforcement and national security operations, the positive results achieved to date in the prevention and repression of subversive and criminal activities constitute all the more a reflection of the personal dedication and professional competence of those public servants, both in the executive and judicial branches of Italian government, who operate on the front line.

The Future

Italians, who tend to be self-critical and oftentimes excessively so, frequently comment that "the only sure thing about Italy is uncertainty" (*L'unica certezza in questo paese è l'incertezza*). This statement is not altogether facetious: it vents recurrent frustrations. Nonetheless, certain trends are readily visible even to those, including the author of this work, who do not possess prophetic lenses.

The Italian sociological makeup, as molded by the weight of history, is such that national cohesiveness and unity of intent will be difficult to achieve in the near future. Internal differences are likely to perpetuate strife, which will be conducive to forms of agitation, subversion, and intermittent political violence. Heterogeneous, unstable, and therefore weak central governments will have to counteract this unrest without the benefit of univocal policies and broad popular support. Likewise, despite considerable progress made in recent years toward the neutralization of organized crime, that antisocial phenomenon—whose most nefarious reflection is the *mentalità mafiosa*—is too entrenched in various sectors of Italian society to be eradicated in the short term. Moreover, Italy's commitment and contribution to Western values and interests will continue to make it a desirable target for clandestine endeavors on the part of the USSR and Soviet-controlled and/or Soviet-inspired agents, all of which can be expected to exploit fully Italian internal weaknesses.

Nevertheless, there is room for more than cautious optimism. Few peoples, if any, have demonstrated through the centuries such a propensity for, and mastery over, the art of survival. No nation other than Italy has achieved worldwide preeminence twice in its history—first in Roman times and then during the era of the Renaissance. It is likely, therefore, that the ingenious Italian character will also overcome the social problems of the modern day.

Appendixes

Appendix 1

CHAMBER OF DEPUTIES:
PERCENTAGE OF ELECTORAL RETURNS

Party*	1948	1953	1958	1963	1968	1972	1976	1979	1983
DC	48.5	40.1	42.4	38.2	39.1	38.8	38.7	38.3	32.9
PCI			22.6	22.7	25.3	26.9	27.2	34.4	30.4	29.9
		31.0								
PSI			12.7	14.2	13.8		9.6	9.6	9.8	11.4
PSU						14.5				
PSDI	7.1	4.5	4.6	6.1		5.1	3.4	3.8	4.1
PRI	2.5	1.6	1.4	1.4	2.0	2.9	3.1	3.0	5.1
PLI	3.6	3.0	3.5	7.0	5.8	3.9	1.3	1.9	2.9
MSI	2.0	5.8	4.8	5.1	4.4				
MSI-DN						8.7	6.1	5.3	6.8
PDIUM	2.8	6.8	2.2	1.7	1.3				
PR							1.1	3.5	2.2
PSIUP					4.4				
PDUP								1.4	
DP							1.5		1.5

*Parties still in existence are listed under their current acronym, even if denominational changes occurred during their history (see Chapter 1). Wedge marks reflect electoral blocs/mergers or schisms, as appropriate. Regional parties and parties that did not obtain parliamentary representation are not listed.

SOURCE: *Il Tempo* (Rome).

Appendix 2

GOVERNMENTS UNDER THE REPUBLICAN CONSTITUTION OF 1948

President	Parties	Formed	Resigned	No. of days	
				Duration	Crisis period (no gov't)
DeGasperi	DC PLI PSLI PRI	5/31/47	5/5/48	347	11
DeGasperi	DC PLI PSLI PRI	5/23/48	1/12/50	599	15
DeGasperi	DC PSLI PRI	1/27/50	7/16/51	535	10
DeGasperi	DC PRI	7/26/51	6/6/53	704	17
DeGasperi	DC	7/16/53	7/28/53	12	20
Pella	DC	8/17/53	1/5/54	141	13
Fanfani	DC	1/18/54	1/30/54	12	11
Scelba	DC PSDI PLI	2/10/54	6/22/55	497	14
Segni	DC PSDI PLI	7/6/55	5/6/57	679	13
Zoli	DC	5/19/57	6/19/58	396	12
Fanfani	DC PSDI	7/1/58	1/26/59	209	20
Segni	DC	2/15/59	2/24/60	374	30
Tambroni	DC	3/25/60	7/19/60	116	7
Fanfani	DC	7/26/60	2/2/62	556	19
Fanfani	DC PSDI PRI	2/21/62	5/16/63	449	36
Leone	DC	6/21/63	11/5/63	137	29
Moro	DC PSI PSDI PRI	12/4/63	6/26/64	205	26
Moro	DC PSI PSDI PRI	7/22/64	1/21/66	548	33
Moro	DC PSI PSDI PRI	2/23/66	6/5/68	833	19
Leone	DC	6/24/68	11/19/68	148	23

Rumor	DC PSU PRI	12/12/68	7/5/69	205	31
Rumor	DC	8/5/69	7/2/70	186	48
Rumor	DC PSI PSDI PRI	3/27/70	7/6/70	101	31
Colombo	DC PSI PSDI PRI	8/6/70	1/15/72	527	33
Andreotti	DC	2/17/72	2/26/72	9	121
Andreotti	DC PSDI PLI	6/26/72	6/12/73	351	25
Rumor	DC PSI PSDI PRI	7/7/73	3/2/74	238	12
Rumor	DC PSI PSDI	3/14/74	10/3/74	203	51
Moro	DC PRI	11/23/74	1/7/76	410	36
Moro	DC	2/12/76	4/30/76	78	90
Andreotti	DC	7/29/76	1/16/78	536	54
Andreotti	DC	3/11/78	1/31/79	326	48
Andreotti	DC PRI PSDI	3/20/79	3/31/79	11	126
Cossiga	DC PSDI PLI	8/4/79	3/19/80	228	16
Cossiga	DC PSI PRI	4/4/80	9/27/80	176	21
Forlani	DC PSI PSDI PRI	10/18/80	5/26/81	220	33
Spadolini	DC PSI PSDI PRI PLI	6/28/81	8/7/82	405	16
Spadolini	DC PSI PSDI PRI PLI	8/23/82	11/13/82	82	18
Fanfani	DC PSI PSDI PLI	12/1/82	4/29/83	149	97
Craxi	DC PSI PSDI PRI PLI	8/4/83	6/27/86	1057	36
Craxi	DC PSI PSDI PRI PLI	8/1/86			

SOURCE: *Il Tempo* (Rome).

Appendix 3

Red Brigades:
Chronology of Major Attacks

(Unless otherwise stated, all actions entail ambush attacks or raids.)

1972
March 3.   Milan. Political abduction of Idalgo Macchiarini, personnel manager of Sit-Siemens. Released same day.

March 13.   Cesano Boscone (Milan). Political abduction of Bartolomeo Di Mino, deputy secretary of the local MSI section. Released same day.

1973
February 12.   Turin. Political abduction of Bruno Labate, provincial secretary of CISNAL metalworkers. Released same day.

June 28.   Milan. Political abduction of Michele Mincuzzi, executive employee of Alfa Romeo. Released same day.

December 10.   Turin. Political abduction of Ettore Amerio, personnel manager of FIAT. Released on December 18.

1974
April 18.   Genoa. Political abduction of Mario Sossi, assistant state attorney. Released on May 23.

June 17.   Padua. Raid on a local MSI section office and murder of Graziano Giralucci and Giuseppe Mazzola, MSI militants.

October 14.   Robbiano di Mediglia (Milan). Murder of Carabinieri NCO Felice Maritano during a gunfire battle.

1975

May 15. Milan. Wounding of Christian Democratic councillor Massimo De Carolis during a raid on his law office.

June 4. Canelli (Asti). Abduction for ransom of Vittorio Vallarino Gancia, a wine producer. Rescued by the Carabinieri the following day.

June 5. Acqui Terme (Alessandria). Murder of Carabinieri trooper Giovanni D'Alfonso and wounding of Lieutenant Umberto Rocca and NCO Rosario Cataffi during a gunfire engagement.

October 21. Rivoli (Turin). Political abduction and wounding of Enrico Boffa, Christian Democratic municipal councillor and personnel manager of Singer. Released same day.

October 22. Arenzano (Genoa). Political abduction of Vincenzo Casabona, personnel manager of Ansaldo Meccanica Nucleare. Released same day.

December 17. Turin. Wounding of Luigi Solera, medical officer of FIAT-Mirafiori.

1976

April 2. Milan. Wounding of Matteo Palmieri, security guard at Magneti Marelli.

April 4. Nichelino (Turin). Wounding of Giuseppe Borello, foreman at FIAT-Mirafiori.

June 8. Genoa. Murder of Francesco Coco, state attorney, and two-man Carabinieri security escort.

September 1. Biella (Vercelli). Murder of Deputy Police Commissioner Francesco Cusano during a document check.

December 15. Sesto San Giovanni (Milan). Murder of Deputy Police Commissioner Vittorio Padovani and Public Security NCO Sergio Bazzega as they made an arrest.

1977

January 12. Belvedere Montaldo (Genoa). Abduction for ransom of Piero Costa, a shipowner. Released on April 3 after payment of 1.5 billion lire.

February 13. Rome. Wounding of Valerio Traversi, inspector general of prison administration in the Ministry of Justice.

February 17. Turin. Wounding of Mario Scoffone, personnel manager of FIAT-Rivalta.

February 19. Cascina Olona (Milan). Murder of Public Security NCO Lino Ghedini and wounding of patrolman Adriano Comizzoli during a document check.

March 12. Turin. Murder of Public Security NCO Giuseppe Ciotta.

April 20. Turin. Wounding of Dante Notaristefano, a Christian Democratic councillor.

April 22. Turin. Wounding of Antonio Munari, foreman at FIAT-Mirafiori.

April 28. Turin. Murder of Fulvio Croce, president of the local bar association.

June 1. Genoa. Wounding of Vittorio Bruno, associate editor of the daily *Il Secolo XIX*.

June 2. Milan. Wounding of Indro Montanelli, editor of the daily *Il Giornale Nuovo*.

June 3. Rome. Wounding of Emilio Rossi, editor of the TG1 television newscast.

June 9. Sesto San Giovanni (Milan). Wounding of Fausto Silini, Christian Democratic militant and foreman at Breda.

June 12. Milan. Wounding of two-man Carabinieri security escort assigned to Mario Trimarchi, chief judge of the local Court of Appeals.

June 21. Rome. Wounding of Remo Cacciafesta, dean of the School of Economics, University of Rome.

June 28. Genoa. Wounding of Sergio Prandi, executive employee at Ansaldo Meccanica Nucleare.

June 30. Milan. Wounding of Luciano Maraccani, executive employee at FIAT-OM.

June 30. Turin. Wounding of Franco Viscaj, executive at FIAT-Mirafiori.

July 11. Rome. Wounding of Mario Perlini, Comunione e Liberazione activist.

July 11. Genoa. Wounding of Angello Sibilla, Christian Democratic regional secretary.

July 13. Turin. Wounding of Maurizio Puddu, Christian Democratic regional deputy secretary.

October 11. Turin. Wounding of Rinaldo Camaioni, executive employee at FIAT-Mirafiori.

October 23. Milan. Wounding of Carlo Arienti, Christian Democratic municipal councillor.

October 25. Turin. Wounding of Antonio Cocozzelli, Christian Democratic municipal councillor.

November 2. Rome. Wounding of Publio Fiori, Christian Democratic regional committee member.

November 8.   Milan. Wounding of Aldo Grassini, executive employee at Alfa Romeo.

November 10.   Turin. Wounding of Pietro Osella, executive employee at FIAT.

November 16.   Turin. Firearm attack on Carlo Casalegno, associate editor of the daily *La Stampa*. He died of his wounds on November 29.

November 17.   Genoa. Wounding of Carlo Castellano, Communist regional committee member and executive employee at Ansaldo Meccanica Nucleare.

December 24.   Rome. Wounding of journalist Mario Pucci and his wife.

1978

January 10.   Turin. Wounding of Gustavo Ghirotti, executive employee at FIAT-Mirafiori.

January 13.   Rome. Wounding of Lello De Rosa, chief of the public relations office at SIP telephone company.

January 18.   Genoa. Wounding of Filippo Peschiera, university professor and Christian Democratic provincial committee member.

January 24.   Milan. Wounding of Nicola Toma, public relations officer at Sit-Siemens.

February 14.   Rome. Murder of Riccardo Palma, Supreme Court judge detailed to the General Directorate of Prisons, Ministry of Justice.

March 10.   Turin. Murder of Public Security NCO Rosario Berardi.

March 16.   Rome. Political abduction of Aldo Moro, president of the Christian Democratic Party and former prime minister, and murder of his five-man joint Carabinieri and Public Security escort.

March 24.   Turin. Wounding of Giovanni Picco, Christian Democratic regional councillor.

April 7.   Genoa. Wounding of Felice Schiavetti, president of the local association of industrialists.

April 11.   Turin. Murder of prison guard Lorenzo Cotugno.

April 20.   Milan. Murder of assistant warden Francesco De Cataldo.

April 26.   Rome. Wounding of Girolamo Mechelli, Christian Democratic regional councillor and president of the region.

April 27.   Turin. Wounding of Sergio Palmieri, executive employee at FIAT-Mirafiori.

May 4.   Milan. Wounding of Umberto Degli Innocenti, manager of the Castelletto plant at Sit-Siemens.

May 4. Genoa. Wounding of Alfredo Lamberti, executive employee at Italsider.

May 9. Rome. Murder of captive Aldo Moro.

May 12. Milan. Wounding of Tito Berardini, secretary of a local Christian Democratic section.

May 15. Bologna. Wounding of Antonio Mazzotti, personnel manager of Manarini.

June 21. Genoa. Murder of Antonio Esposito, assistant deputy police commissioner.

July 5. Milan. Wounding of Gavino Manca, executive employee at Pirelli.

July 6. Turin. Wounding of Aldo Ravaioli, president of the local small industry association.

July 7. Genoa. Wounding of Fausto Gasparino, executive employee at Intersind and former Christian Democratic regional deputy secretary.

July 10. Milan. Wounding of municipal constables Mario Botta and Marcello Moresco during a document check.

July 28. Milan. Wounding of Gino Bufalini, watchman at Villa Ruini.

September 28. Turin. Murder of Pietro Coggiola, executive employee at the Chiavasso plant of Lancia.

September 29. Milan. Wounding of Ippolito Bestonso, executive employee at Alfa Romeo.

October 10. Rome. Murder of Gerolamo Tartaglione, Supreme Court judge detailed to the Ministry of Justice.

October 24. Rome. Wounding of Public Security patrolman Vincenzo Garofalo.

November 17. Turin. Wounding of Public Security NCO Antonio Di Tommasi.

December 15. Turin. Murder of Public Security patrolmen Salvatore Lanza and Salvatore Porceddu assigned to external surveillance of Nuove Prison.

December 21. Rome. Wounding of Public Security patrolmen Gaetano Pellegrino and Giuseppe Rainone assigned to residence security of Giovanni Galloni, Christian Democratic floor leader in the Chamber of Deputies.

1979

January 20. Turin. Wounding of Public Security patrolmen Francesco Sanna and Angelo Cali during a gunfire engagement.

January 24. Genoa. Murder of CGIL labor union representative Guido Rossa, a Communist who had testified against a BR "courier."

March 27. Cittadella (Naples). Wounding of prison guard Giacomo Vegliante.

March 29. Rome Murder of Italo Schettini, Christian Democratic provincial councillor and owner of low-income housing projects.

April 24. Turin. Wounding of Franco Piccinelli, journalist with the TG1 television newscast and Christian Democratic activist.

April 24. Genoa. Wounding of Giancarlo Dagnino, Christian Democratic provincial secretary.

April 30. Genoa. Wounding of Giuseppe Bonzani, executive employee at Ansaldo.

May 3. Rome. Raid and devastation of Christian Democratic committee offices in Piazza Nicosia. Ambush of Public Security patrol called to the scene and consequent murder of NCO Antonio Mea and patrolman Piero Ollanu and wounding of patrolman Vincenzo Ammirata.

May 29. Genoa. Wounding of Enrico Ghio, Christian Democratic regional councillor.

May 31. Genoa. Wounding of Fausto Cuocolo, Christian Democratic regional councillor and dean of the School of Political Science, University of Genoa.

June 8. Turin. Wounding of Giovanni Farina, watchman at FIAT.

July 13. Rome. Murder of Carabinieri lieutenant colonel Antonio Varisco, commander of the unit in support of the court house.

September 24. Rome. Wounding of Public Security patrolman Giuseppe Prizzi during a gunfire engagement.

October 4. Turin. Wounding of Cesare Varetto, executive employee at FIAT-Mirafiori.

October 31. Rome. Wounding of Public Security patrolman Michele Tedesco.

November 9. Rome. Murder of Public Security patrolman Michele Granato.

November 21. Sampierdarena (Genoa). Murder of Carabinieri NCO Vittorio Battaglin and trooper Mario Tosa.

November 27. Rome. Murder of Public Security NCO Domenico Taverna.

December 7. Rome. Murder of Public Security NCO Mariano Romiti.

December 12. Turin. Wounding of Adriano Albertini, foreman at FIAT-Mirafiori.

December 21. Milan. Wounding of hospital attendants Nino Manfredini and Ferdinando Malaterra.

1980

January 8. Milan. Murder of Public Security NCO Rocco Santoro and patrolmen Antonio Cestari and Michele Tatulli.

January 25. Genoa. Murder of Carabinieri lieutenant colonel Emanuele Tuttobene and trooper Antonio Casu and wounding of army lieutenant colonel Luigi Ramundo.

January 29. Mestre (Venice). Murder of Sergio Gori, manager at the Marghera plant of Petrolchimico.

February 12. Rome. Murder of Vittorio Bachelet, vice president of the Superior Council of the Judiciary, professor of administrative law at the University of Rome, and former president of Catholic Action.

February 21. Milan. Wounding of Piero Dall'Era, executive employee at the Arese plant of Alfa Romeo.

February 29. Genoa. Wounding of Roberto Della Rocca, personnel manager of Cantieri Navali Riuniti.

March 16. Salerno. Murder of Nicola Giacumbi, state attorney.

March 18. Rome. Murder of Supreme Court judge Girolamo Minervini and wounding of three bystanders.

March 24. Genoa. Wounding of Giancarlo Moretti, Christian Democratic municipal councillor.

March 28. Genoa. Wounding of Carabinieri NCO Rinaldo Rena as he made an arrest.

March 30. Padua. Raid on an army installation, theft of weapons, and wounding of NCO Gabriele Sisto.

April 1. Milan. Raid on a local Christian Democratic section office and leg-shooting of party activists Nadir Tedeschi, Eros Robbiani, Emilio Del Buono, and Antonio Iosa.

April 16. Rome. Wounding of Savino DiGiacomantonio, Christian Democratic councillor.

May 7. Rome. Wounding of Michele Pirri, Labor Ministry official.

May 12. Mestre (Venice). Murder of Deputy Police Commissioner Alfredo Albanesi.

May 17. Rome. Wounding of Domenico Gallucci, secretary of a local Christian Democratic section.

May 19. Naples. Murder of Pino Amato, Christian Democratic regional councillor, and wounding of two bystanders.

May 20. Milan. Attack on Carabinieri barracks with a grenade launcher and wounding of trooper Maurizio Marcovati.

June 19. Turin. Murder of Pasquale Viale, inmate at the Nuove Prison who was accused of being a spy.

October 27. Nuoro. Murder of prison inmates Biagio Iaquinto and Francesco Zarillo during an uprising lead by jailed red brigadists.

November 12. Milan. Murder of Renato Briano, general manager at Ercole Marelli.

November 13. Civitella Alfetana (L'Aquila). Wounding of Carabinieri trooper Antonio De Crescenzio during an armed robbery.

November 28. Milan. Murder of Manfredo Mazzanti, executive employee at Falk.

December 1. Rome. Murder of Giuseppe Furci, medical officer at Regina Coeli Prison.

December 11. Milan. Wounding of Maurizio Caramello, executive employee at Breda.

December 12. Rome. Abduction of Supreme Court judge Giovanni D'Urso, detailed to the Ministry of Justice. He was released on January 15, 1981.

December 28. Trani (Bari). Wounding of five prison guards during an internal uprising. Nineteen hostages freed by the Carabinieri Special Intervention Group on December 29.

December 31. Rome. Murder of Carabinieri brigadier general Enrico Galvaligi, assigned to the Office for Coordinating the Security of Special Prison Facilities.

1981
January 8. Salerno. Wounding of gun shop owner Domenico Pierri during an armed robbery.

February 5. Milan. Wounding of Salvatore Compare, foreman at Breda.

February 5. Rome. Wounding of jewelry shop owner Bruno Michelini and wife during an armed robbery.

February 17. Milan. Murder of Luigi Marangoni, medical doctor and director of the local hospital.

February 26. Matera. Wounding of prison guard Immacolata Schiuma by two jailed red brigadists.

March 12. Milan. Wounding of Alberto Valenzasca, foreman at Alfa Romeo.

March 27. Rome. Armed robbery of a Banca Nazionale del Lavoro branch office and wounding of a private security guard.

April 7. Rome. Murder of prison guard Raffaele Cinotti.

April 27. Torre del Greco (Naples). Political abduction of Christian Democratic regional councillor Ciro Cirillo, murder of his two-man Public Security escort, and wounding of his secretary. Cirillo was released on July 24.

May 8. La Spezia. Wounding of Public Security patrolmen Enrico Summa and Nicola Bruno during a gunfire engagement.

May 15. Naples. Wounding of Christian Democratic municipal councillor Rosario Giovine.

May 20. Marghera (Venice). Abduction of Giuseppe Taliercio, executive employee at Montedison.

May 22. Rome. Wounding of Renzo Retrosi, director of the provincial labor placement office.

May 29. Rome. Wounding of Giuseppe Magagna, instructor at the technical institute "Teresa Gerini."

June 3. Milan. Murder of security guard Antonio Frasca.

June 3. Milan. Abduction of Renzo Sandrucci, chief of production and labor organization at Alfa Romeo. He was released on July 23.

June 6. Naples. Wounding of Communist councillor Umbero Siola.

June 10. Rome. Raid on a movers' cooperative and wounding of members Alberto Ancora, Giulio Baglione, and Giuseppe Marangella.

June 11. San Benedetto del Tronto (Ascoli Piceno). Abduction of Roberto Peci, brother of "repentant" red brigadist Patrizio Peci.

June 19. Rome. Murder of Deputy Police Commissioner Sebastiano Vinci and wounding of Public Security patrolman Pacifico Votto.

June 19. Rome. Wounding of attorney Antonio De Vita, court-appointed counsel for "repentant" red brigadist Patrizio Peci.

July 6. Mestre (Venice). Murder of Giuseppe Taliercio after 46 days of captivity.

July 16. Pontecchio di Sasso Marconi (Bologna). Wounding of private security guard Giuseppe Archinati during an armed robbery of Banca Cooperativa.

July 30. Rome. Armed robbery of the SIP telephone company payroll and wounding of private security guard Luciano Careddu and one bystander.

August 3. Rome. Murder of Roberto Peci after 54 days of captivity.

October 19. Milan. Murder of Public Security patrolmen Vincenzo Tuminello and Carlo Bonantuono and wounding of patrolman Franco Epifanio and one bystander during a gunfire engagement.

December 17. Verona. Abduction of U.S. Army brigadier general James L. Dozier, deputy chief of staff for logistics and administration of NATO's

Land Forces Southern Europe. He was freed by the Central Operative Nucleus for Security of the State Police on January 28, 1982.

1982

January 6. Rome. Wounding of Deputy Police Commissioner Nicola Simone during an abortive abduction attempt.

April 10. Rome. Wounding of Carabinieri NCO Giulio Gregori and troopers Francesco Valori and Michele Scaringella during an attack on special facilities for the trial of the Rome column of the BR.

April 27. Naples. Murder of Christian Democratic regional councillor Raffaele Delcogliano and his driver Aldo Iermano.

June 8. Rome. Murder of State Police agents Franco Sammarco and Giuseppe Carretta.

June 29. Termini Imerese (Palermo). Murder of assistant warden Antonio Burrafato.

July 13. Naples. Murder of Deputy Police Commissioner Antonio Ammaturo and his driver, State Police agent Pasquale Paola, and wounding of three bystanders.

July 16. Lissone (Milan). Murder of Carabinieri NCO Valerio Renzi.

July 19. Naples. Abduction of hospital x-ray technician Giovanni La Greca for the purpose of assisting wounded red brigadists. He was released on July 24.

August 26. Salerno. Assault on two army vehicles to seize weapons; murder of soldier Antonio Palumbo and State Police agents Antonio Bandiera and Mario De Marco; and wounding of agents Salvatore Manci and Pasquale D'Amelio, soldiers Ventura Talamo and Sergio Garau, and two bystanders.

October 21. Turin. Murder of security guards Antonio Pedio and Sebastiano D'Alleo during an armed robbery of Banco di Napoli.

October 22. Rome. Wounding of State Police agent Luigi Ianuario.

1983

May 3. Rome. Wounding of Gino Giugni, professor of labor law at the University of Rome and labor legislation governmental consultant.

1984

February 15. Rome. Murder of U.S. diplomat Leamon R. Hunt, director-general of the Multinational Force and Observers.

1985
March 27. Rome. Murder of Ezio Tarantelli, professor of economics at the University of Rome and CISL labor union economic adviser.

1986
February 10. Florence. Murder of Republican provincial secretary and arms technology industrialist Lando Conti, a close associate of incumbent defense minister Giovanni Spadolini.

February 21. Rome. Wounding of Antonio Da Empoli, economic counselor to the prime minister.

Appendix 4

Front Line:
Chronology of Major Attacks

(Unless otherwise stated, all actions entail ambush attacks.)

1976
April 29. Milan. Murder of Enrico Pedinovi, MSI provincial councillor.

1977
June 22. Pistoia. Wounding of Giancarlo Niccolai, DC provincial deputy secretary and executive employee at Breda.

June 24. Milan. Wounding of Roberto Anzalone, medical doctor and provincial secretary of the participating physicians in the Medicare program.

1978
May 11. Milan. Wounding of Mario Astarita, general manager of the Milan branch of Chemical Bank.

May 17. Turin. Wounding of Public Security patrolman Roberto De Martini.

July 14. Ciampino (Rome). Raid on railroad police station and wounding of Public Security patrolman Angelo Galloni.

July 19. Turin. Raid on Assicurazioni Generali office and wounding of manager Salvatore Russo.

October 11. Naples. Murder of Alfredo Paolella, professor of criminal anthropology and court-appointed expert.

1979

January 19. Turin. Murder of prison guard Giuseppe Lo Russo.

January 29. Milan. Murder of assistant state attorney Emilio Alessandrini.

February 1. Bagnolo di Cremasco (Cremona). Wounding of Carabinieri NCO Camillo Mangini and trooper Raffaele Giardiello.

February 5. Turin. Wounding of prison guard Raffaela Napolitano.

March 9. Turin. Wounding of Public Security patrolman Gaetano D'Angiullo and one bystander during a gunfire engagement.

March 13. Cologno Monzese (Milan). Wounding of four Carabinieri with an explosive device.

June 22. Naples. Wounding of Stanislao Salemme, retired employee of the Social Security Administration.

July 18. Turin. Retaliatory murder of snack-bar owner Carmine Civitate.

September 21. Turin. Murder of Carlo Ghiglieno, manager of the planning branch at FIAT.

October 5. Turin. Wounding of Piercarlo Andreoletti, managing director at Praxi.

November 30. Naples. Raid on a juvenile delinquents' facility and wounding of prison guard Salvatore Castaldo.

December 11. Turin. Raid on the Industrial Management School and leg-shooting of instructors Diego Pannoni, Vincenzo Musso, Lorenzo Vasone, Angelo Scordo, and Paolo Turin and of students Tommaso Prete, Pietro Tangari, Gianpaolo Giuliano, Renzo Poser, and Giuliano Dall'Occhio.

December 15. Rivoli (Turin). Wounding of Carabinieri NCO Massimo Asnaghi and trooper Giovanni Serra during a gunfire engagement.

1980

February 5. Monza (Milan). Murder of Paolo Paoletti, manager at Icmesa.

February 7. Milan. Murder of William Waccher, an extraparliamentary activist accused of being a spy.

February 26. Viareggio (Lucca). Wounding of bank employee Enzo Bono during armed robbery of Banco del Monte.

March 19. Milan. Murder of Judge Guido Galli.

May 2. Rome. Wounding of Sergio Lenci, architect/designer of the Spoleto prison.

August 11. Viterbo. Armed robbery of Banca del Cimino and murder of Carabinieri NCO Pietro Cursoli and trooper Ippolito Coltellessa.

September 22. Rome. Assault on an army truck and wounding of soldier Giovanni Faga.

1981

February 4. Turin. Gunfire engagement with a Public Security motor patrol during armed robbery of a jewelry store and wounding of two by-standers.

May 5. Mongrendo (Vercelli). Murder of private security guard Antonio Rinaldo during a bank robbery.

November 13. Milan. Murder of Public Security patrolman Eleno Anello Viscari.

1982

January 21. Siena. Murder of Carabinieri troopers Enzo Terzilli and Giuseppe Savastano and wounding of NCO Augusto Barna during gunfire engagement after robbery of a Monte dei Paschi di Siena bank branch.

Appendix 5

Significant Episodes of Transnational Violence Planned or Perpetrated by Third World Groups or Agents

I. In Relation to the Armenian Issue

1977
June 7. Rome. Murder of Taha Carin, Turkish ambassador to the Holy See (Justice Commandos for the Armenian Genocide; JCAG)

1979
December 9. Rome. Bombing of British Airways and El Al offices and consequent wounding of nine bystanders (JCAG).

1980
March 10. Rome. Bombing of Turkish Airlines office causing two deaths and fourteen injuries among bystanders (Secret Army for the Liberation of Armenia; ASALA).

April 17. Rome. Wounding of Turkish ambassador to the Holy See and his body guard (JCAG).

October 3. Rome. Bombing of Turkish Airlines office and consequent wounding of two bystanders (ASALA).

November 10. Rome. Bombing of Swissair and Swiss Federal Railways offices and consequent wounding of seven bystanders (October 3rd Organization).

1981
January 27. Milan. Bombing of Swissair and Swiss Tourist Agency offices and consequent wounding of two bystanders (October 3rd Organization).

October 25. Rome. Wounding of Turkish diplomat Gogberg Eregenekon (ASALA).

II. In Relation to Libyan Affairs

1970
January. Rome. Abortive conspiracy by Libyan expatriates (headed by Abdullah Ben Abdid, a blood-relative of deposed King Idris) to topple Qadhafi's regime.

1971
March 21. Trieste. Seizure of the vessel *Conquistador 13*, which was about to sail for Libya with a party of anti-Qadhafi commandos.

1976
March 6. Fiumicino (Rome). Abortive attempt by three Libyan agents to abduct Major Abdel Moneim Hony, former member of the Libyan Revolutionary Command Council, at Rome's international airport.

1980
March 21. Rome. Murder of Libyan expatriate Salem Mohamed El Rteimi.

April 19. Rome. Murder of Libyan expatriate Gialil Abdul al-Aref.

May 5. Rome. Murder of Libyan expatriate Boujar Mohamed Fouad Ben Arami.

May 21. Rome. Wounding of Libyan expatriate Mohamed Salem Fezzani.

June 11. Milan. Murder of Libyan expatriate Lahderi Azzedin.

June 11. Rome. Wounding of Libyan expatriate Mohamed Saad Bygte.

1981
February 24. Fiumicino (Rome). Wounding of two Libyan expatriates at the airport.

October. Rome. Reported assassination plot by Qadhafi agents against U.S. Ambassador to Italy Maxwell M. Raab.

1984

January 21.   Rome. Lethal assault on Libyan ambassador to Italy Ammar El Taggazy, who died on February 10 (Al Forkan, a dissident group).

September 20.   Rome. Murder of Libyan expatriate Mohammed Khomsi.

1985

January 13.   Rome. Murder of Libyan press attaché Mahkyon Faras (Al Forkan).

March 1.   Rome. Murder of Libyan expatriate Mordechai Fadlum.

1986

February 16.   Rome. Wounding of Abdel Halim Mohamed Reda, an Egyptian resident of Italy, who operates an anti-Qadhafi, Arabic-language private radio station, RTIA.

April.   Rome. Italian judicial and police authorities initiate investigation into a reported plot by Qadhafi agents to assassinate U.S., Egyptian, and Saudi Arabian ambassadors to Italy.

III. In Relation to Palestinian and Middle Eastern Affairs

1964

November 17.   Fiumicino (Rome). Abortive Egyptian intelligence attempt to load a trunk clandestinely aboard the United Arab Airlines flight to Cairo; the trunk contained Mordechai Louk, who had been seized on suspicion of being an Israeli double agent.

1968

July 22.   Fiumicino (Rome). Highjacking after takeoff from the airport of an El Al flight to Tel Aviv by three gunmen (Popular Front for the Liberation of Palestine; PFLP).

1969

August 29.   Fiumicino (Rome). Highjacking after takeoff from the airport of a TWA flight to Athens and Tel Aviv by two gunmen (PFLP).

1971

July 28.   Fiumicino (Rome). Abortive attempt to smuggle booby-trapped luggage aboard El Al flight to Lod airport in Israel (PFLP).

1972

August 5. Trieste. Bombing of transalpine oil terminal and destruction of six oil tanks (joint action by PFLP and Black September Organization [BSO], organized by Mohamed Boudia).

August 16. Fiumicino (Rome). A booby-trapped portable record player carried aboard the El Al flight to Tel Aviv exploded, without causing serious injuries, after takeoff from the airport. It had been presented to two English girls as a parting gift by Arab friends (joint action by Popular Front for the Liberation of Palestine–General Command and BSO).

October 16. Rome. Murder of Jordanian national Abdul Wael Zwater, local Fatah/BSO representative (Israeli intelligence).

1973

April 27. Rome. Wounding of an Italian employee of El Al, Vittorio Olivares, who was suspected of connivance in Zwater's murder (BSO).

June 17. Rome. Accidental detonation of explosives being transported in a vehicle and consequent injury of two BSO operatives.

September 5. Ostia (Rome). Arrest of five Arabs who were planning to fire two Strela SA-7 missiles from a terrace against El Al aircraft taking off from the nearby international airport.

November 23. Italian air space near Mestre (Venice). Explosion of the Douglas C47 jet "Argo 17" and death of its four crew members. The jet had been used by Italian intelligence to return captured terrorists to the Middle East as a form of protective behind-the-scenes diplomacy (Israeli intelligence suspected in Italian media accounts).

December 17. Fiumicino (Rome). In a commando action against the Pan Am flight to Beirut and Tehran, five Palestinians committed 34 murders and 41 woundings (Arab Nationalist Youth Organization for the Liberation of Palestine, probably a PFLP or BSO splinter or affiliate).

1976

October 11. Rome. Seizure of Syrian Embassy and concomitant wounding of councillor Hunen Hatem (Black June Organization).

1980

August 4. Rome. Raid on the Iraqi Embassy resulted in two murders and one wounding.

1981

August 9. Fiumicino (Rome). Bombing of El Al counter at the airport injured three passengers (May 15th Organization for the Liberation of Palestine).

October 9. Rome. Detonation of an explosive device planted in his hotel room killed Majid Abu Shrar, member of Fatah's Central Committee and PLO information officer.

1982

June 17. Rome. Joint murder of Zazih Mattak, member of the PLO's press office in Rome, and Kamal Hussin, PLO representative.

September 10. Rome. Raid on the local synagogue resulted in the murder of one worshipper and the wounding of 36 others (the Abu Nidal network, using the name Black Lebanon Organization).

1983

July 13. Fiumicino (Rome). Arson of a Syrian Airlines Boeing 727.

October 26. Rome. Wounding of Jordanian ambassador to Italy Taysir Alaedin Towkan and his driver (Abu Nidal network).

1984

October 26. Rome. Wounding of United Arab Emirates vice consul Mohamed Al Sowaidi and murder of his Iranian companion Noushine Montassari (Arab Revolutionary Brigades).

November 28. Rome area. Discovery of a plot by Lebanese extremists to bomb the U.S. embassy in Rome.

December 14. Rome. Murder of PLO representative Ismail Darwish.

1985

March 22. Rome. Grenade attack on Jordanian Airlines office and wounding of two employees (Abu Nidal network).

April 1. Rome. Bombing of Syrian Airlines office and wounding of three bystanders.

April 3. Rome. Abortive rocket attack on the Jordanian Embassy (Abu Nidal network).

July 1. Fiumicino (Rome). Explosion in the baggage transit area of the airport caused twelve injuries.

September 16. Rome. Soviet-made F1 grenade, hurled from a motorscooter in the direction of Café de Paris on the Via Veneto, wounded 39 persons, including 19 Americans (the Abu Nidal network, using the name Revolutionary Organization of Socialist Muslims [ORMS]).

September 25. Rome. Bombing of British Airways office caused one death and fourteen injuries (Abu Nidal network/ORMS).

October 7–9.   Mediterranean. Highjacking of Italian cruise liner *Achille Lauro* and murder of American passenger Leon Klinghoffer (connection between the four highjackers and the Palestine Liberation Front).

November 5.   Rome. Dismantling of intercepted parcel-bomb mailed to Iranian ambassador to the Holy See Kosrhw Shahiyan.

December 27.   Fiumicino (Rome). Submachine-gun and grenade attack on El Al counter at the airport resulted in fifteen deaths, including three of the four terrorists, and 75 injuries. The proximity of the El Al and TWA counters partially accounts for the murder of five Americans during the attack (Abu Nidal network).

Notes

Chapter 1

1. The Constitution of the Republic of Italy, Art. 1.

2. Ibid., Art. 5.

3. Ibid., Art. 87.

4. Ibid., Art. 89.

5. Ibid., Art. 92.

6. Ibid., Art. 95.

7. Ibid., Art. 77.

8. Ibid., Art. 105.

9. Special charter regions are Sicily, Sardinia, Val d'Aosta, Trentino-Alto Adige, and Friuli-Venezia Giulia. The first two are large islands with distinctive pre-Italian unification characteristics. The latter three include large populations of French, Germanic, and Slavic ethnic/linguistic stock, respectively.

10. The Constitution, Art. 49.

11. The Lateran Agreements comprise three documents: a treaty that recognized Rome as part of the then–kingdom of Italy, except for an enclave cut out to form the State of the Vatican City ruled over by the Holy See in the person of the Pope: a concordat governing religious relations between the Italian State and the Catholic Church: and a financial agreement.

12. Although all parties rely on ancillary structures, these in no way compare to the efficiency and articulation of the PCI-connected organizations.

13. From the end of World War II to the Soviet invasion of Hungary in 1956. PCI membership exceeded the two-million mark. Thereafter it has ranged from 1.5 to 1.8 million votes with a high peak in the mid-1970s. The PCI's youth organization has been on a decline; from a peak of over 460 thousand in 1950 it dwindled to less than 50 thousand in 1984. For current trends, see *Il Tempo* (Rome), November 20, 1985, p. 20. Membership figures are provided by the parties themselves and are therefore generally believed to be somewhat inflated.

14. Initially the PSI was called the Socialist Party of Italian Workers (Partito Socialista di Lavoratori Italiani). In 1943 it adopted the name Italian Socialist Party for Proletarian Unity (Partito Socialista Italiano di Unità Proletaria), and took its current name in 1947. During the 1966–1969 reunification of the PSI and the Italian Social Democratic Party, the name Unitary Socialist Party (Partito Socialista Unitario) was used. The PSI resumed its current name in 1969.

15. The PSDI first called itself the Socialist Party of Italian Workers—the original denomination of the PSI—and adopted its current name in 1952. After its second break with the PSI in 1969, the PSDI used the name Unitary Socialist Party until 1974, when it resumed its current name.

16. In 1964 a faction of the PSI that did not agree with the party's newly adopted policies of collaboration with the DC and Western alignment went on to form the Italian Socialist Party for Proletarian Unity (Partito Socialista Italiano di Unità Proletaria; PSIUP), which won parliamentary representation in 1968, but was largely absorbed by the PCI in 1972. Another party with political standing to the left of the PCI was the Proletarian Unity Party for Communism (Partito di Unità Proletaria per il Comunismo; PDUP), which elected representatives to Parliament in 1979, but just like the PSIUP was largely absorbed by the PCI in 1984. The PDUP is the offspring of a merger of the Manifesto group, expelled from the PCI in 1969, and of the Democratic Proletarian Unity Party (Partito Democratico di Unità Proletaria; PDUP) a remnant of the PSIUP. Clearly, political denominations tend to repeat themselves.

17. The Constitution, Art. 43.

18. *L'Espresso* (Rome), February 13, 1983, p. 11.

19. Statistics from *La Repubblica* (Rome), February 25, 1984, p. 7 and June 24–25, 1984, p. 11.

20. Statistics from *La Repubblica,* February 25, 1984, p. 7. As in the case of political parties, membership statistics are provided by the unions themselves and are therefore believed to be somewhat inflated.

21. The Constitution, Art. 40.

22. Parties with high returns are favored in the distribution of parliamentary seats beyond the strict ratio between votes received and the availability of parliamentary seats.

23. For an in-depth analysis of the years of the centrism, see Giulio Cesare Re, *Fine di Una Politica* (Bologna: Cappelli, 1971).

24. Statistics from *Il Giornale Nuovo* (Milan), April 18, 1980, p. 18.

25. For detailed data and analytical treatment of Italian internal affairs from 1948 through the late 1970s, see Luigi Preti, *Il Compromesso Storico* (Milan: Rusconi, 1975); Domenico Bartoli, *Gli Italiani nella Terra di Nessuno* (Milan: Mondadori, 1976); Alberto Ronchey, *Accadde in Italia 1968–1977* (Milan: Garzanti, 1977); and Domenico Bartoli, *Gli Anni della Tempesta* (Milan: Editoriale Nuova, 1981).

26. These practices are dealt with in G. Conserva, ed., *Costituzione della Repubblica Italiana* (Rome: Bonacci, 1974).

27. Parties frequently argue that changes in returns brought by local elections with respect to the previous parliamentary ones—even if held recently—reflect the electorate's desire for policy changes as substantiated by its shift in party support, however slight.

28. For a detailed study of party factions, especially within the DC, see Antonino Lombardo, "Sistemi di Correnti e Deperimento dei Partiti in Italia," *Rivista di Scienza Politica* (Bologna), no. 1 (1976).

29. The power exercised by the labor unions is extensively documented in Walter Tobagi, *Che Cosa Contano i Sindacati* (Milan: Rizzoli, 1980).

30. Statistics from *La Repubblica,* March 26, 1985, p. 5 and October 30, 1985, p. 18, and *Corriere della Sera* (Milan), October 21, 1985, p. 4.

31. Statistics from Arnaldo Grilli, *La Criminalità Mafiosa nella Società Postindustriale* (Rome: Edizioni Laurus Robuffo, 1986), p. 48.

32. A combination of unusual circumstances, including the emotional reaction to the sudden death of Secretary-General Berlinguer on June 11, 1984, gave the PCI the largest returns (34.5 percent, as opposed to 33 percent for the DC) in the June 1984 elections for the European Parliament, a political contest that obviously does not directly bear on Italian internal affairs. However, at the next electoral contest—the Italian regional elections of May 1985—the DC once again emerged as the relative-majority party with 35 percent of the vote, and the PCI went down to 30.2 percent. As far back as 1948, this type of vote was termed "the vote of fear," an expression coined by the late Socialist leader Pietro Nenni.

Chapter 2

1. For a discussion of the Ministry of the Interior and its subordinate organs, see Guido Landi and Giuseppe Potenza, *Manuale di Diritto Amministrativo* (Milan: Giuffrè, 1978).

2. The larger regions are served by two Carabinieri legions and the larger provinces are served by two or more Carabinieri groups. The Carabinieri territorial structure is intended to meet the necessities of Italy's subdivision into regions, provinces, and municipalities.

3. For a discussion of all five national police forces and their relationships to the respective parent ministries and to the Ministry of the Interior, see Landi and Potenza, *Manuale di Diritto Amministrativo.*

4. The judicial police function and the status of judicial police officers and agents are discussed in depth in Giovanni Leone, *Manuale di Diritto Processuale Penale* (Naples: Jovene, 1975).

5. Law No. 801 of October 24, 1977, published in the *Official Gazette of the Republic of Italy,* no. 303 (November 7, 1977). For an English translation, see Vittorfranco S. Pisano, *A Study of the Restructured Italian Intelligence and Security Services* (Washington, D.C.: Library of Congress, 1978), appendix I, pp. 35–49. Enabling decrees subsequent to the promulgation of the reform law have not been published in the *Official Gazette* because of their sensitive nature.

6. See Ambrogio Viviani, *Servizi Segreti Italiani 1815–1985,* vol. II (Rome: Adn Kronos, 1985), p. 182.

7. Ibid., p. 183.

8. *Italy at a Critical Crossroads in Her History,* A report by Senator Clairborne Pell to the Committee on Foreign Relations, U.S. Senate, on his trip to Italy, November 1976 (Washington, D.C.: Government Printing Office, 1976), p. 14.

9. For a discussion of Italian nuclear policy supported by extensive documentation, see Achille Albonetti, ed., *L'Italia e l'Atomica* (Faenza: Fratelli Lega Editori, 1976).

10. All five missions are described in detail in the 1985 edition of the Defense White Book: Ministero della Difesa, *La Difesa: Libro Bianco 1985* (Rome). The previous edition was published in 1977.

11. On August 26, 1982, by agreement with the Lebanese government, a reinforced Italian mechanized infantry battalion landed in Beirut as part of a French-Italian-U.S. multinational force in order to insure the orderly and peaceful evacuation of the Palestine Liberation Organization combatants from Lebanon to other Arab countries. The Italian contingent was withdrawn on September 12 after accomplishment of the mission. However, following the Sabra and Shatila civilian population massacres, a larger Italian task force, pursuant to another agreement with the Lebanese government, was again sent to Beirut on September 27 as part of the reconstituted multinational peacekeeping force—this time comprising troops from France, Italy, the United Kingdom, and the United States. The Italian contingent, which at the point of maximum participation consisted of 2,200 men, was withdrawn from Lebanon on February 26, 1984, when the governments of the other contingents decided to disengage. A total of 8,345 Italian soldiers served in Lebanon on a rotating basis.

12. The MFO was established pursuant to the Treaty of Peace of March 26, 1979, between Egypt and Israel; it is usually referred to as the Sinai multinational peacekeeping force. Pursuant to another agreement, signed on June 12, 1982, the administrative headquarters of the MFO are based in Rome. On March 16, 1982, the Italian government agreed to furnish to the MFO a naval contingent with primary responsibility for patroling the Strait of Tiran and its approaches. Italy has also made available three minesweepers and a 90-man detachment.

13. For a detailed overview of Italy's security posture, see Vittorfranco S. Pisano, "The Italian Armed Forces," in Lewis H. Gann, ed., *The Defense of Western Europe* (London: Croom Helm, 1987), pp. 158–87.

Chapter 3

1. The Constitution of the Republic of Italy, Transitory and Final Provisions, Art. XII.

2. The origins of the ON and AN are outlined in Tullio Barbato, *Il Terrorismo in Italia* (Milan: Editrice Bibliografica, 1980), pp. 24–25.

3. For instructive facts and insights, see in particular Miriam Mafai, *L'Uomo*

che Sognava la Lotta Armata (Milan: Rizzoli, 1984). Mafai is a veteran of communist partisan formations and a former PCI functionary and journalist. Her book traces the history of Pietro Secchia, a hard-line member of the PCI leadership whose political activism spanned four decades, from 1930 until his death in July 1973.

4. Statistics from Silvio Bertoldi, *Piazzale Loreto* (Milan: Fabbri, 1983), p. 55. The 30,000 figure is attributed to the Interior Ministry.

5. Ibid., pp. 55–58; Mafai, *L'Uomo che Sognava la Lotta Armata,* pp. 5, 47.

6. The history of the Red Strike Force and its relationship to the PCI are discussed in Mafai, *L'Uomo che Sognava la Lotta Armata,* pp. 48–49; Alberto Ronchey, *Libro Bianco sull'Ultima Generazione* (Milan: Garzanti, 1978), pp. 102–3; Soccorso Rosso, *Brigate Rosse* (Milan: Feltrinelli, 1976), pp. 19–21; and *Europeo* (Milan), supplement to no. 16, April 20, 1981. p. 154.

7. For a reconstruction of this insurgency, including extensive excerpts from police reports, see Walter Tobagi, *La Rivoluzione Impossibile* (Florence: Il Saggiatore, 1978).

8. Statistics from Giovanni De Luna, *Hanno Sparato a Togliatti* (Milan: Fabbri, 1983), p. 31.

9. Mafai, *L'Uomo che Sognava la Lotta Armata,* p. 47.

10. Ronchey, *Libro Bianco sull'Ultima Generazione,* p. 103.

11. Mafai, *L'Uomo che Sognava la Lotta Armata,* p. 55.

12. Both quotations are from Tobagi, *La Rivoluzione Impossibile,* pp. 12–13.

13. The reconstruction of events and pertinent statistics are available in *Il Settimanale* (Rome), July 22, 1980, pp. 16–19, and *L'Espresso* (Rome), June 29, 1980, pp. 32–40.

14. See *L'Espresso,* October 7, 1979, pp. 167–73, and Soccorso Rosso, *Brigate Rosse,* pp. 22–24.

15. Statistics from the deposition of State Police Chief Giovanni Coronas, hearing of June 27, 1980, before the parliamentary committee responsible for investigating the abduction and murder of former prime minister Aldo Moro and terrorism in Italy. See Senato della Repubblica, Camera dei Deputati, VIII Legislatura, *Commissione Parlamentare d'Inchiesta sulla Strage di Via Fani sul Sequestro e l'Assassinio di Aldo Moro e sul Terrorismo in Italia* (hereafter referred to as *Parliamentary Report on Terrorism,*) vol. IV (Rome, 1984), p. 58. At this writing, only part of the hearings have been published as appendixes to the basic report of the committee.

16. CPM document quoted in Soccorso Rosso, *Brigate Rosse,* pp. 35–36.

17. Romano Cantore, Carlo Rossella, and Chiara Valentini, *Dall'Interno della Guerriglia* (Milan: Mondadori, 1978), p. 24.

18. Passages extracted from two BR documents entitled "Red Brigades, No. 6, March 1979, Spring Campaign: Seizure, Trial, Execution of Christian Democratic President Aldo Moro" and "Red Brigades, No. 7, July 1979, From the Field in Asinara."

19. The following books address from different perspectives the origins and/or development of the BR: Soccorso Rosso, *Brigate Rosse;* Alessandro Silj, *"Mai Più*

Senza Fucile!" (Florence: Vallecchi, 1977), pp. 3–96; Vincenzo Tessandori, *BR* (Milan: Garzanti, 1977): Cantore et al., *Dall'Interno della Guerriglia,* pp. 11–137; Barbato, *Il Terrorismo in Italia;* Patrizio Peci, *Io L'Infame* (Milan: Mondadori, 1983); Giorgio Bocca, *Noi Terroristi* (Milan: Garzanti, 1985); Rino Genova. *Missione Antiterrorismo* (Milan: Sugarco, 1985), pp. 61–220; and Liano Fanti, *S'Avanza Uno Strano Soldato* (Milan: Sugarco, 1985).

20. This reconstruction is based primarily on the testimony of State Police Chief Coronas, hearing of June 27, 1980, in *Parliamentary Report on Terrorism,* vol. IV, p. 64. Also consulted were the statements of "repentant" red brigadists Patrizio Peci and Antonio Savasta. See Peci, *Io L'Infame,* pp. 56–59, and Savasta's confession quoted in Genova, *Missione Antiterrorismo,* pp. 126–27.

21. See police report quoted in Genova, *Missione Antiterrorismo,* pp. 159–60.

22. Deposition of State Police Chief Coronas, hearing of June 27, 1980, in *Parliamentary Report on Terrorism,* vol. IV, pp. 68–69.

23. For extensive excerpts from BR security documents, see Tessandori, *BR,* pp. 395–400, and Barbato, *Il Terrorismo in Italia,* pp. 226–27. For additional insights, see deposition of Antonio Savasta, hearing of April 6, 1982, in *Parliamentary Report on Terrorism,* vol. IX, pp. 265–420.

24. Deposition of Patrizio Peci, hearing of February 10, 1981, in *Parliamentary Report on Terrorism,* vol. VII, p. 313.

25. See interviews granted by key police officials, prosecutors, and judges to *Il Giornale Nuovo* (Milan), June 26, 1983; *La Repubblica* (Rome), February 8, 1984; and *L'Espresso,* April 15, 1984. See also pertinent reports in *L'Espresso,* April 7, 1985, p. 9 and April 14, 1985, pp. 22–26.

26. Quoted in Genova, *Missione Antiterrorismo,* p. 40.

27. For background information with particular reference to structures and dynamics on PL, the GAP, the NAP, and lesser formations, see deposition of State Police Chief Coronas, hearing of June 27, 1980, in *Parliamentary Report on Terrorism,* vol. IV, pp. 64–71; Giorgio Bocca, *Il Terrorismo Italiano* (Milan: Rizzoli, 1978), pp. 23–34, 67–76; Cantore et al., *Dall'Interno della Guerriglia,* pp. 46–62, 107–13; Soccorso Rosso Napoletano, *I NAP* (Milan: Libri Rossi, 1976); Silj, *"Mai Più Senza Fucile!"* pp. 99–154; Bocca, *Noi Terroristi,* pp. 43–47, 101–6, 189–95, 240–47; Genova, *Missione Antiterrorismo,* pp. 37–59; and Giampaolo Pansa, *Storie Italiane di Violenza, e Terrorismo* (Rome and Bari: Laterza, 1980), pp. 230–42.

28. The development of the extraparliamentary left as a whole is carefully traced in Mino Monicelli, *L'Ultrasinistra in Italia* (Rome and Bari: Laterza, 1978).

29. Quoted in Federico Orlando, *P 38* (Milan: Editoriale Nuova, 1978), p. 83.

30. For an analysis of the relationship between terrorism and the Autonomy, see *Parliamentary Report on Terrorism,* vol. I, pp. 14–16; Angelo Ventura, "Prolusione all' Università di Padova," in Federico Orlando, ed., *Siamo in Guerra* (Rome: Armando, 1980), pp. 138–55; and Pansa, *Storie Italiane di Violenza e Terrorismo,* pp. 182–216.

31. See Savasta, hearing of April 6, 1982, in *Parliamentary Report on Terrorism,* vol. IX, pp. 315–16.

32. Ibid., vol. I, pp. 119–20.

33. Atti Parlamentari, Camera dei Deputati, IX Legislatura, *Relazione sulla Politica Informativa e della Sicurezza,* May 23–November 22, 1984, p. 23.

34. Quoted in *La Repubblica,* June 13, 1984, p. 6 and April 17, 1985, p. 12.

35. Camera dei Deputati, IX Legislatura, Servizio Prerogative e Immunità, *Risultati Elettorali del 26 Giugno 1983* (Rome, 1983), pp. 44, 180, 214.

36. See deposition of Enrico Paghera, hearing of May 29, 1981, in *Parliamentary Report on Terrorism,* vol. VIII, p. 246.

37. *L'Espresso,* September 8, 1985, pp. 22–23.

38. Atti Parlamentari, Camera dei Deputati, IX Legislatura, *Relazione sulla Politica Informativa e della Sicurezza,* November 23–May 22, 1985, p. 14.

39. *Corriere della Sera* (Milan), February 7, 1985, p. 2.

40. For a comparative analysis of the neo-Fascist terrorist mind-set, see Ronchey, *Libro Bianco sull'Ultima Generazione,* pp. 63–93.

41. The history of New Order/Black Order is traced in Barbato, *Il Terrorismo in Italia,* pp. 24–25, 207–8, 213, 229–30.

42. AN's history is outlined in ibid., p. 25.

43. For a discussion of Third Position, the NAR, and the Popular Revolutionary Movement, see ibid., pp. 30–31, and *L'Espresso,* July 8, 1979, p. 27.

44. Atti Parlamentari, Camera dei Deputati, IX Legislatura, *Relazione sulla Politica Informativa e della Sicurezza,* May 23–November 22, 1984, pp. 26–29; November 23, 1984–May 22, 1985, pp. 20–26; and May 23–November 22, 1985, pp. 26–30.

45. Ibid., May 23–November 22, 1983, p. 29.

46. Ibid., November 23, 1984–May 22, 1985, p. 14.

47. *Corriere della Sera,* February 8, 1985, p. 2.

48. These findings apply to the De Lorenzo, Borghese, Sogno, and Compass Card (Rosa dei Venti) cases, which span the period 1964–1974.

49. In a recent case tried before the Court of Assizes and Appellate Court of Assizes of Rome, a verdict was handed down rejecting all allegations that a secret structure organized for criminal purposes gravitated around the military intelligence service. General Pietro Musumeci, former deputy director of the service, and his assistant, Colonel Giuseppe Belmonte, were also acquitted of charges regarding fabrication of evidence to deviate an investigation into the 1980 Bologna massacre. The two officers were convicted, instead, of financial malfeasance, a nonpolitical crime. See *Corriere della Sera,* March 15, 1986, p. 5, and *La Nazione* (Florence), June 14, 1986, p. 4. The two officers will next have to appear before a Bologna court that is conducting a parallel investigation into the above-mentioned massacre. The trial will also address the matter of possible involvement with terrorism by Masonic lodge P2 (see Chapter 5). Among other VIPs, lodge membership allegedly included high-ranking intelligence officials.

50. Three PCI militants have been victims of the BR (see Appendix 3) and one of AR. Three more have been targeted by other elements of the extreme left.

51. Quoted in Tessandori, *BR*, p. 392.
52. Quoted from *Il Manifesto* in *Il Giornale Nuovo*, April 6, 1978, p. 3.
53. Quoted in Bocca, *Noi Terroristi*, p. 68.

Chapter 4

1. Criminal Code, Art. 605.
2. Ibid., Art. 630 and 289 bis, as amended.
3. Code of Criminal Procedure, Art. 39, as amended.
4. Statistics for the period 1960–1971 are from Ottavio Rossani, *L'Industria dei Sequestri* (Milan: Longanesi, 1978), p. 186; for 1972–1983 from Arnaldo Grilli, *La Criminalità Mafiosa nella Società Postindustriale* (Rome: Edizioni Laurus Robuffo, 1986), p. 289; and for 1984–1985 from *La Repubblica* (Rome), January 2, 1986, p. 6. It might be noted, however, that somewhat lower figures—eighteen for 1984 and nine for 1985—were reported by the Italian radio-television system, TG1, on January 11, 1986, at 8 P.M.
5. The Macchiarini, Di Mino, Labate, Mincuzzi, Amerio, and Sossi kidnappings may be reconstructed, with some variance in detail, from Rossani, *L'Industria dei Sequestri*, pp. 109–22; Romano Cantore, Carlo Rossella, and Chiara Valentini, *Dall'Interno della Guerriglia* (Milan: Mondadori, 1978), pp. 46, 69–74, 81–88; and Giorgio Bocca, *Noi Terroristi* (Milan: Garzanti, 1985), pp. 51–52, 64–66, 73–81. For accounts accompanied by extensive coverage of BR documents related to these kidnappings, see Vincenzo Tessandori, *BR* (Milan: Garzanti, 1977) pp. 75–79, 103–16, 132–37, 141–94. Sossi's kidnapping is also reported in an autobiographical account. See Mario Sossi, *Nella Prigione delle BR* (Milan: Editoriale Nuova, 1979). It is a particularly interesting narration since the author also addresses his state of mind. Among other factors, religion, family commitment, and the vivid memory of his military days in Italy's elite mountain troops—the Alpini—assisted the victim in coping with his captivity.
6. The Gancia, Boffa, Casabona, and Costa kidnappings may be reconstructed from Rossani, *L'Industria dei Sequestri*, pp. 123–27; Cantore et al., *Dall'Interno della Guerriglia*, pp. 99–100, 102, 104; and Bocca, *Noi Terroristi*, pp. 113–17, 145–47. Information that emerged from the recent trial of Costa's kidnappers is drawn from *La Repubblica*, October 2, 1985, p. 14, and *Corriere della Sera* (Milan), November 4, 1985, p. 5.
7. Material details regarding the dynamics of the Moro abduction and captivity reported in the text are drawn primarily from the findings of the parliamentary committee instituted to conduct hearings on the case. See Senato della Repubblica, Camera dei Deputati, VIII Legislatura, *Relazione della Comissione Parlamentare d'Inchiesta sulla Strage di Via Fani sul Sequestro di Aldo Moro e sul Terrorismo in Italia* (Rome, 1983). Also consulted were the statements of a number of terrorists— "repentant" and otherwise—collected in Bocca, *Noi Terrotisti*, pp. 204–28. The texts of Moro's letters and "memorial" appear in the volume containing the minority opinions of members of the above-mentioned committee. See Senato della Re-

pubblica, Camera dei Deputati, VIII Legislatura, *Relazioni di Minoranza della Commissione d'Inchiesta sulla Strage di Via Fani e sul Sequestro e l'Assassinio di Aldo Moro e sul Terrorismo in Italia* (Rome, 1983), pp. 89–175.

8. Information on the D'Urso kidnapping is drawn from Bocca, *Noi Terroristi,* pp. 259–62, and Aldo Bello, *L'Idea Armata* (Rome: Edizioni L'Opinione, 1981), pp. 105–13. The pertinent issues of the Rome daily *Il Tempo* were also consulted.

9. See Bello, *L'Idea Armata,* pp. 114–15.

10. Details regarding the Cirillo, Taliercio, Sandrucci, and Peci abductions are drawn largely from the accounts published in *Il Tempo* during and after their captivity. Additional information is from Bocca, *Noi Terroristi,* pp. 266, 272–75, and Rino Genova, *Missione Antiterrorismo* (Milan: Sugarco, 1985), pp. 93–95, 116–17, 171–72.

11. The entire text of their strategic resolution appears in Giorgio Bocca, ed., *Moro Una Tragedia Italiana* (Milan: Bompiani, 1978), pp. 49–112.

12. For detailed accounts of Dozier's abduction, based on Savasta's confessions, and of the rescue operation, see Genova. *Missione Antiterrorismo,* pp. 97–190. Genova, a State Police official, was directly involved in the rescue.

13. The October XXII Circle, NAP, and UCC kidnappings are dealt with in sufficient detail in Rossani, *L'Industria dei Sequestri,* pp. 7–8, 135–38, 145–46. Saronio's abduction may be reconstructed from data in Mauro Galleni, ed., *Rapporto sul Terrorismo* (Milan: Rizzoli, 1981), pp. 207, 298, 453–54, and Tessandori, *BR,* pp. 347–48.

14. The rightist abductions are discussed in Rossani, *L'Industria dei Sequestri,* pp. 139–41, and Tullio Barbato, *Il Terrorismo in Italia* (Milan: Editrice Bibliografica, 1980), p. 71.

15. Statistics from Rossani, *L'Industria dei Sequestri,* p. 59.

16. Ibid.

17. Statistics from Grilli, *La Criminalità Mafiosa nella Società Postindustriale,* p. 289.

18. Summary made in 1971 by the parliamentary committee after hearings on crime in Sardinia; quoted in Rossani, *L'Industria dei Sequestri,* pp. 31–32.

19. For a highly representative chart of a classical kidnap task force covering the incident from the surveillance phase to the "laundering" of the ransom money, see *Corriere della Sera,* January 5, 1979, p. 7.

20. Rossani's detailed study, which regrettably covers only January 1960 to May 25, 1978, indicates that, out of 329 kidnapping cases involving 334 victims, 28 were murdered and 38 more had not been released at the time of completion of his research. See Rossani, *L'Industria dei Sequestri,* pp. 188–89, 230.

21. Figures from Grilli, *La Criminalità Mafiosa nella Società Postindustriale,* p. 90.

22. *La Repubblica,* March 10, 1984, p. 12.

23. Law Decree No. 625 of December 15, 1979, Art. 13, as converted into law by Law No. 15 of February 6, 1980.

24. See *Corriere della Sera,* July 31, 1984, p. 5, and *Panorama* (Milan), October 13, 1985, p. 84.

25. For details, as well as a photocopy of the communique, see *Corriere della Sera,* December 19, 1983, p. 19.

Chapter 5

1. CENSIS, *Quindicinale di Note e Commenti,* no. 4 (April 1985): 5–29. The study was prepared by Gino Martinali.

2. *L'Espresso* (Rome), February 24, 1985, pp. 6–14 and March 17, 1985, pp. 6–13.

3. The word mafia is still used to express several contrasting concepts: beauty, arrogance, and superiority. According to some scholars, it is of Arabic derivation, originally meaning pride, glory, and strength. As the qualifier of a criminal organization, it was first used in an official document in 1838, before Italian unification. Since 1865 it has repeatedly appeared in postunification police records. Equally enigmatic are the origins of the words 'ndrangheta and camorra, which are currently used to describe Calabrian and Neapolitan organized crime. The word 'ndrangheta is a derivative of the Greek *andragathos,* meaning "valorous and cunning man." It first appeared in its present criminological connotation toward the end of the nineteenth century in a Carabinieri report. Camorra is believed by some etymologists to be a derivative of the Arabic word *kumar,* a gambling game forbidden by the Koran.

4. As early as 1973, "repentant" *mafioso* Leonardo Vitale had made some revelations, which were mistakenly not given full credit. Vitale was subsequently murdered. Buscetta's confessions are corroborated by less detailed statements rendered by "repentant" mafioso Salvatore Contorno and by Vincenzo Marsala, the self-confessed son of a mafia boss from whom he acquired the information in his possession. Buscetta was arrested in Brazil in 1982 and extradited to Italy in 1984. His detailed confessions regarding the mafia are summarized in Lucio Galluzzo, Francesco La Licata, and Saverio Lodato, eds., *Rapporto sulla Mafia degli Anni '80* (Palermo: Flaccovio Editore, 1986). See in particular pp. 45–52. This work includes extensive passages taken from the investigating judge's findings in the ongoing Palermo trial against leading mafia figures.

5. Camorra and 'ndrangheta structures are outlined in Arnaldo Grilli, *La Criminalità Mafiosa nella Società Postindustriale* (Rome: Edizioni Laurus Robuffo, 1986), pp. 191–96, 200.

6. The transformation of mafia-type organizations with particular reference to the Sicilian mafia is discussed in Pino Arlacchi. *La Mafia Imprenditrice* (Bologna: Il Mulino, 1983), and Henner Hess, *Mafia* (Rome and Bari: Laterza, 1984). This matter has also been addressed by the interior minister before the Parliament. See Senato della Repubblica, VIII Legislatura, *Resoconto Stenografico,* March 10, 1982, pp. 20601–12.

7. For a reconstruction of the three-tier system, see Grilli, *La Criminalità Mafiosa nella Società Postindustriale,* pp. 78–82, 89–96.

8. Ibid., statistics on p. 114.

9. Ibid. For a discussion and a graphic representation of the support network, see pp. 113–19.

10. Franz Sesti, *Relazione sull'Amministrazione della Giustizia* (Rome, January 11, 1984), p. 12.

11. Ibid., January 9, 1985, p. 18.

12. *L'Espresso* (Rome), October 28, 1984, p. 29.

13. Ibid., August 18, 1985, p. 24.

14. Statistics from RAI-TV TG1 television newscast of January 11, 1986.

15. Dalla Chiesa's assignment to head the Prefecture of Palermo and the circumstances surrounding his assassination are addressed in detail in Galluzzo et al., *Rapporto sulla Mafia degli Anni '80*, pp. 207–97. The prefect (*prefetto*) is the highest representative of the central government and of the Ministry of the Interior in the province. Responsibilities of the office include law enforcement, a subject matter technically handled by the police commissioner (*questore*), who is also an Interior Ministry official but is subordinate to the prefect.

16. *L'Espresso*, October 14, 1984, p. 11.

17. Galluzzo et al., *Rapporto sulla Mafia degli Anni '80*, pp. 180–206.

18. Politico-criminal alliances of these years are described in Mino Milani, *La Caduta di Gaeta* (Milan: Fabbri, 1983), pp. 45–52, and Indro Montanelli, *Storia d'Italia*, vol. 6 (Milan: Rizzoli, 1979), pp. 416–24.

19. Particularly harsh and well documented was the prepared statement by member of Parliament Taiani, a former magistrate. See Atti Parlamentari, Camera dei Deputati, Sessione del 1874–75. *Discussioni,* June 11, 1875, pp. 4124–35.

20. For Fascist regime antimafia operations in Sicily see Nicola Cattedra, *Prefetto Antimafia* (Milan: Fabbri, 1983), pp. 19–45.

21. Ibid., pp. 47–48, and Hess, *Mafia*, pp. 255–56.

22. *Panorama* (Milan), November 19, 1984, p. 65.

23. See, in particular, Senato della Repubblica, Camera dei Deputati, IX Legislatura, *Relazione della Commissione Parlamentare d'Inchiesta sulla Loggia Massonica P2* (Rome, 1984).

24. Indictments against Gelli have been widely covered in the press. See, for example, *Corriere della Sera* (Milan), September 14, 1982, p. 1, and *La Repubblica* (Rome), December 1–2, 1985, p. 7.

25. Article 18 of the Constitution recites in part: "Secret associations . . . are forbidden." With respect to the P2 lodge in particular, this constitutional dictate has been implemented by Law No. 17 of January 25, 1982.

26. Gelli's background is meticulously investigated in Gianfranco Piazzesi, *Gelli* (Milan: Garzanti, 1983). See, in particular, pp. 197–230 and 281–90.

27. The text of this document appears in a special insert called "Dossier P2" and appended to *La Repubblica,* May 29, 1984.

28. Statement by Lino Salvini, quoted in Piazzesi, *Gelli*, p. 214.

29. Statement by General Rosseti, ibid.

30. For current information, though still subject to judicial verification, see *Europeo* (Milan), March 22, 1986, pp. 18–20.

31. Atti Parlamentari, Camera dei Deputati, *Relazione sulla Politica Informativa e della Sicurezza,* November 23, 1982–May 22, 1983, pp. 11–12; May 23–November 22, 1983, pp. 12–14; and May 23–November 22, 1985, pp. 30–32.

32. Atti Parlamentari, Camera dei Deputati, VIII Legislatura, *Resoconto Stenografico,* March 6, 1980, p. 10889.

33. See Grilli, *La Criminalità Mafiosa nella Società Postindustriale,* pp. 123–24.

34. These links were outlined by the prime minister during a Council of Ministers meeting in early 1982. See *Il Tempo* (Rome), January 22, 1982, p. 1.

35. See *La Repubblica,* February 2, 1986, p. 13 and March 6, 1986, p. 12.

36. See *Ordine Pubblico* (Rome), December 1985, p. 21.

37. See Grilli, *La Criminalità Mafiosa nella Società Postindustriale,* pp. 124–25.

Chapter 6

1. *Il Settimanale* (Rome), March 6, 1980, pp. 40–43.

2. *L'Espresso* (Rome), December 6, 1981, pp. 9–12.

3. *Panorama* (Milan), October 24, 1983, p. 44.

4. *Il Sole-24 Ore* (Milan), November 29, 1983, pp. 1, 3.

5. *Panorama,* November 7, 1983, p. 54.

6. This statement was even printed over two full pages of one of Italy's most circulated nonparty weeklies in the form of an advertisement.

7. Reported in Vinicio Araldi, *Lo Stato Malato* (Rome: Vito Bianco Editore, 1971), pp. 197–98.

8. Oleg Penkovskiy, *The Penkovskiy Papers* (Garden City, N.J.: Doubleday, 1965; New York: Ballantine, 1982), p. 99.

9. See Achille Albonetti, ed., *Il Finanziamento del PCI* (Rome: Circolo Stato e Libertà, 1978). PCI-USSR financial links have also been the object of several detailed investigations by the now-defunct weekly *Il Settimanale.* Pertinent issues were published between June and September 1981.

10. *L'Unità* (Milan edition), November 15, 1979, pp. 8–9.

11. Berlinguer went so far as to acknowledge NATO as a "shield" behind which the PCI could progress on its "individual road to socialism." However, this acknowledgment was left out of the account published in the party's periodical, *L'Unità.* Moreover, *Paese Sera,* a PCI-oriented paper, stressed the "absurdity of concluding that Berlinguer sees in NATO a shield for Italy's advance to socialism" and recalled an earlier statement of the PCI leader alleging that NATO is an alliance that does not work in the interest of freedom for the people. Two weeks before Berlinguer's statement, Giancarlo Pajetta of the PCI Directorate—when asked "What if Italy were attacked by the Warsaw Pact?"—replied: "And why should it be at-

tacked? I do not accept the hypothesis." In 1977, in response to a similar question, Lucio Lombardo Radice of the Central Committee unequivocally opted for the Soviet side, and Armando Cossutta, also of the Central Committee, stated that "it is unthinkable for a party of workers such as ours to go in for anti-Sovietism." Obviously, Berlinguer's campaign statements did not enjoy the full concurrence of the party leadership. For an analysis in English of the PCI stance toward NATO with particular reference to this electoral campaign, see James E. Dougherty and Diane K. Pfalzgraff, *Eurocommunism and the Atlantic Alliance* (Cambridge, Mass.: Institute for Foreign Analysis, 1977).

12. *L'Espresso,* March 1, 1981, p. 59.

13. *L'Unità,* September 26, 1980, p. 3.

14. Statement made during a television interview and widely reported in the press.

15. As advertised on a full page of the PCI's *L'Unità,* January 23, 1983.

16. *L'Espresso,* April 26, 1981, p. 15.

17. Ibid., March 1, 1981, p. 59.

18. Ibid., January 16, 1983, pp. 14–15.

19. For an overview of the vote in virtually all provinces, see *L'Espresso,* March 6, 1983, p. 13. After his statement on December 15, 1981, Berlinguer himself pointed out that there was actually "no break" with the USSR, "but harsh polemics," as reported by *Il Tempo* (Rome), April 4, 1982, p. 16. Substantially the same allegation was made shortly thereafter by Pajetta, as reported by *La Repubblica* (Rome), October 28, 1982, p. 5. Commentators have consequently argued that these statements made possible the large percentage of votes in support of the "wrench," since no "wrench" admittedly took place.

20. Statements reported in *L'Unità* (Venice edition), May 1, 1983, pp. 1, 24, and *La Repubblica,* July 31–August 1, 1983, p. 9 and September 3, 1983, p. 4.

21. Atti Parlamentari, Camera dei Deputati, IX Legislatura, *Discussioni,* November 15, 1983, p. 33.

22. Ibid., p. 28.

23. Ibid., pp. 66–67.

24. Recruitment in Italy is based primarily on the draft system. All male citizens are automatically registered for the draft at age seventeen. The following year they are subject to physical and aptitude examinations. Those who are fit and not entitled to dispensation or deferment for family, academic, conscientious objection, or other reasons are inducted at age nineteen into the army or air force for a twelve-month period, or into the navy, in which case they serve for eighteen months. Reduction of naval service is currently under consideration. Qualified draftees who apply and are selected to serve as reserve officers must spend three additional months on active duty for officer training.

25. Figure from *Panorama,* November 14, 1983, p. 68.

26. Quoted in Renato Proni, *Euromissili: La Tua Scelta* (Milan: Sugarco, 1982), pp. 110–11.

27. Statistics from Speciale Adn Kronos, *XVI Congresso del PCI*, Supplement to no. 43 (Rome, February 21, 1983), p. 6.

28. These statistics are provided by the ARCI itself in an English-language pamphlet published by the International Division and titled *ARCI: Culture, Peace, and Environment*. According to this pamphlet, "The ARCI is the association of all workers, young people, women and citizens who are willing to live together in their cultural, sports and recreational activities, while fighting against all forms of exploitation, ignorance, injustice, discrimination, loneliness, and margination. The ARCI fights for international detente, for peace and cooperation among all countries beyond all frontiers and all barriers, for the limitation of both nuclear and conventional weapons, for the reduction of armies and for disarmament. The ARCI fights at the side of the oppressed and of the peoples struggling for their liberation. [It] fights for a new international order and against the overwhelming action of rich and powerful nations on other countries; against hunger in the world as well as for concrete aids and for the solution of all nutritional, technological, sanitary, financial and cultural problems of developing countries." The organization appears to be almost tailor-made for pacifist militancy and support.

29. The independent but left-oriented *L'Espresso* (October 23, 1983, p. 6) categorized the PCI as "the colossus" within the pacifist movement. Several months earlier, the PCI's official daily, *L'Unità*, noted with satisfaction that the pacifist movement had decided "to institute a permanent general coordination committee as the expression of the regional coordination committees and of the political, social, and cultural forces on the front line for peace and disarmament (and) to request the local entities to provide suitable premises where to meet for discussions" (January 26, 1983, p. 7). Indeed, "the colossus" realized early on the potential political opportunities offered by the material/logistical needs of the pacifist movement and, as will be seen below in greater detail, readily made its structures available. A partial admission of PCI intentions was made by the Communist regional secretary for Sicily, Luigi Colajanni, who stated: "Perhaps at the beginning my party tended to dominate the movement. But today it is no longer so." See *Corriere della Sera* (Milan), December 5, 1983, p. 4.

30. For a discussion of the resurgence of political slogans, see *Panorama*, January 10, 1982, pp. 48–51. The article also provides a list in the vernacular of the most frequently employed peace slogans.

31. The appeal was published in various newspapers. In addition to the march announcement and the list of signatories, it provided the itinerary as well as addresses for where to sign up or make financial contributions. See, for example, the appeal/announcement published in *La Repubblica*, November 20, 1982, p. 6.

32. *Pace e Guerra* (Rome), April 21, 1983, p. 39.

33. *L'Espresso*, October 23, 1983, p. 7.

34. *La Repubblica*, October 23/24, 1983, p. 2. It also reported that a number of march announcements posted in Roman churches were printed by the Catholic organization Charitas without official sanction.

35. An instructive overview of such structures is provided by the "Yellow pages

of the movement" section of the bimonthly bulletin *Pace in Movimento* (Peace in movement), published by the National Coordination of Peace Committees (Coordinamento Nazionale dei Comitati per la Pace). The bulletin lists mailing addresses in care of various entities, including municipalities, municipal organizations, public libraries, political parties, party affiliations, labor unions, research institutes, and even parish churches. A more indirect but nonetheless valuable indication is provided by the pacifist leaflets. For example, the one relative to the June 3, 1984, Vicenza demonstration listed the member organizations of the Vicenza coordination committee, which included—in addition to the Vicenza Committee for Peace—the PCI, DP, CGIL, LOC, Pax Christi, MIR, and National Association of Italian Partisans (Associazione Nazionale Partigiani d'Italia).

36. See, for example, *La Repubblica*, July 23, 1983, p. 1.

37. Ibid., p. 4. The Umbria region is one of the PCI's strongholds.

38. IRDISP, *Quello che i Russi Sanno e gli Italiani non Devono Sapere* (Rome, 1983).

39. Typical coverage in *Notizie Radicali* appears in the March 9, 1985, issue, which includes detailed criticism of the Defense White Book, a list of ecological/green candidates for the various regional, provincial, and municipal councils, and reports on ecological platforms.

40. Estimates in 1982 credited the Non-Violent Movement with 500 members and fifteen branch offices. See *L'Espresso*, December 12, 1982, p. 26. Figures relative to the circulation of its monthly are from *Europeo* (Milan), September 10, 1983, p. 26.

41. See *La Repubblica*, April 17, 1985, p. 16.

42. See *Corriere della Sera*, June 9, 1985, p. 4.

43. The early dissolution of Parliament in 1983 made it necessary for the bill to be reintroduced before the current Parliament. Meanwhile, the PCI unsuccessfully petitioned the Council of Ministers to hold a consultative referendum not having the force of law.

44. See *L'Espresso*, November 10, 1985, p. 33, and *La Repubblica*, May 22, 1985, p. 4, May 26–27, 1985, p. 13, and October 11, 1985, p. 11.

45. See *Corriere della Sera*, June 5, 1985, p. 11.

46. *Panorama*, March 26, 1984, p. 80.

47. *Europeo*, May 17, 1982, p. 13.

48. The history of these camps may be reconstructed from various press sources, including *Corriere della Sera*, March 14, 1983, p. 6 and June 16, 1983, p. 6; *Panorama*, May 16, 1983, p. 84; *La Repubblica*, July 30, 1983, p. 7, August 12, 1983, p. 7, November 8, 1983, p. 11, February 26–27, 1984, March 8, 1984, p. 7, and May 13–14, 1984, p. 5; *L'Espresso*, September 4, 1983, pp. 22–24; and *Europeo*, September 10, 1983, p. 26 and September 24, 1983, pp. 20–21.

49. *Corriere della Sera*, November 14, 1983, p. 2.

50. *Panorama*, May 16, 1983, p. 84.

51. For background information on the CUDIP, see *L'Espresso*, September 4,

1983, p. 4, and *Corriere della Sera,* November 11, 1983, p. 2. Additional data are included in the sources cited above in note 48.

52. *L'Espresso,* December 12, 1982, p. 23.

53. *Panorama,* April 19, 1982, p. 65.

54. *Corriere della Sera,* November 8, 1982, p. 3.

55. For coverage of fiscal objection practices, see *Europeo,* September 10, 1983, p. 26, and *Corriere della Sera,* October 26, 1985, and November 8, 1985, p. 11.

56. See *Agenzia Italiana Stampa* (Rome), January 23, 1984, pp. 4–5.

57. See *La Repubblica,* October 22, 1983, p. 3.

58. Interview with *Panorama,* November 7, 1983, p. 62.

59. See, in particular, *La Repubblica,* August 12, 1983, p. 7.

60. For details, see *La Repubblica,* April 22–23, 1984, p. 5, and *L'Espresso,* August 12, 1984, pp. 7–8.

61. See *Corriere della Sera,* January 15, 1985, p. 5.

62. See *La Repubblica,* July 19, 1985, p. 7. As noted above in note 24, screened conscientious objectors are exempt from military service. However, they are expected to carry out alternative humanitarian service for a duration of two years, to which many self-styled conscientious objectors once again "object."

63. These intentions were also voiced in the communiques issued by the BR during General Dozier's captivity.

64. See *Il Tempo,* May 10, 1982, p. 5.

65. Quoted in *L'Espresso,* September 16, 1984, p. 8.

66. *La Repubblica,* September 11–12, 1983, p. 8.

67. Ibid., September 11, 1984, p. 7.

68. See Atti Parlamentari, Camera dei Deputati, *Relazione sulla Politica Informativa e della Sicurezza,* November 23, 1982–May 22, 1983, p. 27; May 23–November 22, 1983, p. 27; November 23, 1983–May 22, 1984, p. 32; and May 23–November 22, 1984, p. 21.

Chapter 7

1. Three sovereign states are located on the Italian peninsula: the Republic of Italy, the State of the Vatican City, and the Republic of San Marino. Also located on Italian soil are the headquarters of the Sovereign Military Order of Malta, an internationally recognized public entity, those of the Food and Agriculture Organization of the United Nations, and minor offices of other U.N. affiliates. All of these states and international organizations are directly or indirectly exploitable by hostile foreign intelligence services through such means as diplomatic accreditation and international staff personnel.

2. For extensive coverage of known East European espionage cases in Italy from 1945 through the late 1960s, see Enrico Altavilla, *La Battaglia degli Stregoni* (Milan: Rizzoli, 1965), and especially Vinicio Araldi, *Guerra Segreta in Tempo di*

Pace (Milan: Mursia, 1969). For subsequent coverage the daily and periodical press is virtually the only readily accessible source in the public domain that addresses the topic in any depth. The semiannual intelligence reports of the prime minister to the Parliament tend to omit detail, but often provide confirmation of media coverage. In fact, the last three reports attest to the continuing threat posed by the East European Communist countries. See Atti Parlamentari, Camera dei Deputati, IX Legislatura, *Relazione sulla Politica Informativa e della Sicurezza*, May 23–November 22, 1984, pp. 35–36; November 23, 1984–May 22, 1985, pp. 34–38; and May 23–November 22, 1985, pp. 34–36.

3. Soviets expelled in relation to espionage against military offices and installations include Aleksei Solovev (1958), posted as the military attaché's driver; Kir Lemzenko (1966), commercial attaché; Yuri Pavlenko (1967), attaché; Vladimir Alexandrov (1970), military attaché aide; and Ivan Mikhailovich Chelyag (1982), military attaché.

4. The most notorious case of this nature resulted in the expulsion of Soviet trade specialist Genadii Roiko in 1967 and the arrest of four Italian nationals: two businessmen and two Ministry of Foreign Affairs employees.

5. Soviets expelled or arrested—if not in possession of diplomatic immunity—in relation to industrial/technological espionage include Anatoli Gerasimovich Zazulin (1981), posted as comercial attaché, and Viktor Pronin (1982), deputy commercial manager of Aeroflot, the Soviet airline, in Rome. The 1986 expulsions of Viktor Kopytin, first secretary at the Soviet embassy, and Andrei Chelukhin, Aeroflot air-terminal manager in Rome, are also believed to be in relation to such operations.

6. Most Czech cases pertain to industrial espionage. The East German cases entail industrial espionage through commercial channels. Among other military objectives, the Hungarians attempted to infiltrate the Italian War College in Florence.

7. In the late 1940s and early 1950s the Czechs had set up espionage rings coordinated by Italian nationals of communist allegiance who served as links between the ring itself and a Czech case officer. An espionage network organized by the Soviets in Italy, but ultimately responsible for a broader sphere of operations, including Spain, was in place from 1956 through 1967. The Italian field supervisor of the network was former right-wing activist and civilian parachutist Giorgio Rinaldi Ghislieri, who was co opted by the Soviets through misrepresentation and financial inducement.

8. Oleg Penkovskiy, *The Penkovskiy Papers* (Garden City, N.J.: Doubleday, 1965; New York: Ballantine, 1982), pp. 315–16. From April 1961 through August 1962, Penkovskiy furnished Soviet political and military secrets to U.S. and British intelligence services. His personal diaries of this period were posthumously published.

9. Ibid., p. 177.

10. Ibid., pp. 176–77.

11. Alberto Ronchey, *Libro Bianco sull'Ultima Generazione* (Milan: Garzanti, 1978), p. 102.

12. Silverio Corvisieri, *Il Mio Viaggio nella Sinistra* (Rome: Editoriale L'Espresso, 1979), pp. 16–17.

13. A wealth of pertinent excerpts from official party publications appears in Ruggero Guarini and Giuseppe Saltini, eds., *I Primi della Classe* (Milan: Sugarco, 1978). See, in particular, pp. 45–60.

14. See *Foreign Report* (London), July 7, 1976, pp. 6–7. Regarding the PCI's financial dealings with the East European bloc of nations, a bill was introduced in the Chamber of Deputies in July 1983 by the MSI parliamentary group calling for an investigation. Appended to the bill were several lists of companies, including one of companies that "reportedly cooperated with the PCI in dealings with East European countries." Listed among them are Giole SpA of Castiglion Fibocchi and Socam of Arezzo, both connected to Licio Gelli, head of the P2 lodge discussed in Chapter 5. See Atti Parlamentari, Camera dei Deputati, IX Legislatura, Disegni di Leggi e Relazioni, Documenti, *Proposta di Legge,* no. 234, July 21, 1983.

15. Hearing before the Subcommittee to Investigate the Administration of the Internal Security Act and Other Internal Security Laws, Committee on the Judiciary, U. S. Senate, 94th Congress, 2d session, part 2, April 12, 1976, p. 78.

16. The episode is recounted in Gianfranco Piazzesi, *Gelli* (Milan: Garzanti, 1983), pp. 106–14.

17. See *L'Espresso* (Rome), July 15, 1979, p. 48.

18. Ibid.

19. Michael A. Ledeen, "Intelligence, Training, and Support Components," in Uri Ra'anan et al., *Hydra of Carnage* (Lexington, Mass.: Lexington Books, 1986), p. 156.

20. Sejna's revelations to *Il Giornale Nuovo* of Milan (January 11, May 22, and September 18, 1980) are summarized in *Panorama* (Milan), February 9, 1981, pp. 40–42.

21. See *Europeo* (Milan), supplement to no. 16, April 20, 1981, p. 154.

22. See *Il Tempo* (Rome), February 2, 1981, p. 1.

23. Senato della Repubblica, Camera dei Deputati, VIII Legislatura, *Relazioni di Minoranza della Commissione Parlamentare d'Inchiesta sulla Strage di Via Fani e sul Sequestro e l'Assassinio di Aldo Moro e sull Terrorismo in Italia* (hereafter referred to as *Parliamentary Report on Terrorism, Minority Views*), p. 411.

24. See Liano Fanti, *S'Avanza Uno Strano Soldato* (Milan: Sugarco, 1985), p. 187.

25. Hearing before the Subcommittee to Investigate the Administration of the Internal Security Act, 2d session, p. 78.

26. For Pasti's background and statements, see *Il Settimanale* (Rome), August 4, 1981, pp. 20–22, and *L'Espresso,* August 30, 1981, p. 14 and November 2, 1981, p. 65.

27. For background information on all three, see *La Repubblica,* November 9, 1982, p. 5, and *Europeo* (Milan), June 28, 1982, p. 39.

28. See *Corriere della Sera* (Milan), October 25, 1982, p. 1 and November 11, 1984, p. 1.

29. The history of the PSIUP, including its financial sources, is recounted in Silvano Miniati, *PSIUP 1964–1972: Vita e Morte di un Partito* (Rome: Edimez, 1982). The author is a former PSIUP activist.

30. Ages reported in *La Repubblica,* June 2, 1983.

31. See *Panorama,* February 9, 1981, p. 40.

32. Photocopies of pertinent Soviet documents have been published in *OP* (Rome), September 19, 1978, pp. 9–11 and September 26, 1978, pp. 23–24.

33. See Ronald Seth, *Unmasked! The Story of Soviet Espionage* (New York: Hawthorn Books, 1965), p. 269, and *Panorama,* March 14, 1983, p. 79.

34. Ladislav Bittman, *The Deception Game* (New York: Ballantine, 1981), p. 143.

35. Hearing before the Subcommittee to Investigate the Administration of the Internal Security Act and Other Internal Security Laws, Committee on the Judiciary, U. S. Senate, 94th Congress, 1st session, November 18, 1975, p. 15.

36. Bruce E. Henderson and C. C. Cyr, eds., *Double Eagle* (New York: Ballantine, 1983), p. 74.

37. See Bittman, *The Deception Game,* p. 213.

38. Hearings before the Subcommittee on Oversight, Permanent Select Committee on Intelligence, U.S. House of Representatives, *Soviet Covert Action (The Forgery Offensive),* 96th Congress, 2d session, February 6 and 9, 1980, p. 66.

39. Ibid., p. 137.

40. *Il Tempo,* January 17, 1980, p. 1.

41. *L'Espresso,* January 17, 1982, p. 18.

42. See Hearing before the Subcommittee to Investigate the Administration of the Internal Security Act, p. 2, and Josef Frolik, *The Frolik Defection* (London: Leo Cooper, 1975), pp. 59–60.

43. Of the two early incidents in the public record that precede the Bulgarian connection, the first occurred on January 20, 1962, when a Bulgarian Mig 19 crash-landed near Bari after circling around local NATO installations. The pilot, Lieutenant M. Sulakov of the 11th Reconnaissance Squadron stationed in Bergovitza, was in possession of an unexplainably large sum of money. He was repatriated one year later under unclear circumstances. The second incident entailed the expulsion, in 1972, of commercial attaché Dimcho Vazov and company representative Borislav Baltchev, presumably for espionage.

44. A detailed account of the Scricciolo/Elia case was published in all major Italian papers on July 28 and 29, 1983, on the occasion of Elia's second arrest after she had been provisionally released for health reasons.

45. They were Simeon Georgev Diytchnov, Ivan Tomov Dontchev, and Venelin Koumbiev, all three posted in Rome with secretarial rank.

46. The diplomats were Todor Stoyanov Ayvazov, treasurer of the Bulgarian

embassy, and Jelio Kolev Vasilev, military attaché aide; the Balkan Air representative was Sergei Ivanov Antonov.

47. The conspiracy case was brought to trial on May 27, 1985, and the verdict was handed down on March 29, 1986. Three of the four Turks were acquitted under the same formula as the Bulgarians. All defendants have appealed for a full-innocence formula. The fourth Turk was convicted of smuggling into Italy the assault weapon used by Agca, a nine-millimeter semiautomatic pistol. In the course of the trial, the prosecutor cited false documents produced by the Bulgarian government in defense of its three nationals, whom he also accused of lying on various issues, and introduced evidence identifying Antonov as a Bulgarian secret agent. See, in particular, *Corriere della Sera,* February 14, 1986, p. 8; *La Repubblica,* February 23–24, 1986, p. 12; and *L'Espresso,* March 9, 1986, pp. 22–23.

48. Christian Roulette, *La Pista* (Rome: Napoleone, 1985).

49. Atti Parlamentari, Camera dei Deputati, VIII Legislatura, *Discussioni,* December 20, 1982, pp. 44–45.

50. In contrast to a variety of journalistic endeavors of uneven quality to reconstruct the Bulgarian connection with special reference to the papal assassination attempt, a particularly scholarly work was produced by Paul Henze, *The Plot to Kill the Pope* (New York: Charles Scribner's Sons, 1985).

51. John Barron, *KGB* (New York: Readers' Digest Press, 1974), pp. 509–61, and *KGB Today* (New York: Readers' Digest Press, 1983), pp. 437–42.

52. In addition to Barron's works, see listings in Araldi, *Guerra Segreta in Tempo di Pace,* pp. 290–311; *Il Tempo,* December 14, 1982, p. 14; *La Repubblica,* February 16, 1983, p. 11 and February 6, 1986, p. 10; and *L'Espresso,* April 17, 1983, pp. 28–34.

53. Figures from official Italian diplomatic list: Ministero degli Affari Esteri, Cerimoniale, *Ambasciate Estere in Italia* (March 1984).

54. See Araldi, *Guerra Segreta in Tempo di Pace,* pp. 324–25, and George Jonas, *Vengeance* (New York: Bantam Books, 1984), pp. 103–15.

55. Qadhafi's expulsion of the Italian residents was in fact one of the first clamor-inducing acts after his forcible takeover of Libya from pro-Western King Idris in September 1969.

56. Libya's economic and influence operations in Italy are addressed in detail in *Il Mondo* (Milan), January 30, 1981, pp. 10–15, April 28, 1986, pp. 36–43, and May 26, 1986, pp. 44–49.

57. A long series of Libyan provocations against Italy is listed in *Il Giornale Nuovo,* May 13, 1986, p. 2. For background, see also Vittorfranco S. Pisano, "Libya's Multifaceted Foreign Policy: The Italian Application," *Congressional Record,* vol. 127, no. 187, pt. II (December 15, 1981), S15373-375, and Pisano, "Libya's Foothold in Italy," *The Washington Quarterly* (Spring 1982): 179–82.

58. Figures and commentary from *AIS-Agenzia di Stampa* (Rome), February 22, 1986, p. 2. Out of approximately 380,000 aliens whose papers are in order, 112,000 are workers, 93,000 are students, and 71,000 are in Italy for family reasons. See *L'Espresso,* August 25, 1985, p. 26.

59. See Atti Parlamentari, Camera dei Deputati, IX Legislatura, *Relazione sulla Politica Informativa e della Sicurezza,* November 23, 1984–May 22, 1985, p. 30.

60. See U.S. Department of State, Bureau of Public Affairs, *Libya Under Qadhafi: A Pattern of Aggression,* Special Report No. 138 (January 1986), and *Panorama,* September 29, 1985, pp. 48–51.

61. See *Corriere della Sera,* September 1, 1984, p. 7, and *Washington Post,* January 24, 1986, p. C19.

62. Official Italian Records specifically refer to German terrorists Brigitte Mohnhapt, Siglinda Hoffmann, Gabrielle Kroecher-Tiedemann, Elisabeth von Dyck, Rolf Meissler, and Willy Peter Stoll. See Senato della Repubblica, Camera dei Deputati, VIII Legislatura, *Commissione Parlamentare d'Inchiesta sulla Strage di Via Fani sul Sequestro e l'Assassinio di Aldo Moro e sul Terrorismo in Italia* (hereafter referred to as *Parliamentary Report on Terrorism*), vol. I (Rome, 1983), pp. 125–26 and vol. IV (Rome, 1984), p. 203.

63. Ibid., vol. IV, p. 204.

64. Ibid., vol. I, p. 138. Italian participants included Maurice Bignami, Sergio Segio, and Francesca Bellerè.

65. Ibid., vol. IV, pp. 203, 206.

66. For details and analysis, see Vittorfranco S. Pisano, "Euroterrorism and NATO," *Update Report,* vol. XI, issue 1 (Gaithersburg, Md.: International Association of Chiefs of Police, 1985).

67. *Parliamentary Report on Terrorism,* vol. IV, pp. 146–47, 204. According to these official sources, "Feltrinelli made 22 or 23 trips to Czechoslovakia" (p. 174).

68. See, for example, Ronchey, *Libro Bianco sull'Ultima Generazione,* p. 90, and *Panorama,* September 15, 1980, p. 44. Additional names appear for the first time in Claire Sterling, *The Terror Network* (New York: Readers' Digest Press, 1981), p. 317. Sterling cites as her source Czech defector Jan Sejna.

69. See Fanti, *S'Avanza Uno Strano Soldato,* p. 145.

70. See Atti Parlamentari, Camera dei Deputati, VIII Legislatura, *Discussioni,* December 20, 1982, p. 91.

71. See *Panorama,* September 15, 1980, p. 91.

72. See *Parliamentary Report on Terrorism,* vol. IV, pp. 162, 215–16.

73. Their names were eventually acquired and published by *Il Settimanale,* May 5, 1979, p. 33.

74. This disclosure was made by former SID director Vito Miceli on the floor of Parliament on May 19, 1978. See Atti Parlamentari, Camera dei Deputati, VII Legislatura, *Discussioni,* May 19, 1978, pp. 6–9. Since Miceli was elected to the Chamber of Deputies on the rightist MSI slate, some commentators cast doubt on the veracity of the expulsion proposal. Consequently, it should be noted that confirmation of Czech involvement in Italian subversion was given, also on the floor of Parliament, by prime minister Arnaldo Forlani, a Christian Democrat. See Atti Parlamentari, Camera dei Deputati, VIII Legislatura, *Discussioni,* February 3, 1981, pp. 21–22. It is worth noting, moreover, that an accusing finger was pointed at

Czechoslovakia as far back as 1973 by former prime minister Giulio Andreotti, a Christian Democrat. See Atti Parlamentari, Senato della Repubblica, *Resoconti delle Discussioni,* 156th session, May 18, 1973, pp. 7588–7665.

75. See Federico Orlando, ed., *Siamo in Guerra* (Rome: Armando, 1980), pp. 195–96.

76. The entire episode is narrated in detail in Ambrogio Viviani, *Servizi Segreti Italiani 1815–1985,* vol. II (Rome: Adn Kronos, 1985), pp. 149–51. The author is a retired brigadier general who served in a high-ranking counterintelligence position in the SID. He, too, implicitly confirms Miceli's statement. See note 74 above.

77. Classified Matters Office Document No. 41199, reproduced in *Il Borghese,* April 23, 1978, and cited by Sterling, *The Terror Network,* pp. 30, 300.

78. See Miriam Mafai, *L'Uomo che Sognava la Lotta Armata* (Milan: Rizzoli, 1984).

79. See *Il Giornale Nuovo,* November 8, 1980, p. 2.

80. This document, entitled "The KGB Approach: Minister-Plenipotentiary Renzo Rota's Denouncement," is appended to *Parliamentary Report on Terrorism, Minority Views,* pp. 219–366.

81. See *Parliamentary Report on Terrorism,* vol. IV, pp. 300–301.

82. For the full text of the declassified document, see *Parliamentary Report on Terrorism, Minority Views,* pp. 369–96.

83. Ibid., p. 379. Acronyms stand for the Irish Republican Army, Basque Fatherland and Liberty, Armed Nuclei for Popular Autonomy, and Red Army Faction.

84. Ibid., p. 387.

85. See interviews with Imposimato and Priore in *L'Espresso,* February 17, 1985, pp. 8–9, and *Panorama,* April 7, 1985, pp. 36–38.

86. To date it remains unclear whether LARF issued a "solidarity" claim or a "principal's claim."

87. For a discussion of, and chronological material on, the French terrorist scene, see Vittorfranco S. Pisano, *France as a Setting for Domestic and International Terrorism* (Gaithersburg, Md.: International Association of Chiefs of Police, 1985).

88. Statistics provided to the Parliament by the prime minister and reported in *Il Tempo,* February 8, 1985, p. 1.

89. See *Parliamentary Report on Terrorism,* vol. I, pp. 149–50, and *Parliamentary Report on Terrorism, Minority Views,* pp. 384–85.

90. As quoted in Atti Parlamentari, Camera dei Deputati, VIII Legislatura, *Discussioni,* December 20, 1982, pp. 90–94.

91. Michael Ledeen, "From Prague to Rome," unpublished English text of Ledeen's article regarding his interview with Sejna. The article was published in *Il Giornale Nuovo* in January 1980.

92. In addition to Miceli's parliamentary statements, see his interview with *Europeo,* February 9, 1981, p. 10.

93. *Parliamentary Report on Terrorism, Minority Views,* pp. 385–86. The

CESIS report notes that apart from any assessment of Senzani's allegations, he certainly was a "privileged" observer of the clandestine terrorist milieu:

94. Ida Farè et al., *Mara e le Altre* (Milan: Feltrinelli, 1979), p. 25.

95. In February 1985, Socialist prime minister Bettino Craxi reported to the Parliament that 13 fugitives and 44 nonfugitive extremists were located in Nicaragua and Costa Rica; see *Il Tempo,* February 8, 1985, p. 1. In August 1985, the Italian daily press repeatedly made reference to reports that Italian extremists were serving in the Nicaraguan armed forces. This press coverage generated telephone calls and written protests from several individuals whose denial of such service entailed an admission of their militancy in Nicaragua on behalf of a variety of Sandinista regime projects. Moreover, in early 1983 an organization called "National Association for Friendship, Solidarity, and Cultural Exchanges with Nicaragua" had already become operational in Italy with headquarters in Ancona. In a leaflet dated April 9, 1983, it called for "mobilization and commitment to defend the small and heroic people of Sandino." It also stated: "The unique experience of the Sandinista Popular Revolution is endangered by the action of the counterrevolutionary bands trained and financed by the North American Department of State."

96. See *Panorama,* September 15, 1980, p. 45.

97. An unwilling recipient of the Libyan offer, pro-Western former mayor of Comiso Salvatore Catalano, denounced this practice in an interview with *Europeo,* October 15, 1983, p. 21. Libya's interest in Italian/NATO military matters is further evidenced by a 1986 espionage case on that country's behalf involving an Italian air force NCO stationed at the cruise missile installation in Comiso. See *La Repubblica,* February 27, 1986, p. 11.

98. In addition to Libyan overtures and assistance, Italian peace militants in Comiso have been joined by German Greens with suspiciously recent East European visas on their passports. Other references to Communist Bloc clandestine endeavors in relation to the deployment of the Euromissiles in Comiso appear in Renato Proni, *Euromissili: La Tua Scelta* (Milan: Sugarco, 1982), p. 82.

99. Bettino Craxi stated before the Parliament that since the beginning of 1984, Italy has been exposed primarily to "international terrorism." See Atti Parlamentari, Camera dei Deputati, IX Legislatura, *Discussioni,* January 29, 1985, p. 14.

100. For additional details on the development of international linkages and patron-state support for Italian subversion and terrorism, see Vittorfranco S. Pisano, *Terrorism and Security: The Italian Experience,* Report of the Subcommittee on Security and Terrorism, Committee on the Judiciary, U.S. Senate, November 1984, pp. 28–35, 38, 40–41, 43–44, and Pisano, *Terrorism in Italy: An Update Report, 1983–1985,* Report of the Subcommittee on Security and Terrorism, Committee on the Judiciary, U.S. Senate, October 1985, pp. 19–28.

Chapter 8

1. Law Decree No. 59 of March 21, 1978, converted into law by Law No. 191 of May 18, 1978.

2. Law Decree No. 625 of December 15, 1979, converted into law by Law No. 15 of February 6, 1980.

3. Law No. 304 of May 29, 1982.

4. Law No. 398 of July 28, 1984.

5. *La Repubblica* (Rome), January 18, 1985, p. 1.

6. Among those who fled was red brigadist Giovanni Alimonti, a former switchboard operator at the Chamber of Deputies and an obviously useful intelligence source for the BR. See *Corriere della Sera* (Milan), April 24, 1986, p. 6.

7. Law Decree No. 626 of December 19, 1979, converted into law by Law No. 23 of February 11, 1980. It set up the National Committee for Public Order and Security.

8. Law No. 597 of November 23, 1979.

9. Law No. 121 of April 1, 1981, entitled "New Organization of the Public Security Administration."

10. Central offices of the Ministry of the Interior that preceded the Central Directorate for Crime Prevention and carried out similar functions—in some cases with emphasis on subversion rather than terrorism because of requirements at the time—included, in chronological sequence, the Confidential Matters Office (Ufficio Affari Riservati), the Security Service (Servizio di Sicurezza), and the Terrorism Counteraction Inspectorate (Ispettorato per l'Azione contro il Terrorismo).

11. These branch offices are part of the *questura,* that is, the decentralized State Police headquarters at the provincial level headed by the *questore,* or police superintendent.

12. These branch offices combine the functions of the now-defunct Political Office (Ufficio Politico) and the Anti-Terrorism Nucleus (Nucleo Antiterrorismo) of the *questura* (see note 11).

13. For example, the Carabinieri were able to capture the reputed founder of the BR, Renato Curcio, in 1974, by infiltrating into the organization Massimo Girotto, alias Brother Machinegun, who was at one time a Franciscan friar and later a South American revolutionary. Another case could be that of Marco Pisetta, but there is still doubt as to whether he was an actual infiltrator or an informer. See Romano Cantore, Carlo Rossella, and Chiara Valentini, *Dall'Interno della Guerriglia* (Milan: Mondadori, 1978), pp. 63–64, and Vincenzo Tessandori, *BR* (Milan: Garzanti, 1977), pp. 362–64.

14. Terrorist allegations regarding torture are addressed in Giorgio Bocca, *Noi Terroristi* (Milan: Garzanti, 1985), pp. 279–83. The court decisions referred to in the text were handed down by the Tribunal of Padua on July 15, 1983, and by the Court of Appeals of Padua on March 20, 1984.

15. Infiltration constraints are addressed in *Corriere della Sera,* January 23, 1978, p. 2, and *Panorama,* April 19, 1978, p. 55.

16. For a listing and discussion of antimafia measures, see Arnaldo Grilli, *La Criminalità Mafiosa nella Società Postindustriale* (Rome: Edizioni Laurus Robuffo, 1986), pp. 133–48.

17. General references to internal intelligence and security endeavors appear from time to time in the semiannual intelligence reports of the prime minister to Parliament. For the most recent, see Atti Parlamentari, Camera dei Deputati, IX Legislatura, *Relazione sulla Politica Informativa e della Sicurezza,* May 23–November 22, 1985, pp. 30–32.

18. All three reports have been published in *Il Borghese* (Rome), supplement, April 16, 1978, pp. 1–16, and Supplement, April 23, 1978, pp. 18–32.

19. For specific instances of politicized judicial behavior, see Federico Orlando, *P 38* (Milan: Editoriale Nuova, 1978), pp. 202–9, and *Panorama* (Milan), May 30, 1978, p. 57.

20. The political climate of this period is particularly well described in Domenico Bartoli, *Gli Italiani nella Terra di Nessuno* (Milan: Mondadori, 1976), and Alberto Ronchey, *Accadde in Italia 1968–1977* (Milan: Garzanti, 1977).

21. For a totally critical commentary on the Italian intelligence community, see Giuseppe De Lutiis, *Storia dei Servizi Segreti Italiani* (Rome: Editori Riuniti, 1984). This work, which is characterized by the systematic use of the words "perhaps" and "probably" and cites almost exclusively Communist or otherwise left-oriented sources, has been published by the publishing house of the PCI. The central theme of the book is that subversive armed bands have consistently constituted a parallel structure of the Italian intelligence services, whose operations are conditioned by agreements with the United States. For a work that tends to defend the intelligence community, but at the same time provides extensive data, see Ambrogio Viviani, *Servizi Segreti Italiani 1815–1985* (Rome: Adn Kronos, 1985). For a well-balanced commentary that unfortunately covers only the pre-1977 intelligence reform period, see Bartoli, *Gli Italiani nella Terra di Nessuno,* pp. 163–203.

22. Law No. 801, Arts. 7 and 8.

23. Viviani, *Servizi Segreti Italiani 1815–1985,* pp. 148–49. See also interview with General Viviani in *Panorama,* May 18, 1986, pp. 40–45.

Index